The Life of the Author: Charles Dickens

The Life of the Author

This new series aims to transform literary biography from its status as a resource for facts and details to that of a dynamic, innovative aspect of teaching, criticism and research. Outside universities, lives of writers are by far the most popular genre of books about literature, but within them they are neglected as a focus for interpretation and as frameworks for advanced research. *The Life of the Author* will reverse this imbalance by exploring new questions on how and why our conception of the author frames our evaluation and understanding of their work.

New books in this series

The Life of the Author: Charles Dickens
The Life of the Author: John Milton
The Life of the Author: Maya Angelou
The Life of the Author: William Shakespeare
The Life of the Author: Nathaniel Hawthorne

The Life of the Author: Charles Dickens

Pete Orford

Series Editor: Richard Bradford

Registered Offices

John Wiley & Sons, Inc., 111 River Street, Hoboken, NJ 07030, USA

John Wiley & Sons Ltd, The Atrium, Southern Gate, Chichester, West Sussex, PO19 8SQ, UK

For details of our global editorial offices, customer services, and more information about Wiley products visit us at www.wiley.com.

Wiley also publishes its books in a variety of electronic formats and by print-on-demand. Some content that appears in standard print versions of this book may not be available in other formats.

A catalogue record for this book is available from the Library of Congress

Paperback ISBN: 9781119697459; ePub ISBN: 9781119697534; ePDF ISBN: 9781119697497

Cover Design: Wiley

Cover Image: Courtesy of Charles Dickens Museum

Set in 9.5/12.5pt STIXTwoText by Integra Software Services Pvt. Ltd., Pondicherry, India

Contents

Acknowledgements

I am grateful to the many scholars, archivists, students, enthusiasts and friends who have informed, and continue to inform, my ideas and understanding of Dickens and his works. John Drew deserves special mention for his initial encouragement, enduring support, and constant readiness to be a well of information whenever I needed to find 'that one article I vaguely remember we were discussing a few years ago'. My colleagues at the University of Buckingham continue to be a supportive family of scholars, while the library has been a god-send for resources (I also apologise for the many overdue books I've accumulated during the writing of this one).

As ever, the Charles Dickens Museum has been a vital resource for Dickens research, and I am particularly grateful to Louisa Price, Frankie Kubicki, Emily Dunbar and Cindy Sughrue. I also had the pleasure of visiting the archives at the V&A Museum and the Bodleian Library, which was a joy to revisit after several months of isolation in lockdown. Writing a book during a global pandemic was not something I had ever anticipated doing, so thank the maker for reliable online resources like *Dickens Journals Online*, *Victorian Web*, and *Dickens Letters Project*. My thanks also go to the generosity of individual scholars who readily responded to increasingly frantic email queries, including (but not limited to) Emily Bell, Hugo Bowles, Jeremy Clarke, Emma Curry, Michael Eaton, Jenny Hartley, Joanna Hofer-Robinson, Paul Lewis, Leon Litvack, Michael Slater, Catherine Waters, Claire Wood and the ever-welcoming Dickens Fellowship and Dickens Society. I would also like to thank Richard Bradford for inviting me to write this book, and the team at Wiley, especially Liz Wingett, Nicole Allen and Verity Stuart, for their advice and support, as well as the reviewers who provided helpful and encouraging feedback, especially Leon Litvack who courteously took me out to dinner in Rome one evening to politely point out many egregious errors. I shall henceforth be insisting upon receiving all feedback in these conditions.

A number of my postgraduate students at Buckingham got into the curious habit while I was writing this book of apologising anytime they sent me their work to look at, as though it were an inconvenience to me. On the contrary, I thank them heartily for the regular provision of intellectual stimulation both in their writing and our conversations, which were always a joy, both as a welcome break and an inspiration. My role as course director for the Charles Dickens MA has placed me in a privileged position where I can be first in the queue to see a range of exciting work emerging from new Dickens scholars: some of the resulting theses are referenced later in this book, but all the students, cited here or not, have provided me with insight and encouragement, and for that I owe my deepest and sincere thanks.

Finally, and most importantly, my family, who are always there to support me. I dedicate this book to my wonderful, beautiful and absolutely bonkers trio of kids. Cade, Ned and Lirael, the last few years have been unprecedented (I mean, a global pandemic? Really?) – not only have we got through it together, but it has proven to be an experience I will look back on with fond remembrance. I *had* been looking forward to some quiet research leave where I could really power ahead with the book; instead I got lockdowns, online teaching and home-schooling. As a result, this book has been written while simultaneously answering queries such as 'how do you spell potato?', 'what is the square root of 64?' and of course that perennial favourite 'can I have a snack?'. But for every interruption there were ample amounts of hugs, giggles, x-box tournaments and cartoon marathons. It has been glorious. Kids, you keep me grounded, you make me laugh so much, and a smile from you is worth a hundred interruptions. And one day – one day – I will convince you to read a Dickens book.

Introduction

A Life in Brief

> Whether I shall turn out to be the hero of my own life, or whether that station will be held by anybody else, these pages must show.[1]

Charles Dickens is a contradiction. He is the best of men, he is the worst of men; he fills the page with social wisdom, he fills the page with comic foolishness; he is a champion for the poor, he is a champion for his own career; he is the epitome of domestic spirit, he is a scoundrel who abandoned his wife; he is a loving father, he is a demanding and domineering father; he is a dutiful son, he is a resentful son; he is good-hearted and sentimental, he is sneering and satirical. Compared to Shakespeare, that other titan of English literature, we have significantly more information about Dickens's life – too much perhaps. While we are left with a multitude of questions about Shakespeare due to the absence of information, with Dickens we face no less a multitude of questions due to the *abundance* of information. Successive writers and scholars have sifted through the biographies, letters, contemporary accounts and reviews to highlight and suppress different aspects of Dickens, and in so doing we are left with a curiously ambiguous portrait. His friend John Forster, who wrote one of the first biographies of Dickens, described him as 'the most popular novelist of the century, and one of the greatest humourists that England has produced'.[2] Simon Callow declares that Dickens 'is one of the greatest English lives, both humbling and heart-warming, despite titanic flaws.'[3] Peter Ackroyd suggests that 'he embodied the period from which he sprang' yet 'there is a sorrowfulness, a self-contained sorrowfulness, almost a coldness, about aspects of Dickens's life on earth'.[4] Can they all be right? The ambiguity of Dickens's identity is noted by Una Pope-Hennessy who muses he 'was something of an enigma to his contemporaries and remains something of an enigma to us'.[5] Claire Tomalin notes that 'everyone finds their own version of Charles Dickens' who is 'above and beyond every other description, simply the great, hard-working writer'.[6] Edgar Johnson believed that 'Dickens was himself a Dickens

The Life of the Author: Charles Dickens, First Edition. Pete Orford.
© 2023 John Wiley & Sons Ltd. Published 2023 by John Wiley & Sons Ltd.

character, bursting with inordinate and fantastic vitality'.[7] Melisa Klimaszewski and Melissa Gregory note the difficulty of defining Dickens in their biography:

> How to enter the life of Charles Dickens? With his fairly unremarkable birth into a modest middle-class family in Portsmouth in 1812? With his death as a celebrated novelist in 1870? Or perhaps with his writings? His novels? His journalism? His public readings? His cast of thousands? His famous depiction of urban life in Victorian London, the city that shaped him? Or with his afterlife, evident in countless novel, stage, film and television adaptations of his works? Opening any one of these doors on Dickens' life changes our view, from the boy who aspired to success to the celebrated author whose work not only captured his contemporary culture, but also continues to reverberate throughout our own. As a writer with a rich and complicated personal life and a tremendous artistic legacy, there is no obvious beginning to Dickens.[8]

True enough, not every biography starts at the beginning: Ackroyd begins his book at the end, with Dickens's death; Rosemarie Bodenheimer starts hers at the beginning of Dickens's career, not his life; while Tomalin starts her biography in the middle, with Dickens aged 28 attending a court hearing in 1840.[9] Nor is there a unity in focus: Callow makes his book about Dickens's relationship with the stage, believing that 'Dickens's uniquely vivid sense of the theatre informs every page of his writing'; Michael Slater focuses instead on the page and frames his biography around Dickens's 'career as a writer and professional author'.[10] The most recurrent theme across Dickens biographies is the consistent sense of inconsistency, that there is no single portrayal of Dickens which any writer can hope to define. There is so much to say about Dickens – so many positions to adopt, judgements to make, episodes to recount – that ultimately every biography is as conscious of what it is not saying as much as what it is. The Inimitable, as Dickens liked to style himself, has proven to also be The Illimitable.

And thus we come to this book and its purpose. So why are you reading this book? Is it because:

a) Charles Dickens is my favourite author and I want to find out more about him!
b) I feel like I ought to know more about Dickens given how famous he is.
c) I'm struggling to understand Dickens so hoped to get some help.
d) My teacher is making me study Dickens and I need some information for an essay.

Let's face facts, all of the above could be true for different readers. To those of you who answered (d), my condolences. And for those who answered (a) I am giving you a high-five as we speak. But given that any one of these answers could be true, what does that tell us about the way Dickens is perceived today? Any time I mention Dickens to my own children I'm met with groans because they think I'm going to make them read him, or watch a film that doesn't feature cartoon animals or superheroes. People approaching Dickens for the first time today have an equal chance of doing so out of genuine desire or a sense of obligation. In her study of Dickens's reputation around the world, Regenia Gagnier how 'Dickens has served as representative of the "English Book"', which is as true for readers in his own country as it is for readers abroad.[11] We are told that Dickens is a classic writer and so read him either expecting that title to be fulfilled, or actively looking for ways in which we can disprove it and thus react against the hype.

This book cannot tell you who Dickens was; that will be for each reader to decide for themselves. What I can do is tell you about Dickens's life, and explore the key elements which inspired him and his work, to provide a starting point for those wishing to study and understand his works better. I can show you the good and the bad, in both his life and work, so that you can make an informed decision on who Dickens is to you. Over the course of this book I will approach Dickens's life thematically with the intention of showing how we can responsibly incorporate a knowledge of Dickens's biographical experiences into discussion of his works. The book is best understood as a collection of essays, each one taking a key aspect of Dickens's life and focusing upon that, and its impact on his writing. A short case study at the end of each chapter offers an example of how we can then use our biographical knowledge of Dickens to analyse his writing (and, in turn, how his writing can sometimes enable us to better understand his biography). My intention is not purely to retell the narrative of Dickens's life, but to show how our views of that life have changed, and how each new discovery and interpretation helps us to further explore his works. This introduction will first offer a brief overview of Dickens's life, to provide the overarching context for the following chapters where we can focus on key aspects of that life and the lessons we can learn from them.

Early Dickens

Dickens was born in Portsmouth on 7 February 1812 to John and Elizabeth Dickens (née Barrow). Dickens's father was a naval clerk which required him to move as the job required; a further encouragement for moving house was John Dickens's rise in income, and debt, which saw them moving to larger or smaller premises accordingly. As a consequence, the young Dickens lived in a number of different residences across the South East, in Portsmouth, London, and Chatham, before the family moved to London once again in 1822. By this time the family consisted of Dickens, his parents, his older sister Fanny, and his younger siblings Letitia, Harriet, Fred and Alfred (another brother Augustus would be born later in 1827). With the fortunes of Dickens's father looking increasingly bleak, Dickens was employed at Warren's Blacking Factory sometime in 1823, which he felt to be a great betrayal. He had been attending school in Chatham and now he found himself working in a factory while his sister continued to attend a music academy. Further shame came in 1824 when his father was imprisoned for debt in Marshalsea Debtor's Prison. The impact of this upon Dickens would last a lifetime, but the incarceration itself lasted but a few months; Dickens's father was able to secure his own release, and shortly after Dickens ceased working at the factory and went to Wellington House Academy in London from 1824 to 1827.

On completing his education, Dickens worked as a solicitor's clerk for Ellis and Blackmore, and then for a short time for Charles Molloy. He left this employment around 1829 to work as a reporter, first in Doctor's Commons, then in Parliament, where he would note down the proceedings of court in shorthand in order to complete his reports in the evening. This start in journalism developed further over the next five years with positions at the *Mirror of Parliament*, the *True Sun*, the *Morning Chronicle* and *Evening Chronicle*. During this time, he also had his first fictional work published in 1831: 'A Dinner at Poplar Walk', a short comic sketch which he wrote under the pseudonym of Boz. Over the next five years he would balance his work as a reporter with the writing of further sketches, eventually publishing them as one volume in 1836 as *Sketches by Boz*.

While establishing the basis for his literary career, Dickens was also laying foundations for his personal life. After an unsuccessful courtship between 1830 and 1833 of Maria Beadnell, he then met Catherine Hogarth around 1835. Catherine was the eldest of three daughters to George Hogarth, who was the editor of the *Chronicle*. She and Dickens married in 1836. In the same year Dickens commenced work on a proposed series which would evolve into his first novel: *The Pickwick Papers*. Published in monthly instalments, or 'numbers' over the next year and a half, this comic tale was phenomenally popular and established Dickens as a writer. This method of publishing in numbers would prove the model by which Dickens would write all of his subsequent novels. He capitalised on the success of *Pickwick* to secure contracts for more work, such as *Oliver Twist* which was published from 1837 through to 1838, while also exploring playwriting as an additional career. From 1836 to 1839 three plays written by Dickens were performed on the public stage before a fourth one was rejected and Dickens concentrated solely on print. He was also expanding his journalistic experience to adopt the mantle of editor, overseeing *Bentley's Miscellany* (in which *Oliver Twist* was published) from 1837 to 1839. During this time of establishing his career, his family was also developing. It grew with the birth of his son Charley in 1837 and daughters Mamie and Katey in 1838 and 1839 respectively; it also shrank in 1837 with the death of his wife's younger sister Mary Hogarth, who died in Dickens's arms while staying at their house. By the end of the 1830s, Dickens and Catherine had moved from their first family home at Doughty Street to Devonshire Terrace. Professionally, he had now published three novels: *The Pickwick Papers, Oliver Twist* and *Nicholas Nickleby* (1838–1839). Personally, he now had three children: Charley, Mamie and Katey. Both his career and family were firmly under way.

Dickens in the 1840s

Over the course of the next decade Dickens would expand his personal and professional portfolio with five more children and five more novels, in addition to two travelogues and five shorter Christmas books. In 1840 Dickens attempted an experiment, a departure from the model of monthly numbers which his first three novels had been published in. Instead, *Master Humphrey's Clock* would be a weekly serial where he could write several short stories in addition to occasional series. The experiment did not work, and as numbers dwindled Dickens responded by developing one of the threads he had started into *The Old Curiosity Shop* (1840–1841), which eventually accounted for the entirety of each week's issue. This was followed in turn by *Barnaby Rudge* (1841–1842), after which *Master Humphrey's Clock* was wound up. Dickens's reputation now stretched beyond the British borders, and in 1842 he took the opportunity to visit America. It was a long voyage and a gruelling tour, so while Catherine travelled with Dickens, the children stayed behind in London with the actor William Charles Macready and his family. Dickens found the New World to be a dizzying, exciting and disorientating place. He was disillusioned to see it was not the utopia he had hoped, and further aggravated by the lack of international copyright law which allowed publishers in the USA to reproduce his work without paying him a dime. 'I seriously believe', he told Forster of American readers, 'that it is an essential part of the pleasure derived from the perusal of a popular English book, that the author gets nothing for it.'[12] The resulting criticism he raised both in his travel narrative *American Notes* (1842) and his novel *Martin Chuzzlewit* (1842–4) soured Dickens's reputation in America (but only briefly).

Meanwhile Dickens was becoming concerned by his rising costs. Living the life of a gentleman was not cheap, and his constant expenditure on entertainment was making a dent in his income. His household was increasing; Catherine's sister Georgina came to stay with the family and would remain with them as a matriarchal figure for the children for the rest of his life. Being only fifteen years old at the time she first joined them, Georgina would have been unable to contribute to the family income; however, she could and did contribute invisible labour in childcare that effectively saved Dickens money (in later life she would receive a housekeeper's wage in recognition of her role in the household). Dickens wrote *A Christmas Carol* in 1843 which proved a great success, but unfortunately Dickens's insistence on the book having gilt edges and colour illustrations meant that much of its sales was used to cover the costs of production. In 1844 he took the whole family – children and Georgina too – to Italy for one year's holiday. This allowed him to sublet Devonshire Terrace (at a higher rate than what he was paying in Italy) as well as escaping the temptations of London life, as an opportunity to save money. While there he wrote his next Christmas book, *The Chimes* (1843), and also used the experience to produce a second travel narrative, *Pictures from Italy* (1846), but what was more important for Dickens personally is that it gave him chance to breathe, take stock, and plan his next work rather than reacting from month to month – or week to week even – as he had been with his earlier works.

When Dickens returned to the UK in 1845 he thus had ambitions of writing a new type of novel. These ambitions were temporarily delayed by other projects, first writing another Christmas book, *The Cricket on the Hearth* (1845) and then launching and editing the newspaper *The Daily News* at the start of 1846, the pace of which proved too much and prompted Dickens to resign just a few weeks later. Desperate to escape London once more, he took his family away again, this time to Switzerland, where he began work on his next novel *Dombey and Son* (1846–1848), the first one for which we have direct evidence of clear forward planning and structure. He also wrote a fourth Christmas book *The Battle of Life* (1846). Dickens returned to the UK in 1847, and shortly after he established Urania Cottage, a home for 'fallen women', with his friend and philanthropist Angela Burdett-Coutts. He published one further Christmas book, *The Haunted Man*, in 1848, before abandoning that tradition. Dickens ended the decade with the publication of *David Copperfield* (1849–1850), his pseudo-autobiography in which the hero experiences a number of situations not completely dissimilar to the author's own early life. Dickens was now evolving beyond a writer of comic series into a successful and established novelist.

Dickens in the 1850s

In the 1850s Dickens would establish two weekly journals, and write four novels. He would act in a number of amateur dramatic performances and begin public readings of this works. Personally, he would have two more children, lose one of them, and separate from his wife to start a new relationship with a young actress.

The decade began with the publication of *Household Words* in March 1850, 'Conducted by Charles Dickens'. This was a weekly journal which would include contributions from several authors, offering poetry, non-fiction, short stories and a longer serialised work. Dickens was aided in this by his sub-editor W. H. Wills, and together they built up a network of writers and contributors with Dickens at the centre of this new literary circle. Having given up on his solo Christmas books, he now began a new tradition of a Christmas special, in which he and other writers would contribute short stories to an overarching frame narrative, and this tradition would continue up until 1867. Another development of Dickens's growing network was a number of amateur productions he now engaged in. This had begun sporadically in the late 1840s for various charitable endeavours, with Ben Jonson's comedy *Every Man in His Humour* being a recurring favourite; in 1851 they acted in *Not So Bad as We Seem*, written by Dickens's friend and author Edward Bulwer Lytton, and an accompanying farce *Mr Nightingale's Diary* collaboratively written by Dickens and Mark Lemon. It was performed in front of Queen Victoria no less, with further performances across the UK over the next two years.

In 1851 Dickens suffered two personal tragedies: on the 31 March his father died, and then two weeks later on 14 April his daughter Dora, barely eight months old, also died. Professionally, over the first half of the decade he wrote *Bleak House* (1852–1853), *Hard Times* (1854) and *Little Dorrit* (1855–1857). In 1856 he bought Gad's Hill Place, a grand house which his father had pointed out to him as a young boy. This was his second home alongside Tavistock Place in London, which the family had moved into in 1851.

In the second half of the decade Dickens grew increasingly dissatisfied with his domestic life. In 1855 he received a letter from Maria Beadnell, his first love who had rejected his courtship. Dickens was enthralled by the chance to meet her again, only to be disappointed to see that she had inexplicably grown older in the interim. Dickens's disillusionment with women getting older also applied to his wife. The readings and amateur dramatics were offering a new and exciting opportunity for Dickens, while home was proving rather dull. In 1857 his company did a joint performance of Bulwer Lyttons's *Uncle John* and Wilkie Collins's *The Frozen Deep*. The success of the amateur performance inspired them to take it on tour, replacing the women of Dickens's family with professional actresses. In this way he met Ellen Ternan, an eighteen-year-old actress with whom he would begin a relationship that would last the rest of his life. The following year Dickens publicly separated from his wife, though they never divorced; instead Dickens would live a secret life with Ternan outside the public gaze while simultaneously wooing that same public with his reading tours. The decade closed, as it began, with the launch of a new journal: after a disagreement with his publishers, Dickens ceased work on *Household Words* and began the near-identical *All the Year Round*. The first story to appear in it, leading the first issue, was *A Tale of Two Cities* (1859).

Dickens in the 1860s

In the 1860s, Dickens's production of novels would slow dramatically compared to previous decades: just two were produced, with a third (and final) novel written in the early part of 1870 before his death. *Great Expectations* was published in *All the Year Round* from December 1860 through to August 1861. In the same journal Dickens also ran a series of stylised but non-fictional pieces around this time under the title of *The Uncommercial Traveller*. But his main creative output was now the public readings, on which he toured all around the UK. In 1862 he moved to France for a year; in 1863 his mother died. In 1864 he began publication of his last complete novel *Our Mutual Friend* (1864–1865), a monthly serial once again.

Throughout this time his relationship with Ternan continued, with his mistress living in secret locations in South-East England and France. Rumours linking back to comments from Dickens's daughter Katey also suggest that Dickens and Ternan may have had a child in this time, who died.[13] On 9 June 1865, Dickens was travelling back from France with Ternan and her mother when they were involved in a railway accident at Staplehurst in Kent. This would have a lasting effect on Dickens who was frequently uneasy on trains after that date. This was especially unfortunate given that it coincided with the growing success of the reading tours and Dickens's increased travels around the UK and Ireland, before launching an American tour in 1867. On his return to the States, Dickens reconciled with his American audience and apologised for his former comments. The tour was a great success which cemented Dickens's popularity and celebrity status, not least thanks to the amount of merchandise sold, including pictures of the author. It also came at a cost, as the strain of travelling and performing took a toll on Dickens's health, exacerbated by his introduction of new material which enacted Sikes's murder of Nancy in *Oliver Twist*. Consequently, in 1870 Dickens began a farewell tour in the UK, abandoning plans of going to Australia and instead retiring back to Gad's Hill where he commenced work on his final novel *The Mystery of Edwin Drood*. On 8 June 1870 he suffered a stroke at home, and died the following day.

How Does Dickens's Life Inform his Works?

Such is Dickens's life, in a nutshell. Now what do we *do* with it? The use of an author's own biography in the consideration of their writing can offer valuable insight, but also encourage misreading, and there is not always a sure-fire way to distinguish which is which. The purpose of this biography is primarily to consider Dickens's writing in relation to his life. Every writer will be inspired to some extent by their own experience, whether that be through direct referencing of their own life-story, or moments that reflect their personal point of view. At all times we need to remember – forgive me for stating the obvious – that Dickens is writing works of fiction. There is therefore no guarantee that each work is a beacon of truth nor a direct retelling of Dickens's own life experience. Even in those moments where we can see a close parallel with Dickens's life – in fact, *especially* in those moments – we must remember that Dickens's primary concern is writing good fiction. Events and emotions can be exaggerated and reshaped to produce a better reading experience. Chapter 1 will examine this phenomenon in particular with Dickens's hyperbolic reimagining of his childhood in *David Copperfield*. Nonetheless, as much as we should be wary when identifying biographic influences in the work, nor should we jump to the other extreme of refusing to recognise any influence. Whether consciously or subconsciously, it is only logical and practical that Dickens would draw on his own experiences while writing. Topographically, we can see a number of moments where Dickens locates his stories in real-life settings full of detailed minutiae; it is no stretch of the imagination to see him also adopting the same strategy within the space of his own memory.

In the following chapters I will explore his life story by drawing on a key theme, exploring that theme predominately with a specific time period (or focal point) of Dickens's life, but also looking before and after where appropriate, before closing the chapter with one specific work as an example in the case study which closes each chapter, with the aim of showing how Dickens's life can inform reading of his works. In some chapters there will be an overlap between the focal points, in other cases small gaps may occur; the purpose is not to arbitrarily slice Dickens's life into neat slices but to recognise that several major moments in his life will inevitably intersect or coincide. Taking this thematic approach has two potential pitfalls. Firstly, there is a danger of bundling an entire period of Dickens's life under one umbrella. In Chapter 10, for example, I focus on the period 1855–1858 under the heading of Dickens and Separation, which can imply that everything Dickens is doing during that time is informed by his separation from his wife – and while there is some truth in this as the separation was undoubtedly a major event which would have a wide impact, equally we have to allow that there will be several other events and emotions experienced by Dickens in this time that exist independently of that. Secondly, just as there are many themes prevalent in any one time in Dickens's life, so too some themes will span the entirety of Dickens's life rather than just one singular moment. So while Chapter 4: Dickens and Theatre centres around Dickens's professional theatrical career in the late 1830s, his relationship with theatre lasted for nearly his entire lifetime, as a writer, actor, critic and audience member. Readers are therefore invited to keep their wits about them, and to interrogate this text in front of them no less than they would interrogate Dickens's texts. The aim of the book is not to provide you with a final answer that categorically solves the question of Dickens – how boring would that be? – but rather to provide you with the necessary starting information with which you can formulate your own questions, possibly even answers, about Dickens.

How can we meaningfully assess the inspirations upon an author? One of the problems is how ambiguous and nebulous those biographical inspirations can be. By contrast, with literary inspirations we can expect some measure of certainty by searching for and identifying quotations or allusions in the text. Shakespeare, for example, is a regular presence in Dickens's works, as is the *Arabian Nights*, and the Bible; in each case we can point to the original source and find that direct reference to underline the connection. So when Dickens gives Chapter fourteen of *The Mystery of Edwin Drood* the title 'When shall these three meet again?' we can confidently identify it as being informed by Shakespeare's *Macbeth* and the witches' question 'When shall we three meet again?'[14] But when Dickens is drawing inspiration from his life story, there is no easy-to-reference primary source with a fixed text that we can check the quote against. Instead we have to rely on similarities and inferences and attempt to judge how confidently we can assume a direct correlation. The protagonist of *David Copperfield* works as a parliamentary reporter before going on to write novels, just as Dickens did, and this, we can confidently argue, is intentionally drawn from his own experience. But just like David, Pip in *Great Expectations* also experiences several mistakes as a young gentleman as he struggles with his own insecurities about his childhood while trying to impress London society. In both David and Pip we can draw comparisons with Dickens's life, but as to whether they are intentional or not is harder to claim. Even without the sheer abundance of parallels in *David Copperfield*, we are told explicitly by Forster that Dickens was 'partially uplifting the veil' of his life in *David Copperfield*.[15] With *Great Expectations* however the link is hazier: Pip is a blacksmith, not a boy in the blacking factory, and he becomes a gentleman, not a writer. There are certainly going to be facets drawn from Dickens's experience but to what extent that is intentional or subconscious is up for debate without concrete external evidence. But when a character is experiencing emotions or situations that the author has also experienced, it is not unreasonable to presume the author is allowing their former views and ideas to inform the character's response.

In my previous research I spent a lot of time looking at the many, many, MANY solutions to Dickens's last unfinished novel *The Mystery of Edwin Drood*.[16] I have seen first-hand the way in which subsequent readers can look upon the same text and confidently draw completely different conclusions. Often, in the case of *Drood*, they will not just propose a theory but also argue emphatically that what they are proposing is exactly what Dickens intended. Over two hundred solutions later, and Edwin is dead, alive, roaming Cloisterham in disguise or working in Egypt. Clearly, they cannot all be right. Our endless theorising over *Drood* highlights the subjectivity of interpretation, and the danger of overconfidently presuming to know Dickens's intentions. As much as Dickens drew inspiration from his own experiences, as any writer will, we must always remember his primary intention is to write an interesting piece to read. Dickens's exaggeration of his own childhood misery in the backstory of *David Copperfield* could be a deliberate method of working through his angst and exploring the darkest parts of his psyche – OR, it could simply be that as a writer he saw opportunity to heighten the emotion further and develop the melodrama of the piece to further wring a reaction from his readers. Both can be true, to varying degrees, and we would be wise to remember this as we look within his works for potential parallels. Similarly, Dickens populates his novels with a multitude of characters who all hold different views and outlooks upon the world; not all of these ideas can be shared directly by the author. We should be wary of confidently stating that a character is voicing Dickens's own opinion when the novels will inevitably contain another character stating the opposite opinion.

Nor should we maintain this caution for the fictional works of Dickens only. Dickens's non-fiction is highly stylised, and shows an equal awareness of pacing, structure and how best to engage the reader. A good example of this is his 1853 essay 'Gone Astray'. In this essay Dickens recalls how once, when he 'was a very small boy indeed, both in years and stature, [he] got lost one day in the City of London.'[17] Now, did this actually happen? The simple answer is we do not know, but it may have. Dickens often adopts a persona in his non-fictional writing – sometimes he even adopts a name for this alter-ego: Boz in his early works, and the Uncommercial Traveller in his later works. The immediate danger therefore when reading Dickens is assuming that 'I' automatically equals Dickens. Conversely, Dickens was a writer who regularly observed the world around him and used that to populate his work with fine detail, and so there will always be elements of truth and his own observations present in his works: we just cannot always say for certain which parts are fact and which are fiction. In 'Gone Astray', the descriptions of London are clearly drawn from experience, but is it the experience of a young Dickens, being recalled by the older author, or is it the experience of that older Dickens, either retracing the steps of his younger self and adding further details, or fabricating the entire story and using contemporary details to flesh it out? Then there is the question of audience: Dickens is writing this to be read by the public, so how does that awareness of audience affect the veracity of what he is saying? If this were a private letter to his friend we might have more confidence that it is an actual memory being recalled; but for a public audience, there is that sense of performance and distance. Dickens, as we know, spent a lot of time in London as a young man working at the factory and living apart from his family while his father was in prison. It may well be that the experiences in 'Gone Astray' stem from this time, in which case Dickens would certainly not be prepared to tell his audience about his time in the factory, and therefore while the experience of walking London alone in his youth may be true, the framing narrative of being on a trip and separated from an adult may be a necessary fabrication to keep Dickens's secret safe.

At several points I will draw connections between Dickens's life and work just as many have done before me. Forster is very forceful in identifying real-life inspirations for several character in Dickens's work and referring readers to Dickens's writing as a form of autobiography: 'readers may remember how vividly portions of his boyhood are reproduced in his fancy of the Christmas-tree' he writes, referring to an 1850 article in *Household Words*, also referring his readers to Dickens's 'thoughtful little paper on Nurse's-stories' which was written in 1860. It is also Forster who consistently insists upon *David Copperfield*'s regular repackaging of Dickens's own memories. Of all biographers, Forster knew Dickens best, and was well-placed to comment on the veracity of certain details. We, unfortunately, do not have his intimate knowledge to be able to say with the same confidence which bits are and are not real. Hence whenever I discuss parallels in the text, I would warn the reader to bear in mind my questions above about 'Gone Astray.' As readers we can make reasonable assumptions about parallels between Dickens's life and work; we can identify interesting points in his writing that seems to reflect and comment upon situations he himself experienced. But we must always be aware of that capacity for exaggeration, or reshaping of his own life for dramatic purpose.

Dickens in (and out) of Context

Do we need to know about Dickens to understand his works? Certainly not. Some might even argue that knowledge of the author only confuses the directness of the work. Barthes's *Death of the Author* champions the idea that 'writing is the destruction of every voice, of every point in origin'.[18] Regardless of the moment the book was written, the moment we read it we recreate it anew as a contemporary text: 'The reader is the space on which all the quotations that make up a writing are inscribed without any of them being lost; a text's unity lies not in its origin but in its destination.'[19] In addition to thinking about Dickens's life, we also need to acknowledge how our own life informs our reading of a text, for it is our experiences, our opinions, which will which shape our understanding. Staff at the Charles Dickens Museum in London inform me there have been a number of occasions where international visitors have asked whether Dickens himself was at home that day, prompting an awkward conversation in which the staff have to break the news that Dickens is, in fact, dead. But is it really such an extraordinary misconception to have? Others have keenly pointed out that in countries around the world there are slums approximating the levels of poverty Dickens wrote and campaigned about; but in patronisingly nominating other countries as modernday counterparts of Victorian slums, there is a staggering lack of self-awareness. While the Western World may choose to content ourselves with the thought that Dickens is writing about the past, in turn implying that the problems of Victorian England no longer exist in its modern-day counterpart, the reality is that Dickens remains increasingly relevant in an era of foodbanks and a cost of living crisis.

There is thus a danger that over-contextualising the works can end up historicising them and consigning them as artefacts of the past rather than texts to be enjoyed and engaged with in the present. Some screen adaptations have attempted to imagine Dickens's stories outside of their original setting: Disney's 1988 film *Oliver & Co* moved Oliver Twist and Fagin from Victorian London to 1980s New York; Alfonso Cuarón's 1998 film of *Great Expectations* also relocated the story to New York, this time in the modern day, with the Kent marshes where Pip grew up replaced by the Gulf Coasts of the US. Adaptations such as these show how the characters Dickens created maintain relevance and universality beyond their original context.

At the same time, Dickens studies have regularly taken an interest in topography – the mapping of locations onto the text. Dickens is frequently associated with London – when he tried writing *The Chimes* in Genoa in 1844 he found the process very difficult to start without the familiar surroundings and walks to provide him with inspiration:

> Put me down on Waterloo-bridge at eight o'clock in the evening, with leave to roam about as long as I like, and I would come home, you know, panting to go on. I am sadly strange as it is; and can't settle.[20]

His novels are full of specific details about the city and its locations; street names and districts are cited to firmly place the story within its environs. Jeremy Tambling notes that the sheer amount of writing Dickens sets within and about London 'shows that the novelist not only knew and used London but that it was an obsession for him.'[21] Dickens and London have a reciprocal relationship: the city inspired him, but his legacy is that now we can visit London through the lens of his novels. Visitors to London can and do explore Dickens's city and the 'real-life' locations of his stories: there is the cemetery where Scrooge saw his own grave, the church where Little Nell sought sanctuary, the steps where Nancy met Mr Brownlow and unwittingly secured her own doom. Like the biography, this must also be taken with a pinch of salt: yes, Dickens is inspired by the landscape around him, but he is not bound by it, nor is he above changing details to suit the needs of the story first and foremost.

Recently there has been growing awareness of Dickens's debt to the wider world beyond London, and recognition of how his time in Portsmouth, Chatham and Gad's Hill also informed his works. Rochester has an annual Dickens festival celebrating the author's links to the city, inspiration for Cloisterham in his final novel. Walking down the streets of Rochester you can see several plaques informing you of the corresponding locations in *The Mystery of Edwin Drood*. Often these signs blur fact and fiction; the shop next to the gatehouse (where Dickens housed his antihero John Jasper) has a plaque proclaiming 'THIS WAS THE HOME OF MR TOPES, THE CHIEF VERGER OF THE CATHEDRAL IN "THE MYSTERY OF EDWIN DROOD."' Well, no. Both Mr Topes and his wife, who is not mentioned, are fictional characters and therefore have never set foot in the building, but it is where Dickens imagined them living in his story, and over time that boundary between fiction and reality has become blurred. Yet beyond the location of his characters, what is more significant is the region's location of the author, and an awareness of how Dickens would have walked that street, looked upon the gatehouse and its environs, and imagined his characters inhabiting the space.

If the South East of England is making a claim to Dickens, so too is his impact and inspiration being claimed further afield. In Michael Hollington's edited collection *The Reception of Charles Dickens in Europe* a team of scholars have charted the critical history of Dickens from his own time to the present day in Germany, Russia, France, Spain, Portugal, Italy, Austria, Switzerland, the Netherlands, Denmark, Finland, Iceland, Norway, Sweden, the Czech Republic, Slovakia, Croatia, Poland, Bulgaria, Estonia, Latvia, Lithuania, Romania, Greece, Hungary and Georgia.[22] Gagnier has researched the circulation of Dickens even further afield, including New Zealand, Australia, Africa, China, Japan and India.[23] Today the Dickens Fellowship boasts branches not only across the UK but also in Ireland, France, Italy, Norway, Denmark, America, Japan, New Zealand and Australia. America in particular has a number of Dickens Fellowship branches and Pickwick Clubs who are proud of the direct links between Dickens and their location thanks to his American tours. No doubt if Dickens had made it to Australia there would be similarly enthusiasm identifying of places he visited there too – as it is, the emigration of two of his sons – Alfred in 1865, and Edward (nicknamed Plorn) in 1868 – provides a connection for Australian fans of Dickens to bring the author closer to their home. It would be easy to dismiss this fervour to find places connected with Dickens as either the naïve act of enthusiasts or the cynical ploy of tourism boards, but let us not be hasty. Like Monet's garden, visiting the sites which inspired Dickens can allow us a moment of contact with a man now dead for a century and a half; his remains may be limited to Westminster Abbey but his footprint is all over the world for us to retrace. Is it essential that we visit the Coliseum to see 'Its solitude, its awful beauty, and its utter desolation' just as Dickens described in order that as readers we can understand *Pictures from Italy* better? Of course not.[24] But does visiting the Coliseum enhance our reading of it – and, moreover, does reading Dickens's description of it enhance our visit to it? Yes, absolutely. In that same spirit, this biography offers to take the reader through the footsteps of Dickens's life to better understand and enhance our experience of the works.

To return to Barthes, while I readily accept the potential and capacity for readers to create their own context of Dickens's writings beyond the life and times of the author, equally I cannot help feel that some writers like Dickens offer resistance to the idea of the death of the author. By 'writers like Dickens' I am not referring to his fame or status, though admittedly that helps: it is hard to ignore an author when often we are reading the book specifically because of who it is by. But the predominant reason I query whether Barthes's ideas apply to Dickens is in his narrative style. In every Dickens novel the narrator is as much a character as the people he is describing. Only three of his novels attempted first-person narrative, but even in those Dickens's own views come through. When we read the works, we are frequently being made to look upon the world through Dickens's eyes. He made himself a personality in his lifetime – the reading tours, the international visits, and the banner under his journal titles of 'Conducted by Charles Dickens', all ensured that his audience knew who they were reading. He was as much a part of the sales pitch as his books. Today, Dickens's fame is secured, and often readers approach his works for his reputation. He was certainly not a one-hit wonder. Many classic novels are now more famous than the authors – we talk about *Dracula* and *Frankenstein* more often than Stoker and Shelley. Dickens, on the other hand, is a name that everyone knows, often more than the individual works he wrote. To read a Dickens book today then is to read it knowing full well that it *is* a Dickens book. The author, the man, the persona, all loom over our understanding and appreciation of the book. And often after reading the book we find ourselves wanting to know more about the man who produced it. And ultimately, dear reader, that is what this book is for.

Notes

1 Charles Dickens, *David Copperfield*, ed. by Nina Burgis (Oxford: OUP, 1981), Ch. 1, p. 1.
2 John Forster, *Life of Dickens*, Volume One (London: Chapman & Hall, 1872), p. 1.
3 Simon Callow, *Charles Dickens* (London: Harper Press, 2012), p. 350.
4 Peter Ackroyd, *Dickens*, Abridged Edition (London: Vintage, 1994), pp. xiv–xv.
5 Una Pope-Hennessy, *Charles Dickens* (London: Chatto & Windus, 1945), p. xi.
6 Claire Tomalin, *Charles Dickens* (London: Penguin, 2012), p. 416.
7 Edgar Johnson, *Charles Dickens: His Tragedy and Triumph* (Harmondsworth: Penguin, 1977), p. 7.
8 Melisa Klimaszewski and Melissa Gregory, *Brief Lives: Charles Dickens* (London: Hesperus, 2008), p. 7.
9 Rosemarie Bodenheimer, *Knowing Dickens* (Ithaca: Cornell University Press, 2007).
10 Callow, p. 351; Michael Slater, *Charles Dickens* (New Haven: Yale, 2012).
11 Regenia Gagnier, 'The Global Circulation of Charles Dickens's Novels', *Literature Compass*, Vol. 10, No. 1 (2013), pp. 82–95 (p. 84).
12 Charles Dickens, Letter to Forster, 3 May 1842, in Madeline House, Graham Storey and Kathleen Tillotson (eds.), *The Letters of Charles Dickens*, Volume Three 1842–1832 (Oxford: Clarendon Press, 1974), pp. 231–234 (pp. 231–232).

13 Gladys Storey, *Dickens and Daughter* (London: Frederick Muller, 1939).

14 Charles Dickens, *The Mystery of Edwin Drood*, ed. by Margaret Cardwell (Oxford: OUP, 1982), p. 121.

15 Forster, Volume One, p. 21.

16 Pete Orford, *The Mystery of Edwin Drood: Charles Dickens' unfinished novel and our endless attempts to end it* (Barnsley: Pen & Sword, 2018).

17 Charles Dickens, 'Gone Astray', *Household Words*, No. 177 (13 August 1853), pp. 553–557 (p. 553).

18 Roland Barthes, 'The Death of the Author', in Roland Barthes, *Image, Music, Text*, trans. Stephen Heath (Glasgow: Fontana, 1977), pp. 142–148 (p. 142).

19 Barthes, p. 148.

20 Charles Dickens, 'Letter to John Forster', in Kathleen Tillotson (ed.), *The Letters of Charles Dickens*, Volume Four 1844–1846 (Oxford: Clarendon Press, 1977), pp. 199–200 (p. 200).

21 Jeremy Tambling, *Going Astray: Dickens and London* (Harlow: Pearson Education, 2009), p. 1.

22 Michael Hollington (ed.), *The Reception of Charles Dickens in Europe* (London: Bloomsbury, 2013).

23 See Gagnier.

24 Charles Dickens, *Pictures from Italy*, ed. by Pete Orford (Oxford: OUP, 2023), p. 107.

1

Young Dickens

Focal Point: 1812–1817

Case Study: David Copperfield

Author biographies will inevitably start with a whimper. No-one is born as an author, after all; the skies do not crack, nor do angels sing to announce the moment. Charles Dickens's infancy, compared to the rest of his biography, is not the story of a writer. There are elements of his childhood which can arguably be considered the most normal or universal part of his experience, distinct from the ever-growing reputation and public awareness of his work as a writer that would commence in the 1830s. But rather than being seen as a generic childhood, Dickens's youth is frequently framed by the traumatic episode of his father's imprisonment for debt and his own employment in Warren's Blacking, a factory which produced boot-blacking. Fred Barnard's 1904 illustration conveys the traumatised young Dickens, slumped in a heap either of exhaustion or despair at his worktable [see Figure 1.1]. The inspiration for seeing this as such a prominent part of Dickens's biography stems predominantly from Dickens himself albeit through a tangled web of indirect sources: there is his friend John Forster's biography, which is drawn from Dickens's own brief autobiographical fragment, as well as the refashioning of that fragment by Dickens as the background to his hero's adventure in *David Copperfield*. The relationship of Dickens and Copperfield, creator and creation, will be discussed in due course. However, while the blacking factory certainly provides the headlines for Dickens's youth, it can be seen that Dickens's later anxieties in life stem from the *entirety* of his childhood, precisely because of their lack of grandeur. It is not simply what he *did* experience, in Warren's Blacking, but also what he did *not* experience in his youth – namely, an unbroken education and university experience, or the travel and culture a richer man's son might encounter – which provided the basis for a number of associated insecurities for the adult Dickens to counter while he attempted to establish himself as a gentleman. Throughout Dickens's life there is a hunger, a need to expand his knowledge, skills and reputation: this would manifest as an adult in his renewed vigour to

The Life of the Author: Charles Dickens, First Edition. Pete Orford.

Figure 1.1 Fred Barnard, 'Dickens at the Blacking Warehouse', 1904.

read and develop a library; to learn new languages and travel the world; and his eagerness to become a newspaper editor and man of letters.

But before this extraordinary series of experiences comes the everyday: to repeat, Dickens's childhood began quite normally. He was born in Portsmouth on 7 February 1812 in the family home at 1 Mile End Terrace. His father, John Dickens, was a clerk for the Navy Pay Office, and his mother, Elizabeth Dickens (née Barrow) had moved to Portsmouth shortly after their marriage in 1809 for John's work. They had originally met in 1805 in London, through Elizabeth's brother Thomas, who worked in the office with John in Somerset House. The couple married in 1809 and moved to Portsmouth, where in 1810 their daughter Frances – Dickens's older sister – was born, commonly known in the family as Fanny. John's parents were servants, while Elizabeth's father was, like her husband, a Navy Pay clerk; in 1810 he was found guilty of embezzlement. Such was the family that Dickens was born into: son to a Navy clerk, grandson to servants and another navy clerk charged with embezzlement, and younger brother to a sister two years old. Dickens's full name at his christening was Charles John Huffam Dickens, named respectively after his maternal grandfather, his father, and his godfather Christopher Huffam, who was a gentleman and head of a firm in Portsmouth.

One of the defining traits of Dickens's early life is being on the move. Dickens and his family relocated according to his father's job (and later, in response to his growing debts): Table 1.1 shows at a glance just how much the young

Table 1.1 Dickens's Childhood Homes.

Location	Year entered
Mile-end Terrace, Portsea	1812
16 Hawke Street, Portsea	1812
39 Wish Street, Southsea	1813
Norfolk Street, London	1815
Sheerness	1816
No 2 Ordnance Terrace, Chatham	1816
The Brook, 18 St Mary's Place, Chatham	1821
16 Bayham Street, London	1822
4 Gower Street North, London	1823
Little College Street, London (while family are in Marshalsea)	1824
Lant Street, London	1824
Little College Street, London (again)	1824
Johnson Street, London	1824

Dickens moved home during his first twelve years. Michael Slater suggests, not unreasonably, that the repeated act of relocation, and resultant unsettledness, 'affected Dickens in his later life when he seemed to have some sort of need for constant changes of environment.'[1] This need for change extends beyond environment and into the need for new activities and interests; Dickens's unsettled childhood may well have cultivated the restless spirit that would characterise the older Dickens.

As a navy clerk, Dickens's father was working in interesting times, with Britain engaged in naval conflict with France and the USA. He moved where the job required him to move, but there is also an element of levelling up, with Hawke Street and Wish Street both being larger properties than Dickens's birth-home of Mile End Terrace. Those early years in Portsea and Southsea, both in Portsmouth, might be presumed not to have made a significant impact on the young Dickens simply because of the limited awareness of his infancy, but in his later recollections, Dickens displays a remarkable memory and eye for detail from events of this time. In Forster's biography he notes 'the small front garden to the house at Portsea' which Dickens often recalled, 'where, watched by a nurse through a low kitchen-window almost level with the gravel-walk, he trotted about with something to eat, and his little elder sister with him.'[2] The recollection of this small garden has a nostalgic glow of a simpler life, almost rural in comparison to what would follow. In 1815 they moved to London, Dickens's first experience of the big city. Only a year later they moved again to Sheerness for a brief period, before settling in Chatham, where the family would remain until 1822, a relative period of stability for Dickens. During this time, he began his education, first privately, then at a dame school, then at William Giles's school. Giles, 'a young Baptist minister', took kindly to Dickens; sixteen years later in 1838 Dickens wrote to Giles with copies of his works so far inscribed 'From his old and affectionate pupil', and in the accompanying letter Dickens professed to Giles 'a vivid remembrance of your old kindness and excellence'.[3] Giles in turn had sent Dickens 'a silver snuff-box with admiring inscription to 'the inimitable Boz' 'halfway through the publication of *The Pickwick Papers*.[4] Taken all in all, it suggests that Dickens's time at Giles's school was a happy one which fostered genuine respect and affection between teacher and pupil. When John Dickens next moved job again in June 1822, it is thought that Dickens stayed behind in Chatham to complete the school term before joining them in London.

Who were Dickens's household companions during his early childhood? His parents had several more children after Fanny and Charles: Alfred, born in 1813 and died the same year; Letitia, born in 1816; Harriet, born in 1819; Frederick, born in 1820; and another Alfred, born in March 1822, shortly before the family moved to London (see Table 1.2). Nor were they alone; there would also have been the servants of course, including Mary Weller who is believed to have told the Dickens children ghost stories, and in doing so provided inspiration for Dickens's many phantasmagorical tales, as well as being immortalised in the surname of Pickwick's beloved servant Sam Weller. In addition, Dickens's aunt Mary Allen (his mother's sister) had moved in with the family in Wish Street after being widowed, and she would remain in the household until her second marriage in 1821. Her new husband, Matthew Lamert, had a son from a previous marriage – George Lamert – who would prove to have a significant influence on Dickens, both positive and negative.

Table 1.2 The Dickens Siblings.

Frances (Fanny)	1810–1848
Charles	1812–1870
Alfred	1813–1813
Letitita	1816–1893
Harriet	1819–1824
Frederick	1820–1868
Alfred	1822–1860
Augustus	1827–1866

George Lamert was ten years older than Dickens, yet the two struck up a friendship. George's father and his new bride moved to Ireland, and George stayed in England and lodged with the Dickens family. Living in London, it is widely believed that Lamert took Dickens to the theatre, and also built a toy theatre for him too, fostering an interest in the stage that would last the rest of Dickens's life. Lamert had just attended Sandhurst for military training, but now stepped into an entirely different sphere of employment, going into business with his brother-in-law William Edward Woodd who had just purchased Warren's Blacking. With money proving tight for the Dickens family, Lamert suggested to John Dickens that Charles might find employment at the factory. It was by no means unusual for a child of Dickens's age to enter employment, and from an adult's perspective it can be seen as an act, if not of benevolence, then at least not of malice. Dickens recalled that Lamert 'had kindly arranged to teach [him] something in the dinner hour; from twelve to one', as well as offering to keep him separate from the other boys in the factory, but neither of these suggestions lasted very long:

> But an arrangement so incompatible with counting-house business soon died away, from no fault of his or mine; and for the same reason, my small work-table, and my grosses of pots, my papers, string, scissors, paste-pot and labels, by little and little, vanished out of the recess in the counting-house, and kept company with the other small work-tables, grosses of pots, papers, string, scissors and paste-pots downstairs.[5]

Note how even Dickens concedes the dropping of these arrangements were done 'from no fault of his or mine'; similarly, the moving of the small boy from his isolated position in the counting-house to join the rest of the boys can be equally interpreted as a well-intentioned end to his self-imposed segregation. But from Dickens's perspective, this was a gross betrayal.

One particular reason for Dickens's ire was that his older sister Fanny was able to continue her education even when he could not. She had been admitted to the Royal Academy of Music, and Dickens's parents had their hopes pinned on her, so understandably kept her in education. In contrast, Dickens was a young boy of eleven, just finished school and with no clear plan; if there was an opportunity for the family to increase their income, it was one they had to accept. For Dickens this meant finding himself in an alien environment, doing physical labour while his sister trained in the arts. Years later, when writing *Little Dorrit* (in which Mr Dorrit is a long-standing inmate of the Marshalsea) Dickens gives the titular character, Amy, an older sister called Fanny, who works as a dancer at the theatre while Amy works penitently and diligently to help her father. As poor as both sisters are, there is nonetheless a broad distinction made between the poor life of Amy and the glamour of Fanny's. When Amy visits her sister at the theatre, Fanny is amazed:

> The notion of you among professionals, Amy, is really the last thing
> I could have conceived![6]

Fanny's condescending tone, and implicit sense of Amy not belonging in this
realm, may very well be a lingering resentment on Dickens's part for the
real-life Fanny and his own sense of not belonging. It is also pertinent to
remember a more favourable portrait of a younger child and his older sister
Fanny in *A Christmas Carol*. Scrooge's older sister comes to his school to 'bring
[him] home' now that father says circumstances have changed: 'Father is so
much kinder than he used to be [...] And you're to be a man!'[7] In both fictional
instances, the younger sibling is bearing the brunt of their father's actions.

If the young Dickens hoped his time in the factory would soon end, he was
disappointed. His father's debt troubles increased, and shortly after Dickens
began working in the factory, his father was committed to Marshalsea Debtor's
Prison. Dickens's mother and siblings subsequently moved in to the Marshalsea
with his father, while Dickens remained on the outside, lodging in London and
walking to and from work alone. His trauma of this era is not borne from
poverty so much as shame and isolation. Dickens's recollections of his time in
Warren's is full of pain and remorse, which is elaborated further in *David
Copperfield*, but it is important to note that the job itself was not a bad one. It
paid, and was certainly much safer than several other employments for young
boys. The horror of the role lies entirely in Dickens's shame and self-awareness
of his social descent. Dickens recalled that the other boys in the factory 'always
spoke of me as "the young gentleman"'.[8] This is both praise and damnation:
recognition of his different status, alongside potential mockery for his perceived superiority. It is this that isolated Dickens, this sense of distinction between he and his co-workers, felt no less by him: shame, not poverty, was the
overwhelming horror informing Dickens's memory of this time.

Much of the details of Dickens's time in the blacking factory have been significantly redefined by Michael Allen's recent work. Allen noted how 'the story
of Charles Dickens's childhood is dominated by a single narrative' – Dickens's
own.[9] This was recorded first in a short fragment of autobiography, since lost,
but used by Forster in his subsequent biography, and of course in *David
Copperfield*, but in both cases this narrative as dictated by Dickens had been
neither corroborated nor challenged, so Allen went to historical sources for
clarification, and found several inaccuracies. For example, Forster refers to
Dickens's cousin as James Lamert, not George. As Allen notes, 'it is just possible that Dickens, when it came to writing his fragment of an autobiography,
simply forgot his cousin's name', which seems at odds with our perception of
Dickens's infallible memory but could be explained if 'the young boy didn't
often use his cousin's first name'; or it might be that George preferred to use a

different name.[10] An error in a name is not a fundamental fault, but it high-lights immediately the danger of taking Dickens's own word as gospel. More importantly, the chronology in Forster is wrong. Forster's biography tells us that Dickens went to work in the factory *after* his father's imprisonment, but Allen's re-examination of the historical documents now suggests he was working there *before*. Dickens's autobiographical fragment recalls the factory being at Hungerford Stairs, but the legal documents show the factory had moved out of these premises in 1824 – Dickens must have been working there in 1823. This re-examination of Dickens's testimony is not intended as an attack on him, who in his later reflections is trying to articulate the memories of an eleven-year-old boy from a time of personal trauma; but it does show how naïve we have been in automatically assuming Dickens's account to be true without corroborating it. With this awareness in mind, we can re-evaluate Dickens's narrative with a better awareness of the author's personal bias – his is a subjective account, not an objective one.

Sending the young Dickens to work in a factory was clearly not ideal, but nor was it demonic. This is no longer the narrative of a child sent to work while the father is incarcerated, but a child assisting the father in the aim of staving off incarceration. The family was in dire straits and, at eleven years old, Dickens was of an age to be working. Significantly, it potentially reframes Lamert's interven-tion as a kindly one, but that is not how Dickens saw it. The same cousin who had built him a toy theatre and been a companion through his childhood was forever rewritten as the treacherous destroyer of Dickens's dreams.

If shame defined Dickens's time in the factory, it was shame that got him out of it. Not his own, but his father's, who saw Dickens working in the factory window and felt the shame of his son being so prominent in the position. Dickens recalls that his father and his cousin argued and its probable cause being 'my employment at the window.'[11] Dickens Snr had previously had no issue with his son working there – but being *seen* to work there was too much. It also helped that John Dickens's mother had died and left an inheritance of £450. Charles was free – but further aggravation awaited when his mother wanted him to stay on:

> My mother set herself to accommodate the quarrel, and did so next day. She brought home a request for me to return next morning, and a high character of me, which I am very sure I deserved. My father said I should go back no more, and should go to school. I do not write resentfully or angrily: for I know how all these things have worked together to make me what I am: but I never afterwards forgot, I never shall forget, I never can forget, that my mother was warm for my being sent back.[12]

It is not so much what he says, but how he says it. It is all very well saying he does not write resentfully or angrily, but his repeated assertion that he will never forget betrays the impact of his mother's eagerness to send him back to the factory. And yet, once again, let us reconsider this objectively – he had a position, and a wage, so Dickens's mother was not being unreasonable in suggesting he stay on, especially given the financial insecurity experienced by her husband and father. But if her decision was practical, it was not maternal, and ignored both the misery Dickens felt, and the shame.

Dickens's Self-reflections in the 1840s

In 1838 Dickens was asked by J. H. Kuenzel to provide a few biographical details for an article he was writing for *Konversationslexikon*, a German publication. The account Dickens provides in his letter to Kuenzel is brief and offers the basic information which would inform the public biography of Dickens until after his death:

> I was born at Portsmouth, an English Seaport town principally remarkable for mud, Jews, and Sailors, on the 7th of February 1812. My father holding in those days a situation under Government in the Navy Pay Office, which called him in the discharge of his duty to different places, I came to London, a child of two years old, left it again at six, and then left it again for another Sea Port town – Chatham – where I remained some six or seven years, and then came back to London with my parents and half a dozen brothers and sisters, whereof I was second in seniority.
>
> I had begun an irregular rambling education under a clergyman at Chatham, and finished it at a good school in London – tolerably early, for my father was not a rich man, and I had to begin the world. So I began in a Lawyer's office[.][13]

This is the official story which would resurface in Dickens's obituaries, and it contains a notable omission. That second paragraph in particular jumps from his Chatham education to his London education with no mention of the factory work he engaged in. Even when he admits to his father not being rich, and having to begin the world, he reimagines that beginning as the lawyer's office, not the blacking factory. This was the lie, the secret, which would cause Dickens such anxiety. That gap in his resumé might be contested at any time by a former workmate emerging, or a schoolmate querying dates. The more famous Dickens became, the more scrutiny he faced. As a result, the contradiction of his success and security was that it brought even more insecurity and fear of failure.

Often when we look to interpreting Dickens's childhood we turn to his pseudo-autobiography *David Copperfield*, which proves both insightful and misleading. I shall be using it here with a cautious eye, for as a commentary on Dickens's childhood it tells us two stories: one is the elements there drawn from Dickens's own life, and the other is the framing and reshaping of it by the adult Dickens. Ultimately, *Copperfield* is a work of fiction, and as much as Dickens draws on aspects of his early life in telling David's story, he is not beholden to the truth, and even when he is drawing on actual events, he is still spinning his version of those events. It is particularly telling that in creating David's story, he does not simply repeat his own life but actually makes the circumstances so much worse. David's father dies before he is born, subsequently to be replaced by his villainous stepfather Mr Murdstone who beats David, actively suppresses his imaginative qualities, and ultimately sends him to work in the blacking factory not out of financial desperation but as a further means of punishment combined with the opportunity to remove David from the family home. It hardly requires Sigmund Freud to read several layers of subconscious angst in this narrative. The blacking factory becomes categorically a form of torture, intended only to demean and dispirit the child. There is no sense of community spirit in the factory, or of playfellows for the child. Murdstone is particularly keen to remove David from the family home so that he can instead focus on his own child, David's young stepbrother, who is showered with praise in equal measure to the scorn poured on David. Dickens was not simply revisiting the past, but rewriting and massively exaggerating it. He is inviting pity for his character and his difficult upbringing; if we do choose to read David as a pseudonym for Dickens, then what Dickens is doing here is presenting his childhood as a subject that demands sympathy. Given time, the less savoury memories of his younger life have developed into demons. To what extent is this a conscious decision though? Is the older Dickens, as an experienced writer of fiction, recognising on some level that his own childhood is not sensational enough and requires these additional elements of heightened drama?

Copperfield was written in the late 1840s, at a point when Dickens was firmly established as a great success and, consequently, when aspects of his childhood were causing him ever growing concern. A chance encounter between Forster and 'Mr. Dilke [...] who had been a clerk in the same office in Somerset-house to which Mr. John Dickens belonged' in which Dilke mentioned Dickens had 'had some juvenile employment in a warehouse near the Strand' consolidated Dickens's worst fears that his new society would discover the truth of his childhood.[14] After being confronted by Forster about it, Dickens 'was silent for several minutes' and some weeks later sent Forster what has since become known as the autobiographical fragment, in which he first told Forster about his childhood.[15] But the wider world would remain in ignorance of this until after Dickens's death, when Forster reproduced the fragment in the biography of his friend. *David Copperfield* is therefore as much, if not more of, a product of the 1840s as it is of Dickens's childhood.

Slater notes that Dickens was 'playing with fire' in drawing on his own life for this novel, as several contemporaries recognised autobiographical elements in the text.[16] Journalists recognised Micawber as a parody of Dickens's father; while the trope of a young reporter becoming a novelist ensured a wider awareness of connections to Dickens's own career path. Equally, however, there were elements that were not recognised as autobiographical – David's fervent romancing of Dora, mimicking Dickens's doomed attempts to woo Maria Beadnall, were considered as purely fanciful. And therein lies the rub: parts of the book based on fact can be dismissed as pure fiction, while other parts that are heavily fictionalised can be mistaken for fact. Dickens congratulated himself for his 'very complicated interweaving of truth and fiction' in the early parts of the novel, and we have been trying to unpick that weaving ever since.[17]

Forster is keen to stress the idea of Copperfield as Dickens: 'the poor little lad, with good ability and a most sensitive nature, turned at the age of ten into a "labouring hind" in the service of "Murdstone and Grinby", and conscious already of what made it seem very strange to him that he could so easily have been thrown away at such an age, was indeed himself.'[18] But this is not true. David was never Dickens; he was only ever Dickens's own interpretation of himself. Dickens was not 'thrown away' as David was, but put into employment to help the family by a cousin with good intentions for him. If the blacking factory was a tragedy, then the author was Dickens himself who reframed this time as melodrama, a dark secret of shame out of which England's great author was born. It is a terrific narrative, and all the more beguiling for that reason, but we must be conscious that we are being told this tale of woe by a master story-teller.

Case Study: Charles Dickens and *David Copperfield*

Compare these two passages, the first from John Forster's *Life of Dickens*, and the second from *David Copperfield*.

> No words can express the secret agony of my soul as I sunk into this companionship; compared these every-day associates with those of my happier childhood; and felt my hopes of growing up to be a learned and distinguished man, crushed in my breast. The deep remembrance of the sense I had of being utterly neglected and hopeless; of the shame I felt in my position; of the misery it was to my young heart to believe that, day

by day, what I had learned, and thought, and delighted in, and raised my fancy and my emulation up by, was passing away from me, never to be brought back any more; cannot be written.[19]

––––––––––

No words can express the secret agony of my soul as I sunk into this companionship; compared these henceforth every-day associates with those of my happier childhood – not to say with Steerforth, Traddles, and the rest of those boys; and felt my hopes of growing up to be a learned and distinguished man crushed in my bosom. The deep remembrance of the sense I had, of being utterly without hope now; of the shame I felt in my position; of the misery it was to my young heart to believe that day by day what I had learned, and thought, and delighted in, and raised my fancy and my emulation up by, would pass away from me, little by little, never to be brought back any more; cannot be written.[20]

Reading the two passages, one after the other, it is undeniable that they represent different drafts of the same story. *Copperfield* introduces a few details relevant to the book's narrative, in the mention of David's school friends Steerforth and Traddles, and makes occasional changes to the tense, but ultimately we are reading the same narrative twice over. *Copperfield* was published, like all Dickens's novels, in a serial form, so this chapter would have first appeared in print in August 1849. Forster's *Life of Dickens* was published in three volumes, with this passage appearing in the first volume, published in 1872. However, Forster tells us the passage comes from an autobiographical fragment, now lost, written *before* the publication of *Copperfield*. There is some debate as to when precisely – Forster dates it to sometime after 'March or April of 1847', Ackroyd believes it to be 'just after Fanny's death' in 1848; and Slater imagines various drafts appearing between 1847 and 1849.[21] In turn, the events described in the fragment of course relate to Dickens's childhood in 1824. We are therefore looking at two pieces of writing which account for three different time periods – the 1820s, when the events occurred; the 1840s, when the events were first written about; and the 1870s, when Forster subsequently edited and published the fragment and the world first learned about Dickens's origins.

It is vital that we remember this order when we consider the two texts and their influence upon another: the fragment, as written by Dickens, predates *Copperfield*, but the fragment, as published by Forster, postdates *Copperfield*. Forster based his biography upon his own recollections and letters from Dickens, but also regularly supplements it with reference to Dickens's fiction. Describing Dickens's childhood home in Chatham, Forster refers the reader to *David Copperfield*, in which Dickens imagines David reading a small library of his father's books 'in a little room upstairs':

From that blessed little room, Roderick Random, Peregrine Pickle, Humphrey Clinker, Tom Jones, the Vicar of Wakefield, Don Quixote, Gil Blas, and Robinson Crusoe, came out, a glorious host, to keep me company. They kept alive my fancy, and my hope of something beyond that place and time,—they, and the Arabian Nights, and the Tales of the Genii,—and did me no harm; for whatever harm was in some of them was not there for me; I knew nothing of it.[22]

Forster states that this is 'one of the many passages in *Copperfield* which are literally true'.[23] Fact and fiction are frequently interwoven in Forster's narrative both to inform the story of Dickens's life and, to an extent, justify the prolonged discussion of Dickens's childhood in his biography by asserting its relevance to his written works.

Thus, when we look at the similarity of the fragment and *Copperfield*, there are two explanations. One is that Dickens himself turns directly to the fragment as source material when writing *Copperfield*, and the other is that Forster turns to *Copperfield* as source when editing the fragment, to make the parallels clearer. In the instance of the two passages cited together earlier, the first explanation is the likelier one, but in other instances in Forster, the second explanation should not be fully discounted. The comparison of *Copperfield* to Dickens's own life, as reported in Forster, should be treated with caution, recognising both where Dickens himself has edited his earlier experiences to fit his later fiction, and where Forster has interpreted events of the past shaped by that fiction. But also we need to look at the autobiographical fragment itself as a piece of rhetoric; in writing about his childhood and presenting it to his friend Forster, with the possibility at that stage of wider publication, Dickens was not simply reporting, but framing the narrative to show himself as victim, and the time at Warren's shows that bias of narrative most of all.

With that caveat, consider now the description of Dickens's, then David's, workplace.

The blacking warehouse was the last house on the left-hand side of the way, at old Hungerford-stairs. It was a crazy, tumble-down old house, abutting of course on the river, and literally overrun with rats. Its wainscoted rooms, and its rotten floors and staircase, and the old grey rats swarming down in the cellars, and the sound of their squeaking and scuffling coming up the stairs at all times, and the dirt and decay of the place, rise up visibly before me, as if I were there again.[24]

Murdstone and Grinsby's warehouse was at the water side. It was down in Blackfriars. Modern improvements have altered the place; but it was the last house at the bottom of a narrow street, curving downhill to the river, with some stairs at the end, where people took a boat. It was a crazy old house with a wharf of its own, abutting on the water when the tide was in, and on the mud when the tide was out, and literally overrun with rats. Its panelled rooms, discoloured with the dirt and smoke of a hundred years, I dare say, its decaying floors and staircase, the squeaking and scuffling of the old grey rats down in the cellars, and the dirt and rottenness of the place are things, not of many years ago, in my mind, but of the present instant. They are all before me, just as they were in the evil hour when I went among them for the first time, with my trembling hand in Mr Quinion's.[25]

Note immediately the similarity of details: the crazy old house, abutting on the water, described as 'literally overrun with rats' in both narratives, word-for-word. But beyond, the tone of the description speaks as much about Dicken's response as it does about the building itself. The emphasis upon the rundown state of the building: discoloured, rotten, decaying – this becomes a place of neglect, a place where the young Dickens is sent to be forgotten, his young hopes dashed. There is almost an element of snobbery in his revulsion at how decrepit everything is, but what speaks volumes about his memory of the place is that it is depicted as this forlorn post where all hope is abandoned. Note also the tension between the past and present. In the passages above, Dickens says these visions of the building's degradation 'rise up visibly before me, as if I were there again.' In the correlating *Copperfield* passage he expands further on this, claiming them to be 'things, not of many years ago, in my mind, but of the present instant. They are all before me, just as they were in the evil hour when I went among them for the first time'. This is far more emotive, and speaks more emphatically of the continuing influence this experience had upon Dickens. George Lamert, and Dickens's parents, may have considered this an opportunity for the boy in difficult circumstances, but for Dickens himself the moment is interpreted solely as a betrayal, a punishment and an abandonment. In the fragment he makes this entirely clear. He calls the moment when Lamert first makes the suggestion to his parents to be 'an evil hour for me, as I often bitterly thought', and he writes further of his crushing disappointment that Lamert's suggestion was never countered:[26]

It is wonderful to me how I could have been so easily cast away at such an age. It is wonderful to me, that, even after my descent into the poor little drudge I had been since we came to London, no one had compassion enough on me – a child of singular abilities, quick, eager, delicate, and soon hurt, bodily or mentally – to suggest that something might have been spared, as certainly it might have been, to place me at any common school. Our friends, I take it, were tired out. No one made any sign. My father and mother were quite satisfied. They could hardly have been more so, if I had been twenty years of age, distinguished at a grammar school, and going to Cambridge.[27]

Dickens's indignation is clear: the talk of being cast away reinforces the sense from the previous description of the factory as a place to be abandoned and neglected. Contrasted with this is Dickens's own fervent belief in his 'singular abilities': it is not simply that the blacking factory was a terrible place to be, but that it was a particularly terrible place for Dickens, of all people, to be. The reference to being 'twenty years of age, distinguished at a grammar school, and going to Cambridge' speaks of Dickens's preferred upbringing, had he had the opportunity. Again, it is important to note that this fragment is written by Dickens in the 1840s, not the 1820s when it happened, so that longing for a university education may well be informed by his subsequent moving among literary circles, and a sense of his own shortcomings in that society, rather than accurately portraying his hopes when still a child.

The outrage felt by Dickens when writing about his time at Warren's is palpable in the autobiographical fragment, especially in the betrayal of his parents who 'were quite satisfied' with arrangements. We will never know if this outrage was simmering throughout the 1820s and 1830s, or if it came bursting out in a rage in the 1840s as he began to reflect back on his life in comparison to the upbringing of his friends. It is certainly clear that shame, not poverty, dictates his response. Dickens was a successful man in the 1840s, and a poor upbringing might only speak further of his triumph in rising to the top. But the shame of neglect, of not being sent on to school and university; this is what truly enrages him. So it is unsurprising to see that when Dickens fictionalises his autobiography for *David Copperfield* he does not simply retell the horrors of his childhood, but dramatically increases the woes of his protagonist to make the narrative even more tragic. Dickens grew up in a loving family, with a father imprisoned for debt; David's father dies before he is born, to be replaced by a wicked step-father who beats him, and his mother dies during his childhood, leaving David penniless and abandoned by the villainous Murdstone. Dickens gives free rein to his imagination to allow the depth of his own shame to dictate the atrocities David has to endure. We will never know the exact details of the conversation between Dickens, his father and Lamert when Warren's was first proposed; all we have instead is the exaggerated version between Murdstone and David:

'I suppose you know, David, that I am not rich. At any rate, you know it now. You have received some considerable education already. Education is costly; and even if it were not, and I could afford it, I am of opinion that it would not at all be advantageous to you to be kept at a school. What is before you, is a fight with the world; and the sooner you begin it, the better.'

I think it occurred to me that I had already begun it, in my poor way; but it occurs to me now, whether or no.[28]

Forster makes an explicit link between the 'crisis of [Dickens's] father's affairs in fact which is ascribed in fiction to Mr. Micawber's', confirming the idea many readers have since suspected that the optimistic, but unpractical, Mr Micawber is a fictionalised rendering of Dickens's father.[29] But in this moment it is Murdstone who represents the demonic side of Dickens's father as perceived by the young Dickens himself. Murdstone claims to be taking David out of school because he cannot afford it, but this is shown to be untrue given the life Murdstone and his sister are now leading in David's home, once the property of his father, then his mother, and now owned by Murdstone, not David. Murdstone then confirms that he would still not send David to school even if he could afford it. It is possible in this to read the reasoning and excuses of Dickens's father, rendered into monstrosities from Dickens's perspective. For Dickens's father education would have been costly, but John Dickens may well have tried to present the sending of his son to Warren's as an opportunity rather than necessity, for his own pride as well as his son's. In *Copperfield* the moment is one that screams of resentment and unfair treatment. Once again there is the awareness of the narrator reflecting on himself back then in the final line 'it occurs to me now'. The moment may be from David's past, but the anger comes from the present. So too with the autobiographical fragment we need to look at the events described as belonging to the 1820s, and the tone and narrative belonging to the 1840s.

The story of Dickens's childhood is therefore a narrative told, and retold, many times – and that retelling has confused rather than clarified. In *David Copperfield* we are not presented with Dickens's past, but rather with Dickens's interaction with his past. The narration is unreliable, but reveals more than Dickens meant to reveal. In his exaggerations and lamentations, Dickens betrays his own embarrassment and insecurity. Whatever is untrue or exaggerated, Dickens's shame is real. This sense of shortcomings in his upbringing would prompt him to forever push himself. In the next chapter we will see how upon reaching adulthood, Dickens began his frantic climb to the top of the literary sphere.

Notes

1 Michael Slater, *Charles Dickens* (New Haven: Yale, 2011), p. 4.

2 John Forster, *The Life of Charles Dickens*, Volume One (London: Chapman & Hall, 1872), pp. 2–3.

3 Forster, p. 12; Charles Dickens, Letter to the Rev. William Giles, August 1838, in Madeline House and Graham Storey (eds.), *The Letters of Charles Dickens*, Volume One 1820–1839 (Oxford: Clarendon Press, 1974), p. 429.

4 Forster, Vol. 1, p. 13.

5 Forster, Vol. 1, p. 32.

6 Charles Dickens, *Little Dorrit*, ed. by Harvey Peter Sucksmith (Oxford: OUP, 1979), Ch. 20, p. 227

7 Charles Dickens, 'A Christmas Carol', in Robert Douglas-Fairhurst (ed.), *A Christmas Carol and Other Christmas Books* (Oxford: OUP, 2008), Stave 2, p. 33.

8 Forster, Volume One, p. 38.

9 Michael Allen, *Charles Dickens and the Blacking Factory* (St. Leonards: Oxford-Stockley, 2011), p. 1.

10 Allen, p. 89.

11 Dickens in Forster, Vol. 1, p. 48.

12 Dickens in Forster, Vol. 1, p. 49.

13 Charles Dickens, Letter to J H Kuenzel, July 1838 in *Letters*, Vol. 1, pp. 423–4 (p.423).

14 Forster, Vol. 1, p. 27.

15 Forster, Vol. 1, p. 27.

16 Slater, p. 29.

17 Dickens, 'Letter to John Forster', 10 July 1849, in Graham Storey and K. J. Fielding (eds.), *The Letters of Charles Dickens*, Volume Five 1847–1849 (Oxford: Clarendon, 1981), p. 569 (p. 569).

18 Forster, Vol. 1, p. 28.

19 Forster, Vol. 1, p. 33.

20 *Copperfield*, Chapter 11, p. 133.

21 Forster, p. 27; Ackroyd, p. 305; Slater, p. 278.

22 *Copperfield*, Ch. 4, p. 53.

23 Forster, Vol. 1, p. 9.

24 Dickens in Forster, Vol. 1, p. 31.

25 *Copperfield*, Ch. 11, pp. 132–3.

26 Dickens in Forster, Vol. 1, p. 30.

27 Dickens in Forster, Vol. 1, p. 31.

28 *Copperfield*, Ch. 10, p. 131.

29 Forster, Vol. 1, p. 16.

2

Dickens the Reporter

Focal Point: 1827–1836

Case Study: The Pickwick Papers

Dickens's Early Career

Charles Dickens's professional writing career began as a reporter; in fact it is believed that his first involvement with the press was as early as 'some time after March 1825 and before October 1826', when he would have been only thirteen or fourteen years of age.[1] This sounds quite a remarkable feat and it warrants some explanation. His father John had retrained as a reporter after his release from the Marshalsea debtor's prison, working for *The British Press*, and it is this paper to which Dickens contributed 'penny-a-line stuff'.[2] This type of writing is as functional as the name suggests: brief reports detailing smaller incidents, mostly crimes, deaths, accidents and fires that did not warrant the headlines or the attention of the permanent staff. Our knowledge of this writing is due solely to a brief note in the biography of Samuel Carter Hall; though the articles themselves will have survived, they were published anonymously and so we have no way of conclusively identifying any of Dickens's early writing from the many other articles in *The British Press*; nor could we realistically expect to find any great undiscovered literature even if we could deduce which were Dickens's.[3] The work he was doing as young teenager was reporting first and foremost, where his own voice had to play second fiddle to the facts. It provided extra income while Dickens was still a schoolchild at Wellington House Academy; but the fact that after leaving school Dickens then sought employment as a clerk rather than a journalist suggests that the writing fever had not gripped him yet.

His employment as a lawyer's clerk seems to have come primarily from his mother's efforts (the same mother who Dickens forever recalled as wanting him to stay employed at Warren's Blacking factory). Her aunt, Elizabeth Charlton, kept a boarding house at which one of the tenants was 'a young

The Life of the Author: Charles Dickens, First Edition. Pete Orford.
© 2023 John Wiley & Sons Ltd. Published 2023 by John Wiley & Sons Ltd.

solicitor called Edward Blackmore.'[4] Dickens's mother sought employment for him, and Blackmore provided it. Dickens would work at the firm of Ellis and Blackmore from May 1827 through to November 1828; a short time relative to his writing career, but an informative one. His fiction would later revel in the world of the law, from the trial of Pickwick vs Bardell in *The Pickwick Papers*, through the infamously complicated case of Jarndyce vs Jarndyce in *Bleak House*, right through to the character of Mr Grewgious, solicitor, in his final work *The Mystery of Edwin Drood*. As with his previous work for *The British Press*, Dickens was writing for a living, but the nature of that writing was reporting and fact, rather than rhetoric and fancy. A solicitor's clerk was a promising position for a young man, with good prospects for progression; and it would certainly have been a more positive outlook for the Dickens family than the blacking factory and debtor's prison just a few years before. But it was not to be: Dickens left Ellis and Blackmore to work for another solicitor, Charles Molloy, then after just a few months left the profession completely to try something new.

We do not know precisely why he left. It is entirely plausible that Dickens was seeking something more creative at this time; although it's equally possible, being just sixteen years of age, that he was still undecided about what he wanted to do. A few years after this he would apply to audition for the stage, so he was by no means fixed on a writing career; even if he had been, he was in no position to simply write his first novel and expect immediate success and financial security. Whatever the reason, on leaving Molloy, Dickens trained to be a reporter. In this decision he was following in his father's footsteps, and like his father he sought the help of John Barrow, Dickens's uncle. Barrow had trained Dickens's father in shorthand, and now he did the same for Dickens too. By 1829 Dickens was working as a freelance reporter in Doctors' Commons. To clarify (and to repeat a refrain every academic has had to say of themselves countless times), they were not *that* kind of Doctor. In this instance, 'Doctor' refers to their academic qualifications: they were doctors of law. The Doctors' Commons were three courts: they did not deal with sensational crimes but on more routine legal issues like contesting wills, although Slater notes they also dealt with 'people accused of misbehaving in church or at vestry (parochial) meetings' who 'were punished with fines which they much resented and periods of excommunication about which they cared nothing at all.'[5] Similar to the reporting he had done earlier for *The British Press*, Dickens was not dealing with the sensational, landmark stuff of national import, but instead was getting an insight into the everyday despairs and frustrations felt by those in the court and confounded by the court itself. He writes of this in *David Copperfield*, where 'Night after night' David would 'record predictions that never come to pass, professions that are never fulfilled, explanations that

are only meant to mystify.'[6] David feels that he 'wallow[s] in words'; an interesting image that reflect on the young Dickens in his early writing career.[7] He
was making a living by his pen, but his words were having no effect, reporting
on things that were left unpassed, unfulfilled and mystifying.

After working freelance in Doctors' Commons, Dickens began reporting in
Parliament, working for *The Mirror of Parliament* in 1831 and *The True Sun*
soon after. The time spent recording and reporting upon the words of others
may not have offered him the same creativity of his later career, yet the experience proved fundamental to it. In addition to the life experience he was gaining listening to the steady flow of cases and speeches each day, he was also
unknowingly changing the way he thought about words. To be a reporter,
Dickens needed to be adept in shorthand. The system his uncle taught him
was Gurney's Brachygraphic system, which is fiendishly difficult to interpret,
and this both explains and is exacerbated by the system generally falling out
of use. Dickens would use it to the end of his career though, even teaching it
in turn to Arthur Stone in 1859. The implications of Dickens's adeptness in
Gurney's system went largely unnoticed until Hugo Bowles's ground-breaking
work in *Dickens and the Stenographic Mind*, in which he shows how learning
to write in shorthand effectively rewired Dickens's approach to letters and
sounds in a way that would continue to echo through his career: 'he acquired
an unusual, letter-based mode of processing language which would later
come to influence certain aspects of his writing process', providing him with a
'cognitive advantage'.[8]

The Gurney system allocates a symbol to represent each letter of the alpha-
bet. When taking down dictation, the writer drops out all of the vowels, and just
records the consonants. Hence 'Marley was dead: to begin with' would become
'Mrly ws dd: t bgn wth'. This would then be written using the symbols of the
Gurney system, which is further complicated in that symbols were not written
separately, but joined together to make a new symbol unique to that particular
cluster. Dickens would therefore have been sat in Doctors' Commons reducing
the language to these clusters of consonants all day. But then comes stage
two. To prepare the report, Dickens would then have to consult his notes and
decipher them, inserting the missing vowels. Would 'dd' be 'dead', or 'died', or
'deed'? This would require additional mental gymnastics as Dickens worked
from his own memory supplemented by the context of the writing. Bowles
argues that writing in this manner encouraged Dickens to see patterns between words based upon their consonants; moreover, some consonant clusters
appear repeatedly through Dickens's writing with a frequency far above the
norm: 'For example, Dickens uses the ICC [initial consonant cluster] /tr/ for
the beginnings of the surnames *Trabb*, *Traddles*, *Trent*, *Trotter* and *Trotwood*,
while the Victorian corpus contains only the single surname *Travis*.'[9] In *The*

Pickwick Papers we can see Dickens's wordplay at work with the curious inscription Mr Pickwick discovers on a stone that reads:

+

BILST

UM

PSHI

S. M.

ARK

Reading the letters together we can quickly decipher, as Mr Blotton does, 'the simple construction of "BILL STUMPS, HIS MARK;" and that Mr. Stumps, being little in the habit of original composition, and more accustomed to be guided by the sound of words than by the strict rules of orthography, had omitted the concluding "L" of his Christian name.'[10] Pickwick and his friends treat this idea with contempt, the joke being that Pickwick has instead proclaimed the stone as an ancient treasure of great archaeological interest and presented it as such to the Royal Antiquarian Society. While Pickwick is triumphant within the narrative, the reader is in no doubt that Blotton's reading is correct, but to interpret the cluster of letters into that meaning requires a different way of thinking about words; a way that would be familiar to the reporter Dickens who had spent his working life staring at, and interpreting, such clusters.

Dickens was now a young man, and developed an interest in a banker's daughter, Maria Beadnell, which was not to be requited. The family aspirations were also growing; in 1832 they moved to 18 Bentinck Street in Marylebone, where they would perform amateur dramatics, including some written by Dickens himself. In 1833, with the support once again of his uncle John Barrow, Dickens began reporting for the *Morning Chronicle* and later its sister paper, the *Evening Chronicle*. He would write for the *Chronicle* for the next three years, but not solely as a reporter. Since 1833 he had begun to write occasional short fictional sketches in the press, under the pseudonym of 'Boz'. This name comes from his youngest brother, Augustus, born in 1827, who Dickens nicknamed Moses. Unable to pronounce his own nickname, the young Augustus unintentionally coined 'Boz', which Dickens would subsequently use as his pen-name. So Dickens began a double life, reporting for the press while writing these fanciful tales of modern life. Of course, the pseudonym soon proved to be an open secret, but for the wider world, the name of Dickens remained unknown even while people were enjoying and praising *Sketches by Boz*.

The sketches build upon Dickens's reporting career while allowing his imagination free rein at last. They present scenes from London and the parishes that would be familiar to his readers, but written about with a charm and fancy for which he would become famous. The first, 'A Dinner at Poplar Walk' (later renamed

'Mr. Minns and his Cousin') is one of the more narrative-based sketches, telling a short farcical tale about the bachelor Minns who is invited to his cousin Mr Budden's house in the hope that Minns might patronise Budden's son, only for a catalogue of things to go wrong. The final paragraph is not so far removed from the sort of brief reporting Dickens might have written elsewhere:

> It was somewhere about three o'clock in the morning, when Mr Augustus Minns knocked feebly at the street door of his lodgings in Tavistock Street, cold, wet, cross, and miserable. He made his will next morning, and his professional man informs us, in that strict confidence in which we inform the public, that neither the name of Mr Octavius Budden, nor or Mrs Amelia Budden, nor of Master Alexander Augustus Budden, appears therein.[11]

The sketches started as a disparate set of individual pieces published sporadically across several publications: *Monthly Magazine, Bell's Weekly Magazine* and the *Morning Chronicle*; but they grew in popularity, and when George Hogarth asked Dickens in 1835 to write a sketch for the *Evening Chronicle* Dickens pushed for more, and an agreement was instead made for him to produce a series of sketches. From this point their identity as a coherent group began to develop, eventually being anthologised and published in a volume format: Boz became a celebrated newcomer on the literary scene.

The success of the sketches led to Dickens being commissioned to write a new series, designed to accompany and showcase the comic illustrations of the artist Robert Seymour, who was a much bigger name than Dickens at this point. However, through a combination of tragedy and Dickens's own tenacity, the project would prove to be the success that made his name famous, not Seymour's. Originally, the idea was that Seymour would produce illustrations that played to his strengths, namely humorous portrayals of sporting gentlemen having mishaps. *The Pickwick Papers*, or to give it its full title, *The Posthumous Papers of the Pickwick Club containing a faithful record of the perambulations, perils, travels, adventures and sporting transactions of the corresponding members*, thus presented the hero Samuel Pickwick and his three friends – the poet Mr Snodgrass, the helpless sportsman Mr Winkle, and the hopeless romantic Mr Tupman – as they travelled around Southeast England getting into various farcical mishaps. The work would be published in a serial format, with each issue appearing monthly. The title page of the first monthly number on April 1836 announced that the papers were 'Edited by Boz', with 'Four illustration by Seymour': note how Seymour only needs his surname listed, while Dickens is still being presented by his pseudonym, and credited as an editor rather than author, as though the adventures were writing themselves. Indeed, this was essentially the plan, that Dickens's words would just be filler for the illustrations. Dickens clearly had other ideas, as the early numbers already show deviations from the plan: Pickwick begins his adventure in London before venturing to Rochester, where Tupman attends a ball and Winkle is mistakenly challenged to a duel; hardly the stuff of sporting mishaps.

The work would undergo a more radical change yet when Seymour committed suicide on 20 April 1836, just a few weeks after the first number had been published. The project might easily have ground to a halt there and then; there were a few illustrations provided already by Seymour for the second number, but ultimately this work built around Seymour's illustrations had now lost its artist. Moreover, the sales for the first number had been disappointing. But Dickens took the opportunity to push forward. A new illustrator would be appointed, and to save costs he suggested that the number of illustrations be reduced from four a month down to two; this in turn meant there was more space for Dickens to fill with his text, increasing the pages from 24 to 32.[12] The dynamics now shifted; it was Dickens's project, not Seymour's, with the new artist Hablot Knight Browne accompanying him with illustrations, rather than Dickens writing to complement the illustrations. Shortly after, Dickens introduced a new regular character – Sam Weller – a cheeky, lovable cockney who would become Pickwick's servant and introduce a master–servant dynamic reminiscent of Don Quixote and Sanzo Pancha (and later echoed in P. G. Wodehouse's Jeeves and Wooster).

The Pickwick Papers was a phenomenal success, one that would bring fame and fortune to Dickens, and also become the benchmark which his later works would forever be compared to in his lifetime. But it is not true to say that he then left reporting to engage full-time in fiction writing: journalism and the serial press would continue to be a part of his career for the rest of his life. While *Pickwick* was published in self-contained monthly instalments, his next book *Oliver Twist* was published in the pages of *Bentley's Miscellany*, nestled among the other fiction and articles: his future novels would all be published in one of these two formats, either as self-standing monthly numbers, or as smaller, weekly instalments published in a magazine. It was only when the final number was published that the complete work would be available to buy as a book (much like buying a DVD box-set after the last episode of a TV series has aired). Even as a novelist then, Dickens continued to be a presence in the serial press. Furthermore, his involvement with *Bentley's* was not merely as contributor, but editor as well, from January 1837 through to 1838. It is clear then that Dickens's launch as a novelist was by no means seen as confirmation of his career, but rather that Dickens continued to explore different avenues of working in the press. This model of literary journalism alongside his novel-writing would be one that would persist throughout his career. Today we think of Dickens primarily as a novelist, but in his lifetime readers would be experiencing his writing in a number of formats and publications.

Later Journalistic Endeavours

Dickens's career began in the press, but even after his success as a novelist was confirmed, he continued to work in various fields of the press. After the publication of his third novel, *Nicholas Nickleby*, Dickens tried a new model for his writing: a weekly miscellany containing several works of fiction, some of which would be standalone stories, others being printed in two or three parts, and others still being the first of a promised series of themed stories. It was replicating the format of various existing miscellanies, but the difference in this instance is that Dickens was writing it all. *Master Humphrey's Clock* appeared in print from April 1840 through to November 1841; the concept for the work was that Master Humphrey had a small circle of friends who all enjoyed writing, with their endeavours being stored in the bottom of a grandfather clock, from which Master Humphrey would select a handful of tales each week to share with his readers. Humphrey was 'editor' in the same way Boz had been for *Pickwick*. Not only did Dickens write all the stories, he also wrote the letters to the editor too. In this instant, the experiment failed: his readers wanted more novels from him and sales were dwindling. Dickens introduced Mr Pickwick into Master Humphrey's inner circle, but even this was not enough; however, a new tale in the journal, *The Old Curiosity Shop*, proved more popular, so much so that Dickens dropped all framing narrative in future instalments and *Master Humphrey's Clock* consisted solely of the next instalment of *The Old Curiosity Shop*; and when that ended the journal then published his next novel *Barnaby Rudge*, after which a short postscript informed the reader of Master Humphrey's death, and the closing of the journal. Dickens's readers had made it clear that what they really wanted was more novels.

Dickens nonetheless persisted with journalism alongside his fiction writing. In 1842 he wrote up his travels in America as *American Notes*, and four years later produced another travelogue on Italy, *Pictures from Italy*. Initially conceived as another book, this Italian travelogue first appeared in a newspaper, primarily because Dickens had been approached once more to be an editor, for a new publication *The Daily News*. As a newspaper, this was unlike other journals Dickens had edited, or would go on to edit, with a greater focus on reporting and correspondence. In addition to adding his own accounts of travel, he also contributed several letters discussing capital punishment. Ultimately, the project was a bad fit for Dickens and he walked away from the paper in February 1846, just a few weeks after launching it, having found the pressures of daily publication too much, and having also felt affronted by what he considered to be the intrusive nature of the publishers Bradbury and Evans, who second-guessed some of his appointments to the team and frequently expressed concern about profits and expenses. It was William Bradbury in particular who received the bulk of his ire, with Dickens writing that 'his interposition between me and almost every act of mine at the newspaper office, was as disrespectful to me as injurious to the enterprise'.[13] There has been much debate about why Dickens agreed to edit in the first place, and some consideration of whether it was always intended to be a short appointment, to launch the paper under a celebrity editor and then pass the torch once it had made its own name; but even if this is true there is no doubt his leaving the paper was still earlier than expected. Editing *The Daily News* offered Dickens a steady income – even at this point he was concerned about finances and security – but moreover it offered the status of being a man of letters. To be an editor, rather than just an author, had an element of prestige to it.

Dickens's next attempt to edit a journal would prove far more successful and enduring. This time he would learn from the past and play to his strengths. *Household Words* would be a weekly miscellany including a mix of serialised fiction and imaginative articles: Dickens would *not* be writing it all himself, as he had for *Master Humphrey's Clock*, but the house style was definitively Dickensian. The majority of pieces were published anonymously (the occasional exceptions being where a major piece of fiction was serialised, and the author's previous works were used as a form of advertisement and recommendation). The first issue, published on 30 March 1850, offers a varied mix of pieces:

'A Preliminary Word' (by Charles Dickens)
Lizzie Leigh Chapter One (by Elizabeth Gaskell)
'Valentine's Day at the Post Office' (by Charles Dickens and W. H. Wills)
'Abraham and the Fire-Worshipper' (by James Hunt)
'The Amusements of the People' (by Charles Dickens)
'An Incident in the Life of Mademoiselle Clairon' (by George Hogarth)
'The Wayside Well' (by William Allingham)
'A Bundle of Emigrant's Letters' (by Caroline Chisholm and Charles Dickens)
'Milking in Australia' (Samuel Sidney and John Sidney)
'Metal in Sea-Water' (author unknown)

The format for each issue would be one piece of major fiction running through as a serial, with individual non-fiction articles supporting it. In 1859 Dickens ceased editing *Household Words* after a disagreement with the publishers, and started a new journal *All the Year Round* which operated on exactly the same model. Both journals were published in two columns, and each article began immediately where the other finishes, be it halfway down a column or right at the bottom, so that readers were encouraged to read the whole thing rather than flicking through and browsing each page individually. With the articles all published anonymously, you could never be sure who you were reading, although several authors would later republish their work in subsequent anthologies of their writing or, in the case of the serialised fiction, as a novel, but ultimately there was only one name readers could be guaranteed to see each week. There, directly under the title of the journal each week was the phrase 'Conducted by Charles Dickens'. Dickens was now not only a novelist, but a conductor of other writers and their work as well, and while there was more variety of writing in the main serialised fiction each week, the smaller articles all worked to the journal's style, creating works of imagination in the Dickensian vein. It is important to note however that, as much as Dickens loomed over the project, both journals launched and supported the careers of several prominent authors and their works, seeing the debut of *North and South* and *Cranford* by Elizabeth Gaskell; and of several works by Dickens's friend Wilkie Collins, including his two most famous novels *The Woman in White* and *The Moonstone*, not to mention Dickens's own novels *Hard Times, A Tale of Two Cities* and *Great Expectations*.

Dickens would continue to edit, or conduct, *All the Year Round* until his death. He was greatly supported in both this, and *Household Words* before it, by his subeditor W H Wills, which is discussed further in Chapter 9. The key point to be made for now is that journalism was not just Dickens's gateway into writing, but an essential part of his career for the majority of his life. John Drew's work *Dickens the Journalist* made an important intervention in stressing the significance of Dickens's journalistic writing, and Drew's subsequent work in setting up the *Dickens Journals Online* site, which offers free access to the entirety of *Household Words* and *All the Year Round*, allows us to once more explore these miscellanies and their vast horde of articles.[14] Dickens began as writer of 'penny-a-line stuff', and ended as the conductor of his own journal.

Case Study: Reporting the Eatanswill Election in *the Pickwick Papers*

There is some ambiguity over what should be considered as Dickens's first novel. The sketches were his first foray into published fiction, but there is no overarching narrative to connect the various tales and observations. This then presents *The Pickwick Papers* as the next candidate, and its overwhelming success certainly makes it the one most regularly cited as his first work of fiction. Yet as we have seen from the manner of *Pickwick*'s origin, this was not originally conceived as a novel, but as a running series of humorous anecdotes to accompany Seymour's illustrations. The beginning of the story is open-ended and linear, as Pickwick and his friends stumble from one town – and disaster – to the next. It is only as the story develops that a larger narrative emerges and a sense of a novel, rather than a series, emerges.

When we read *Pickwick* then, it is better to appreciate the first half of it as a series of sketches, and mini-adventures, written in the style of Boz's previous sketches and once again approximating the sense of reportage. The announcement on the title page that Boz is the editor allows the narrator to adopt the tone of reporter and historian, compiling the papers of Mr Pickwick and commenting on them as he relays them. While the framing narrative meant that the novel was set in the recent past, the actions were also increasingly contemporary, as Dickens used the serial format to allow his characters to move through the year at the same pace as his readers. In January, readers could see how Pickwick and his friends had enjoyed Christmas; in March the story told us how Sam Weller had sent a card for Valentine's day; each month then the reader was treated to an update of what the characters had been doing for the past four weeks.

The rambling, picaresque nature of the narrative provides many changes of scene and small episodic interludes, each one contributing to the sense of Dickens, or Boz, as roving reporter. The cricket match of Dingley Dell, or the miliary manoeuvres at Rochester, could easily have been separated out and written as another sketch by Boz, rather than an integral part of a tightly meshed narrative. The conceit of *Pickwick* not only allowed Dickens to continue in the same vein as his earlier sketch-work, but to present a wide panorama of English life, from the aforementioned cricket match to the court report on the trial of Bardell vs Pickwick which clearly draws upon his own experience in Doctors' Commons. Any one of these moments displays how Dickens's journalistic background influences his writing, but for now, as an example, let's consider the arrival of Pickwick and his friends at Eatanswill in time for the local elections, and see how Dickens's reporter heritage can be seen in his narrative of events there. The elections are discussed in Chapter 13, titled 'Some Account of Eatanswill; of the State of Parties therein; and of the Election of a Member to serve in Parliament for that ancient, loyal, and patriotic Borough', which appeared in the fifth monthly number, first published in August 1836. The opening of the chapter reinforces the illusion of the events being a real historical moment noted down by Pickwick, with the narrator demonstrating his investigative journalism skills:

> We will frankly acknowledge, that up to the period of our being first immersed in the voluminous papers of the Pickwick Club, we had never

heard of Eatanswill; we will with equal candour admit, that we have in vain searched for proof of the actual existence of such a place at the present day. Knowing the deep reliance to be placed on every note and statement of Mr Pickwick's, and not presuming to set up our recollection against the recorded declaration of that great man, we have consulted every authority, bearing upon the subject, to which we could possibly refer. We have traced every name in Schedules A and B, without meeting that of Eatanswill; we have minutely examined every corner of the Pocket Country Maps issued for the benefit of society by our distinguished publishers, and the same result has attended our investigation.[15]

This opening has no direct purpose to the plot of the story. Dickens could easily have cut the entire passage with no harm done to our understanding of the narrative. No, its significance is in the tone; it is entirely stylistic, placing the succeeding events in the frame of a newspaper article, of a pseudo-historical moment being presented before the reader. Dickens no sooner invents a location than he starts stressing to his readers that it is invented. The narrator's endeavours to find the town in question, and his fervent desire to pre-emptively counter any queries on his reader's part, has a sense of damage control about it, as though he is trying to avoid a scandal. The name itself is fairly obvious as a joke, and Malcolm Andrews compares it to the equally preposterous 'Guzzledown' in William Hogarth's series of election paintings done in the 1750s.[16] For *Pickwick*'s narrator, it is presumed that Pickwick himself has deliberately changed the name to avoid offence to its inhabitants (ironically, since the publication of *Pickwick*, Ipswich and Sudbury have both proudly announced themselves as the real-life inspiration for Eatanswill). The narrator, having displayed his credentials by listing all the efforts he has made to ascertain the truth, draws a line under it, saying 'We will not, therefore, hazard a guess upon the subject, but will at once proceed with this history': the insistence upon the falsity of the name inversely implies the truthfulness of the events, which are now proclaimed as 'history'.[17]

What makes the Eatanswill elections particularly interesting in *Pickwick* is that they in turn are being reported upon by the town's two papers, who then become part of the narrative too: Dickens is reporting on the reporters. This allows the chapter to not only focus on the absurdity and hypocrisy of the politicians, but also of the papers whose job it was to impartially report on them:

Of course, it was essentially and indispensably necessary that each of the powerful parties should have its own chosen organ and representative: and, accordingly, there were two newspapers in the town – the Eatanswill Gazette and the Eatanswill Independent; the former advocating

Blue principles, and the latter conducted on grounds decidedly Buff. Fine newspapers they were. Such leading articles and such spirited attacks! – 'Our worthless contemporary, the Gazette' – 'That disgraceful and dastardly journal, the Independent' – 'That false and scurrilous print, the Independent' – 'That vile and slanderous calumniator, the Gazette;' these, and other spirit-stirring denunciations were strewn plentifully over the columns of each, in every number, and excited feelings of the most intense delight and indignation in the bosoms of the townspeople.[18]

'Fine newspapers' is clearly intended to be ironic, but is entirely true. Both the *Gazette* and the *Independent* are doing precisely what they intend to do, to excite the townspeople with 'spirit-stirring denunciations' and sway the course of the election. Those reporting on events were trying to influence and shape those events. But Dickens did not just turn his wry eye to the papers en masse, but to the individuals working for them too. When Pickwick meets Mr Pott, the editor of the *Gazette*, it soon becomes apparent that he holds a high opinion of himself and his work, which Dickens delights in attacking. Though Pott proclaims 'The press is a mighty engine, sir,' there is little in his actions or mannerism to confirm this idea. His attempt to discuss it further quickly descends into an incoherent and endless ramble, brought to a close only by Pickwick interrupting:[19]

> 'But I trust, sir,' said Pott, 'that I have never abused the enormous power I wield. I trust, sir, that I have never pointed the noble instrument which placed in my hands, against the sacred bosom of private life, or the tender breast of individual reputation; – I trust, sir, that I have devoted my energies to – to endeavours – humble they may be, humble I know they are – to instil those principles of – which – are –'[20]

When Mr Pott then volunteers to read out a selection of his previous articles to Pickwick that evening, the result is hardly positive, with Pickwick falling asleep, but Dickens's reporting of it delights in showcasing the same truth-twisting and subjectivity that the *Gazette* and *Independent* are clearly guilty of: 'We have every reason to believe that he was perfectly enraptured with the vigour and freshness of the style; indeed Mr. Winkle has recorded the fact that his eyes were closed, as if with excess of pleasure, during the whole time of their perusal.'[21] Dickens could simply have said 'Mr. Pickwick fell asleep', but instead, the objective truth of Pickwick falling asleep while Pott drones on is repackaged and presented as a favourable review of 'the vigour and freshness' of Pott's writing. It is written almost as though it could be Pott himself reporting on the evening, championing the quality of the *Gazette*'s writing. The subtlety of Dickens's narrative here is that the joke relies entirely upon the reader understanding what is actually happening, rather than what is being reported. It is teaching good critical media skills, to unpick the bias in the narrative, sift out the personal opinions, and identify the key facts: Pickwick's eyes were closed the entire time.

The reporting style can also be seen later in the chapter when election day begins and the tense slips between past and present. Pickwick and his friends are unable to see exactly what is happening over the crowd, so their host Mr Perker, who is the assistant to the Blue candidate Samuel Slumkey, offers an unfolding narrative of events, exactly as we might hear today from a roving reporter as the story unfolds:

> 'He has come out,' said little Mr. Perker, greatly excited; the more so as their position did not enable them to see what was going forward.
> Another cheer, much louder.
> 'He has shaken hands with the men,' cried the little agent.
> Another cheer, far more vehement.
> 'He has patted the babies on the head,' said Mr. Perker, trembling with anxiety.
> A roar of pleasure that rent the air.
> 'He has kissed one of 'em!' exclaimed the delighted little man.
> A second roar.
> 'He has kissed another,' gasped the excited manager.
> A third roar.
> 'He's kissing them all!' screamed the enthusiastic little gentleman.[22]

Note that Perker himself cannot see what is happening either; everything is inferred by the sound of the crowd and Perker's confident interpretation of that. Just like the *Independent* and *Gazette*, there is an interplay between reporting and influence: Perker can confidently say what is happening because he already knows what Slumkey's plan is, and the noises are simply confirming when each action occurs. At the same time, it shows great perception on Perker's part that he is able to interpret *which* action occurs, based solely upon the enthusiasm of the crowd's roar and his ability to pick out individual comments on words among the tumult. But note also how, as each sentence becomes shorter, and the emphasis falls more upon the sounds from the crowd and Perker's words, that the tense shifts towards the present: The 'roar of pleasure that rent the air' is followed by 'A second roar' and 'A third roar' with no reference to the past tense; likewise, Perker's commentary shifts from telling us what Slumkey has *done* to what he is *doing*: 'He's kissing them all!' The result is that we hear about events faster than they are unfolding, catching up to switch from past to present and to be there on the scene as it is happening. Dickens's reporting style places us there in the moment.

The same technique is used later on in the trial of Bardell vs Pickwick, where Dickens frequently relinquishes the narrative to the dialogue between characters, such as this moment between the judge and Mr Winkle:

> 'What's your Christian name, sir?' angrily inquired the little judge.
> 'Nathaniel, sir.'
> 'Daniel, – any other name?'
> 'Nathaniel, sir – my Lord, I mean.'
> 'Nathaniel Daniel, or Daniel Nathaniel?'
> 'No, my Lord, only Nathaniel: not Daniel at all.'
> 'What did you tell me it was Daniel for, then, sir?' inquired the judge.[23]

The bulk of the dialogue in this passage is presented direct without comment. We are told the judge asks the first question angrily, but after that it is entirely open to us to infer in what tone the subsequent lines are being uttered. It is straight reporting, exactly such as Dickens would have done as a parliamentary reporter. The fact that there is confusion over Winkle's name is presumably a problem with which Dickens could sympathise, straining to hear every word while furiously scribbling it down in shorthand, it is entirely likely he might mishear a name only to then correct it a moment later. In Winkle's interrogation Dickens is reporting the sort of moment he would have witnessed first-hand and written about a dozen times before, not only in the content, but also the format and presentation.

What this chapter has aimed to show is how journalism was not simply a subplot in Dickens's career but a major contributor to it. From his early start as a reporter to occasional sketch writing, editing, and eventually founding and running his own journals, Dickens maintained an interest and presence in the periodical press which was crowned by his novels. To truly appreciate his novels today they should be read as they were first released, in instalments. Then we can appreciate how even in the midst of his fiction, Dickens took the opportunity to respond to contemporary events and national mood. Whether fiction or non-fiction, Dickens was reactive in his writing, each work a comment and reply to the events and time in which he was living.

Notes

1 John Drew, *Dickens the Journalist* (Houndmills: Palgrave, 2003), p. 6.

2 Samuel Carter Hall, cited in Drew, p. 6.

3 See Samuel Carter Hall, *Retrospect of a Long Life, from 1815 to 1833* (London: Bentley, 1883), Vol. 1, p. 111.

4 Michael Slater, *Charles Dickens* (New Haven: Yale, 2011), p. 27.

5 Slater, p. 32.

6 Charles Dickens, *David Copperfield*, ed. by Nina Burgis (Oxford: OUP, 1981), Ch. 43, p. 535.

7 *Copperfield*, Ch. 43, p. 535.

8 Hugo Bowles, *Dickens and the Stenographic Mind* (Oxford: OUP, 2019), p. 20.

9 Bowles, pp. 126–127.

10 Charles Dickens, *The Pickwick Papers*, ed. by James Kinsley (Oxford: OUP, 1986), Ch. 11, p. 168. Subsequent references to this edition unless specified.

11 'A Dinner at Poplar Walk' in Charles Dickens, *Sketches by Boz*, ed. by Paul Schlicke and David Hewitt (Oxford: OUP, 2021), p. 315.

12 Robert Patten, *Dickens and his Publishers* (Oxford: Clarendon Press, 1978), p. 65.

13 Dickens, 'Letter to F. M. Evans', 26 February 1846, in Kathleen Tillotson, *The Letters of Charles Dickens*, Volume Four 1844–1846 (Oxford: Clarendon Press, 1977), pp. 505–506.

14 *Dickens Journals Online*, www.djo.org.uk.

15 *Pickwick*, Ch. 13, p. 177.

16 Malcolm Andrews (ed.), Charles Dickens, *The Pickwick Papers* (London: Everyman, 1998), p. 788.

17 *Pickwick*, Ch 13, p. 178.

18 *Pickwick*, Ch. 13, pp. 178–179.

19 *Pickwick*, Ch 13, p. 182.

20 *Pickwick*, Ch. 13, p. 182.

21 *Pickwick*, Ch 13, p. 185.

22 *Pickwick*, Ch. 13, p. 190.

23 *Pickwick*, Ch. 34, p. 525.

3

Dickens's Angels

Focal Point: 1830–1837

Case Study: The Old Curiosity Shop

While the last chapter focused on the beginnings of Dickens's writing career, that same period also witnessed Dickens's initiation in love and romance. In the 1830s Dickens would meet and woo Maria Beadnell, ultimately without success, before meeting his wife Catherine Hogarth, and her two younger sisters Mary and Georgina, all three of whom would have a significant influence on Dickens's life and work. This chapter will explore Dickens's dynamics with these women and the way in which the Victorian ideal of the angel in the house resurfaces through Dickens's writings, especially in the character of Little Nell in *The Old Curiosity Shop*.

Maria Beadnell: First Crush

Dickens met Maria Beadnell in 1830. It was his first crush, and like so many before him, he fell hard. His letters to her are enthusiastic and idealistic, and ultimately suggestive of a superficial attraction, wherein Dickens placed this poor girl on a pedestal and imagined her to be a goddess. Looking back on the infatuation twenty-five years later, Dickens impressed upon Forster the strength his feelings had over him during that young courtship:

> I don't quite apprehend what you mean by my overrating the strength of the feeling of five-and-twenty years ago. If you mean of my own feeling, and will only think what the desperate intensity of my nature is, and that this began when I was Charley's age [Dickens's son was 18 at this time]; that it excluded every other idea from my mind for four years, at a time of life when four and four are equal to four times four; and that I went at it with a determination to overcome all the difficulties, which fairly lifted

The Life of the Author: Charles Dickens, First Edition. Pete Orford.
© 2023 John Wiley & Sons Ltd. Published 2023 by John Wiley & Sons Ltd.

me up into that newspaper life, and floated me away over a hundred men's heads: then you are wrong, because nothing can exaggerate that.[1]

As Dickens suggests in this letter, his aspirations for Maria and his career were linked: his desire to prove himself worthy of this girl spurred him on to succeed in his work, but equally the promise of a beautiful, young wife – the daughter of a banker no less – would be a gratifying step towards becoming a gentleman. The security of career and respectability of a marriage were both a development in maturity, and an opportunity to confirm himself as a reputable young man. His courtship of Maria would last from 1830 through to 1833, which coincides with his progression from freelance reporter in Doctor's Commons to a member of paid staff for *The Mirror* and *The True Sun*. Not only that, but he moved out of the family home and into Buckingham Street, where he lodged with a law student called James Roney. In career, accommodation and love, Dickens was attempting to establish himself. Maria Beadnell is best considered then not solely in terms of her own attributes, but in what she represented as the next step in Dickens's maturity: a banker's beautiful daughter offered all the attractions of a better and more prosperous life.

However, this idea of a young man seeking stability should be balanced with the wild and romantic exaggerations of his courtship. He wrote poetry, and even the most ardent Dickens enthusiast treats these early verses with a weary sense of vicarious embarrassment. For example, this acrostic poem goes full-tilt to express the despair Dickens feels without Maria, and the sheer bliss that she alone can provide.

My life may chequered be with scenes of misery and pain,
And't may be my fate to struggle with adversity in vain:
Regardless of misfortunes tho' howe'er bitter they may be,
I shall always have one retrospect, a hallowed one to me,
And it will be of that happy time when first I gazed on thee.
Blighted hopes, and prospects drear, for me will lose their sting,
Endless troubles shall harm not me, when fancy on the wing
A lapse of years shall travel o'er, and again before me cast
Dreams of happy fleeting moments then for ever past:
Not any worldly pleasure has such magic charms for me
E'en now, as those short moments spent in company with thee;
Life has no charms, no happiness, no pleasures, now for me
Like those I feel, when 'tis my lot Maria, to gaze on thee.[2]

It's a bit much. But the only reason we can now read this poem is because Maria Beadnell kept it, so as superficial and cringe-inducing as it may appear, clearly for two young people courting it worked, at least enough for Maria to be flattered and wish to hold on to it. Equally, the album in which she stored it also has letters penned by *other* admirers, so her interest in the poem may well speak less of her appreciation for the author, and more for the pride of her effect on the opposite sex. Of course, as Dickens's career progressed the letter would become even more prized, and eventually Maria Beadnell would meet Dickens again, with disappointing results. As will be discussed in Chapter 10, Dickens was horrified to see the young girl of his dreams and imagination grown up, and the balance of power was shifted to Maria awkwardly revelling in her past charms over Dickens, which no longer maintained their attraction. In the 1830s however, when Dickens was but a young reporter, it was a very different story: he was enthralled, and it was she who held the advantage.

Concerns of his father's financial insecurity held sway, and eventually Maria rejected Dickens. He was heartbroken. Forster was the first of many to publically compare Maria Beadnell to the character of Dora in *David Copperfield*, that disastrous first marriage David has in which neither really know one another or choose wisely in selecting their partner: 'I used to laugh and tell him I had no belief in any but the book Dora, until the incident of a sudden reappearance of the real one in his life.'[3] But Maria echoes through other Dickens's characters too: Flora Finching in *Little Dorrit* is a scathing portrait of the older Maria, whose nostalgic wallowing in her girlish affections for Arthur Clennam are portrayed as grotesque and ridiculous. But there is another potential echo too in the cold and distant Estella in *Great Expectations*, who looks down upon the coarse and uneducated Pip. As considered in Chapter 1, we have to be careful when reading what the older Dickens has to be said about his early life, as his own personal sense of shame or resentment can potentially exaggerate and distort true events. But if we take the perception to be true, then there is much in Pip's own self-loathing of his coarse hands and lack of upbringing which may well indicate Dickens's own regrets and remorse over his chequered childhood while trying to woo this banker's daughter in all her finery.

Dickens's unsuccessful courtship of Maria ended on 18 March 1833. In a letter he wrote 'nothing will ever afford me more real delight than to hear that you, the object of my first, and my last, love, are happy.'[4] Slater calls the tone of this letter 'self-consciously noble'; but it is also unconsciously self-pitying.[5] Dickens also writes:

> The result of our past acquaintance is indeed a melancholy one to me. I have felt too long ever to lose the feeling of utter desolation

and wretchedness which has succeeded our former correspondence. Thank God! I can claim for myself and feel that I deserve the merit of having ever throughout our intercourse acted fairly, intelligibly and honourably.[6]

There is a familiar amount of guilt-tripping and passive blame in this passage, seen elsewhere in Dickens's description of his parents' role in the blacking factory episode. Though Dickens suggests Beadnell's happiness is his sole aim, to call her his last love is a poor attempt to invoke guilt and pity, and ultimately is proved untrue by his subsequent marriage to Catherine, and later affair with Ellen Ternan. Nonetheless, the proclamation of Maria Beadnell as his first love is the true significance here. There may well have been earlier, fleeting crushes for all we know of, which Dickens has not recorded in his letter to Maria for obvious reasons. But this is certainly his first significant infatuation; one which lasted two years and involved several letters, meetings, and hopes and aspirations on Dickens's part. She was not the last, but she certainly made an important first impression on Dickens.

Catherine Hogarth

After Dickens ended his courtship of Maria in March 1833, there was a brief respite of just over a year before he met his future wife, Catherine Hogarth. This was during the time when his work as Boz was underway, leading to his work at the *Morning Chronicle* and its sister paper, the *Evening Chronicle*, edited by George Hogarth. It was he who approached Dickens to write a sketch for the first issue, and who ended up raising the young writer's salary in exchange for a series of sketches. George Hogarth proved to be a supportive editor in Dickens's fledgling career, and he invited the young man to his home, where Dickens met Hogarth's daughters Catherine, Mary and Georgina. Catherine would have been seventeen or eighteen years of age when they first met, Dickens being three years older. His earlier courtship of Maria offered him the advantage of experience, and with it a sense of caution and moderation which comes through in his letters. The earliest surviving letter we have from Dickens to Catherine is from May 1835 when the couple were already engaged, and as such it has a surer footing from the start, with Dickens addressing her as 'My dearest Kate'.[7] But in subsequent enquiry after her health, we can see Dickens mediating between the same enthusiastic passion seen in his earlier courtship of Maria, and a more tempered, rational limitation of his feelings to maintain a sense of decorum.

> If I were to say on paper how interested I am in the slightest word that concerns you, much more on so important a point as your health, it would look like egotism: were I to express half my solicitude in your behalf it would appear like profession without sincerity, and were I to endeavour to embody the least of the feelings I entertain for you in words, it would be a useless, and hopeless attempt. For each and all my dear Girl you must give me credit, until time has enabled me to prove the sincerity and devotion of the affection I bear you.[8]

This is an improvement on the poetry he was sending to Maria; he expresses his emotion in a more sincere, grounded way without falling prey to hyperbole, but still manages to express the depth of his feelings. He acknowledges that what he has to say may well sound like exaggeration, but impresses upon Catherine that those feelings are sincere, and that word 'devotion' shows more permanence and sobriety in his affections than the wild and passionate words to Maria. However, if Dickens was controlling his words, he was also seeking to control Catherine's response. Later that same month he writes a letter of reproach to his future bride. He writes it 'with the greatest pain' but argues it is 'a duty to myself as well as to you' to hold her to account for what he considered to be unacceptable behaviour:[9]

> The sudden and uncalled-for coldness with which you treated me just before I left last night, both surprised and deeply hurt me – surprised, because I could not have believed that such sullen and inflexible obstinacy could exist in the breast of any girl in whose heart love had found a place; and hurt me, because I feel for you far more than I have ever professed, and feel a slight from you more than I care to tell.[10]

Dickens goes on the attack. On the one hand, this speaks of his confidence, which allows him to feel he can remonstrate Catherine honestly and openly like this, compared to the sugared and superficial praise he lavished on Maria. But on the other hand, there is a great deal of insecurity betrayed in this too: Dickens is determined not to be trifled with. 'If three weeks or three months of my society has wearied you' he continues, 'do not trifle with me, using me like any other toy as suits your humour for the moment'; Dickens was worried about Catherine's feelings being insincere or fleeting, and this anxiety can justifiably be linked to his previous experience with Maria.[11] We can see a similar tone to that which Dickens used in his later letters to Maria, quoted earlier: that same sense of passive blame, and accusations of cruelty or indifference compared to Dickens's own apparent sincerity. Slater suggests that Dickens was 'not prepared to tolerate anything savouring of the tormenting behaviour in which Maria had allowed herself to indulge', and thus the letters to Catherine bear that same note of chastisement as Dickens tries to resolve the issue in its early stages rather than letting it develop and worsen.[12] However, in her biography of Catherine (a much-needed intervention that shows Mrs Dickens's experience of the marriage), Lilian Nayder wonders whether the coolness of Catherine was a similar tactic, and if 'Catherine attempted to shape the behaviour of her fiancé and mould his priorities to her own.'[13] There are several letters from Dickens during their courtship in which he excuses himself from seeing her because of writing deadlines; it is entirely understandable why Catherine might not be pleased by this and seek to curb it. The coolness with which she bids him farewell is certainly shown to have an impact on Dickens, and to have instilled a fear in him that her feelings could not, should not, be taken for granted. The popular narrative, inevitably given the stratospheric fame of Dickens, is one of the budding author dazzling this young girl, but ultimately Catherine had the more respectable family, and with an editor for a father had a more impressive literary heritage than this rookie reporter. Dickens wrote to his uncle Thomas Barrow that his future wife was 'the daughter of a gentleman who has recently distinguished himself by a celebrated work on Music; who was the most intimate friend and companion of Sir Walter Scott, and one of the most eminent among the Literati of Edinburgh.'[14] In becoming Mrs Dickens she may justifiably have considered it a meeting of equals; but Dickens's subsequent treatment of her, and growing control over the marriage, would prove this wrong.

For now, though, the marriage was one of great promise and hope. We must be forever cautious about letting later events prejudice our interpretation of earlier ones. The Dickens marriage would end in acrimony and scandal; but despite Dickens's subsequent assertions that he always had doubts, the letters which survive from this time show two people who genuinely care about each other. Even Dickens's early warning to Catherine seen previously demonstrates a care and investment in the strength and foundations of their future relationship. Whatever his feelings might be about the older Mrs Dickens, in these early years she was decidedly his 'dearest Kate'. The couple were married on 2 April 1836, the same month in which the first instalment of *The Pickwick Papers* would be published.

Again, it is tempting, but unwise, to see the coincidence of this timing as foreboding in retrospect. After all, it means that even while marrying Catherine, Dickens was preparing his first major work of fiction, and entering into that regular schedule of serial publication. Given that he began work on *Oliver Twist* while still completing *Pickwick*, and that in turn he began writing *Nicolas Nickleby* while still completing *Oliver*, this means that the first three years of the Dickens marriage were set to the backdrop of Dickens's emerging career as a novelist, and the regular monthly schedule of writing and publishing instalments. The stratospheric success of *Pickwick* in particular not only propelled Dickens's fame as an author, but also redefined the balance of power between him and his new wife, who was no longer married to a young reporter and budding writer, but a literary phenomenon. Even before *Pickwick*, while the pair were still engaged, there are signs of Dickens prioritising his writing. In November 1835 he wrote to excuse himself from coming to see her as he was working hard on *Sketches by Boz*: 'Necessity and necessity alone, induces me to forego the pleasure of your companionship' he pleaded, arguing that 'your future advancement and happiness is the main-spring' of all these writing endeavours.[15] Clearly Catherine was not convinced. Dickens stresses his absence is 'about my working as a duty, and not as a pleasure' but ultimately once he realises she does not accept this, he writes 'why then, my dear, you must be out of temper and there is no help for it.'[16]

So yes, reading these early disputes can certainly offer further justification for Dickens's later separation and sense of a doomed marriage, but again it needs to be balanced. There are other examples that show greater harmony between Dickens professional and personal life. Henry Burnett recalls visiting Dickens's home in Doughty Street during the writing of *Oliver Twist*:

> One night in Doughty Street, Mrs. Charles Dickens, my wife and myself were sitting round the fire, cosily enjoying a chat, when Dickens, for some purpose, came suddenly from his studio into the room. 'What, you here!' he exclaimed; 'I'll bring down my work'. It was the monthly portion of *Oliver Twist* for *Bentley's*. In a few minutes he returned, manuscript in hand, and while he swas pleasantly discoursing he employed himself in carrying to a corner of the room a little table, at which he seated himself and re-commenced his writing. We, at his bidding, went on talking our little nothings – he, every now and then (the feather of his pen still moving rapidly from side to side), put in a cheerful interlude.[17]

In later years there's evidence of Dickens becoming rather particular about where he wrote, and the exact conditions required, so it is rather remarkable that in this instance he would choose to move and sit in with the others while working. Far from being antisocial, it is very social of Dickens to prefer to be in company while he is writing. We must wonder whether other occasions ever happened, either with other guests, or when it was just Catherine and Dickens home alone together. Nearly a decade later, in 1846, when Dickens was busy in his new role as editor of the *Daily News*, and attempting to write his travel narrative *Pictures from Italy*, there is evidence of Catherine's continued support and involvement in his writing career. The letters, which Dickens had sent home from Italy to Forster and other correspondents with the intention of then using as source material, have been transcribed, and while the handwriting is not confirmed it most closely resembles Catherine's hand. Nayder notes too that when Dickens was unwell, and needed to write the preface for *Barnaby Rudge*, that he dictated it to Catherine.[18]

Thus, with retrospect, while the start of Dickens's marriage alongside the simultaneous start of Dickens's novel-writing career can seem ominous, given our knowledge that the writing would prove more successful and enduring than the marriage (and receive the greater share of Dickens's care and attention), nonetheless the details of Dickens effectively working with or alongside Catherine show a more optimistic view of his work–life balance at the start of their relationship. Indeed, if we are looking for fictional counterparts, then it is plausible to propose that if Maria Beadnell were the inspiration for *David Copperfield*'s Dora, then Catherine must have seemed – at least initially – to be an Agnes for Dickens, far more pragmatic and reliable than her predecessor.

Their honeymoon was in Chalk, a small village near Rochester (where Pickwick and his friends travelled to in the first monthly number). Their first child, Charles Dickens Jnr, was born in January 1837 – nine months after their wedding. This certainly set the pace for their family life as Catherine would spend much of her young adulthood either pregnant or with a young child. This again is an area which is deeply coloured by Dickens's later accusations against his wife for failing in her duties as a mother. To look at the facts, we know that Catherine was unable to produce milk for Charley, and whereas today this would simply require a young mother to use formula milk, in this age the only alternative available was to find a nurse who would breast-feed the child instead. Dickens would later write of such an arrangement in *Dombey and Son*, with the surrogate mother seen by the father as a purely practical solution:

> 'You have children of your own,' said Mr Dombey. 'It is not at all in this bargain that you need become attached to my child, or that my child need become attached to you. I don't expect or desire anything of the kind. Quite the reverse. When you go away from here, you will have concluded what is a mere matter of bargain and sale, hiring and letting: and will stay away. The child will cease to remember you; and you will cease, if you please, to remember the child.'[19]

For Dombey, as a man, there is no emotional turmoil involved in hiring this woman to be a surrogate mother to his child; Dickens emphasises Dombey's coldness throughout the novel so it is hoped that this too is intended as view-point to be criticised, not celebrated. And yet even so there seems to be a failure on his part to fully comprehend just how upsetting it must have been for Catherine. It would be entirely understandable for her child being nursed by another woman to prove traumatic and distressing for Catherine, and a perceived slight on her womanhood. Her sister Mary wrote, in a remarkably naïve and insensitive tone, that they had 'got a very nice Nurse for [Charley] but poor Kate looks upon her now with very jealous eyes.'[20] Nayder suggests the inability to produce milk was a consequence of post-partum depression; alternatively, it could well have been the cause or exacerbation of such depression: 'in failing to nurse Charley, Catherine felt that she was failing as a mother'.[21] The same issue would arise with future children too, and this, combined with the amount and frequency of children, could hardly have failed in having a significant and detrimental impact on Catherine. It is interesting to speculate how different her life might have been had she *not* married Dickens, and whether that other life might not have proved a happier one for her.

Mary Hogarth

The next significant young woman to have an impact on Dickens was not a romantic entanglement, but rather his sister-in-law Mary. Four years younger than Catherine, Mary was seventeen when she became Dickens's sister-in-law, the same age Catherine had been when she met Dickens, and it is not unreasonable to presume that Mary and her parents would have been looking for her to find a match just as her older sister had. There were several occasions when Mary came to stay with her sister and her new husband, to go out and enjoy London social life. Mary writes enthusiastically of her clever brother-in-law:

> I am sure you would be delighted with him if you knew him he is such a nice creature and so clever he is courted and made up to by all the literary Gentleman and has more to do in that way than he can well manage ...[22]

Mary's letter is one of a young woman, enraptured by her sister's new life and her new husband as much as the excitement of London life. One can reasonably presume Dickens would by no means have been displeased by his sister-in-law's admiration of him, and he and Catherine took her on a number of excursions and evenings out. In April 1837, the couple and their eldest child Charley had moved into 48 Doughty Street, preserved today as the Charles Dickens Museum. Dickens was truly becoming a young gentleman, with a good property and a burgeoning reputation. As a novelist he was completing *Pickwick* and had commenced *Oliver*; as a journalist he was not only continuing to write shorter pieces of journalism, but was also editor of *Bentley's Miscellany*; furthermore, he had also embarked on what would be a short-lived professional playwriting career. No wonder Mary was delighted with him. On 6 May 1837 she was staying with them in London, and had accompanied the pair to the theatre where Dickens's own play *Is She His Wife?* was being staged. On their return, Mary collapsed, dying the next day of suspected heart failure. Dickens was devastated.

Once again, I am at pains to point out the impact of Dickens narrating his own life. The primary reason we have to believe that Dickens was devastated is drawn from what he writes about it. In contrast little is said of how Catherine felt upon the death of her own sister; attention is always pored first and foremost on Dickens's response. As Nayder notes, this is 'the consequence of approaching the Hogarth women in relation to Dickens rather than in relation to each other'.[23] Our tendency to do so is explained partially by his greater prominence, but also by his control of the narrative. Immediately after the event, Dickens wrote to those of his associates who had met Mary to share the news, and while each letter differs in length and exact details, all of them are very specific about *where* she died.

> ... despite our best endeavours to save her, expired in my arms at two o'clock this afternoon.[24]

> She had been with us to the theatre the evening before; was taken suddenly ill in the night, and breathed her last in my arms at the time I have mentioned.[25]

> It is my melancholy task to inform you that Mrs Dickens' sister whom you saw here, and at the dinner on Wednesday, died in my arms yesterday afternoon.[26]

> I am most sorry to inform you that Mrs Dickens' sister whom you saw here, after accompanying us to the Theatre on Saturday Evening in the best health and spirits, was suddenly taken ill, and died in my arms yesterday afternoon.[27]

> She was at the Theatre with us on Saturday Night well and happy, and expired in my arms a few hours afterwards.[28]

There is something quite ghoulish about how Dickens takes possession of the moment here. He is, ultimately, not the main character in the narrative of Mary's death, nor was his connection to her comparable to that of her relations: Mary is not *his* sister, and it would have fallen to Catherine to inform her family. Their suffering, and the impact on them, was considerably great: Mrs

Hogarth was inconsolable, and Catherine said to be stoic and supportive, although she later suffered a miscarriage, with the grief of Mary's death considered a likely cause. Therefore, Dickens is ultimately on the fringe of events when compared to the Hogarth family, yet he seizes the narrative and presumes to be more greatly affected. Those to whom he wrote the letters above were not particularly close to Mary – some had only just met her that week – but their further distancing from her allowed Dickens to reiterate by contrast his relative closeness to her, and it is no coincidence that each letter reinforces the fact that Mary died in *his* arms. In a subsequent letter on the 17 May to his friend Thomas Beard, Dickens is more explicit in his feelings on events: 'Thank God she died in my arms, and the very last words she whispered were of me.'[29] Why 'Thank God'? Dickens could not lay a greater claim of connection to Mary than her own family, but he could – and did – lay a greater claim on proximity to her last moments.

Just as his outpourings of love for Maria Beadnell had verged on the ridiculous in his excessiveness, so too his mourning for Mary went to similar extremes. He wore her ring for the rest of his life. He took charge of the funeral arrangements, and expressed a fervent desire to one day be buried alongside her (a desire which was ultimately unfulfilled). For the only time in his entire career, he took an unscheduled break from writing, with no instalment for *Pickwick* or *Oliver* appearing at the end of that month. Years later he would still be reminded of her. While visiting the Niagra Falls, he was struck by the thought of 'the dear girl whose ashes lie in Kensal-Green' who he wished could be with them now, 'but she has been here many times, I doubt not, since her sweet face faded from my earthly sight'.[30] Just as his early letters all proclaimed his stake in her moment of death, so his future actions continued to reassert his own pain and the prominence of his suffering and connection to her. This speaks as much about Dickens, if not more so, than it does about Mary. She, like Catherine, is destined to be forever written about in relation to him, a secondary character in his narrative, and even her death is reduced to the catalyst for his outpourings of grief. His letter to Beard on 17 May continues:

> I solemnly believe that so perfect a creature never breathed. I knew her inmost heart, and her real worth and value. She had not a fault.[31]

Once more we are confronted with the spectre of what might have been. Had Mary lived, would she have prompted such praise from Dickens? How much of this outpouring is inspired by her death rather than her life? Ultimately, such questions are redundant: she *did* die, and Dickens *was* affected by it. She was still only seventeen at her death, and as such was preserved forever in Dickens's memory at that age. Maria Beadnell and Catherine both grew older to shatter Dickens's early admiration of them, but Mary was forever young, without fault, 'so perfect a creature'.

Case Study: Perfecting the Moment of Mourning in *The Old Curiosity Shop*

There are many moments in Dickens's literature which we could turn to for echoes of Mary's death. The very next instalment of *Oliver Twist* written after her death introduces the character of Rose Maylie, eventually revealed to be Oliver's aunt, and sister to his mother who has died long ago. Dickens's subsequent fiction returns ever and again to a pure and innocent child heroine – both Florence Dombey in *Dombey and Son* and the titular character of *Little Dorrit* are applauded for their steadfast goodness and innocence. Such characters draw inspiration not solely from Mary, but equally from the broader Victorian cultural trend of the angel in the house, or the ill-fated daughter Cordelia in Shakespeare's *King Lear*, a play which Dickens much admired. Child mortality was not a unique phenomenon but an unfortunately widespread and shared experience; Dickens would later experience this as a father with the death of his child Dora in 1851 at just eight months old. It is not surprising then to see both innocent child heroes and child deaths in his fiction, and we cannot conclusively draw them to one single inspiration. Treading forward then with caution and perspective, let's consider Dickens's most famous and infamous child death – Little Nell in *The Old Curiosity Shop*. Popular anecdote tells how crowds gathered at the docks in New York awaiting the latest shipment of the most recent number, begging those on board for news of Little Nell's fate (though no direct source for this anecdote has ever been uncovered), while Oscar Wilde is famously said to have pronounced 'one must have a heart of stone to read the death of Little Nell without laughing'.[32] Both these stories are so widely reported as to become apocryphal; both are true reflections of how we react to this infamous moment in Dickens's story. It is a victim of its own success, so notorious that it is widely accepted everyone will know the heroine dies at the end of the tale – a Victorian spoiler born from its own fame (in much the same way that yes, we all know Bruce Willis's character is a ghost, and actually the Planet of the Apes was Earth all along).

Dickens's decision to kill his heroine has proved less controversial than the manner in which he writes of it. The book is steeped in pathos, a sentimental style popular at the time but which has fallen out of favour since.[33] This is why the book was such a success in Dickens's lifetime, and such cause for consternation and wry remarks ever since. The description of her in death elevates her to something more than human – almost angelic:

> She was dead. No sleep so beautiful and calm, so free from trace of pain, so fair to look upon. She seemed a creature fresh from the hand of God, and waiting for the breath of life; not one who had lived and suffered death.[34]

There is a veritable crowd at her bedside to mourn over her passing, who 'moved so gently, that their footsteps made no noise; but there were sobs from among the group, and sounds of grief and mourning.'[35] The sobs may be involuntarily; but the silence of their footsteps is intentional, as this group is there primarily to be an audience to the *real* victim, Nell's grandfather, who is identified as the one who suffers most from pure little Nell's death. He rounds on those gathered there to speak jealously and possessively, and assert his authority as the one with the most claim to Nell:

> You plot among you to wean my heart from her. You never will do that – never while I have life. I have no relative or friend but her – I never had – I never will have. She is all to me. It is too late to part us now.[36]

Whether consciously or subconsciously, this echoes Dickens's own extreme passion and insistence of his devotion to Mary Hogarth – clearly Dickens himself was fully aware of the parallels between Mary's death and Nell's as a whole, telling Forster that 'Dear Mary died yesterday, when I think of this sad story.'[37] But he is doing more than thinking of it, he is dwelling and wallowing in it, seeing what he can do it to intensify the sorrow of it all. In this outburst of Nell's grandfather, he turns grief into a competition. While writing Nell's death, and reflecting on Mary's, he also told Forster 'Nobody will miss her like I shall' – but it is not clear if he is referring to Nell or Mary: either is possible.[38] The parallels to Dickens's reaction to Mary's death can also be seen in the focus upon touch, and last touch in particular. As Mary died in Dickens's arms, so Nell reaches out her hand to her grandfather:

> The old man held one languid arm in his, and had the small hand tight folded to his breast, for warmth. It was the hand she had stretched out to him with her last smile – the hand that had led him on, through all their wanderings. Ever and anon he pressed it to his lips; then hugged it to his breast again, murmuring that it was warmer now; and as he said it, he looked in agony, to those who stood around, as if imploring them to help her.[39]

Just as Dickens had exaggerated the trauma of Warren's Blacking when he wrote *David Copperfield*, so too the experience of Mary's death is heightened in this fictional scenario to hyperbolic levels. The key addition here, which Dickens craves, is an audience to the event. Nell's grandfather looks 'in agony, to those who stood around'; just like his many letters describing Mary's last moments, Dickens wants people to witness this moment of grief, and by witnessing they enhance the moment. This borders on the pathological, but it also calls upon Dickens's theatrical experience; here he is setting a scene, and any good scene needs an audience, not only in the seats but on the stage as well to control and dictate the reaction. The scene is confirmed as sad because those watching are weeping and sobbing. Seen as an extension of Dickens's experience of Mary's death, there is something rather needy, if not sinister, in this elaborate fantasising of the moment as high art. But it gets worse.

At the time of writing *The Old Curiosity Shop*, Dickens was great friends with the celebrated actor William Charles Macready. Macready's enduring claim to fame today is that he restored Shakespeare's *King Lear* to the stage – for the previous century and a half, actors had all performed a heavily adapted version written by Nahum Tate, in which Lear and Cordelia do NOT die, with Cordelia ending up happily married to Edgar. Macready's restoration of the original was celebrated then for the more downbeat ending, and Cordelia's death in particular is one which, as I have noted, has been cited as a likely influence upon several of Dickens's heroines.[40] But in a tragic case of life imitating art, Macready's own daughter died soon after. And it was while Macready was mourning the death of his daughter, that Dickens was working on *The Old Curiosity Shop* and building up to Nell's death. Ever one to seek approval and feedback from his peers, Dickens sent advance copies of instalments to Macready to ask for his reaction. This would seem to show a staggering lack of tact and consideration on Dickens's part, to send fictional writings of a child's death to a mourning father, especially in the abrupt and emotive way in which Dickens described the process in one letter to Macready in January 1841: 'I am slowly murdering that poor child, and grow wretched over it.'[41] Macready's notes in his diary show that each instalment was having a profound emotional impact on him:

> I saw one print in it of the dear dead child that gave a dead chill through my blood. I dread to read it, but I must get it over.
>
> I have read the two numbers; I never have read printed words that gave me so much pain. I could not weep for some time. Sensation, sufferings have returned to me, that are terrible to awaken; it is real to me; I cannot criticise it.[42]

This is high literary praise and a stark contrast to Oscar Wilde's later dismissal. But as pleasing as this response might be to Dickens professionally, we have to ask ourselves why he would subject his friend to this experience given the recent loss of his child. It is possible at this point to say a word in defence of Dickens's bizarre actions here; the same which can be said of what seems to be an over-egged death scene deserving the scorn of Wilde and others after him: *The Old Curiosity Shop* is from a different era, and that element of pathos which we find so mawkish and cloying now, was seen as pure and enriching then. Much like wallowing in sad songs when our hearts are broken, there is a healthy benefit to be gleaned from taking our emotions to the extreme and indulging in a scene like Nell's death where description leaps to the hyperbolic. While a modern reader can see the writing as decadent and pandering to Dickens's ego, it's also possible to argue that the more he heightens the language and exaggerates the emotion, the more befitting it becomes of Mary's death. Likewise, sending these remarkable episodes to Macready in his time of mourning could potentially be seen as a kindness, encouraging him to cry through his pain, to exorcise his suffering and put his loss into words as a means to articulate, and ultimately contain, his despair in order to move on to hope. Dickens proclaims this himself in *The Old Curiosity Shop* as he addresses how any of us can make sense from the loss of a child:

> Oh! It is hard to take to hear the lesson that such deaths will teach, but let no man reject it, for it is one that all must learn, and is a mighty, universal Truth. When Death strikes down the innocent and young, for every fragile form from which he lets the panting spirit free, a hundred virtues rise, in shapes of mercy, charity, and love, to walk the world, and bless it. Of every tear that sorrowing mortals shed on such green graves, some good is born, some gentler nature comes. In the Destroyer's steps there spring up bright creations that defy his power, and his dark path becomes a way of light to Heaven.[43]

If Dickens was writing from his own experience, he was not alone in having that experience. Many parents, if not most, would suffer the loss of a child in the nineteenth century, but the frequency of the event en masse made it no easier to bear each individual moment. If Dickens is indulging his darker fantasies here, wallowing in the saddest of emotions, it is not simply self-gratification that he is pursuing but rather he is tapping in to a widespread and shared pain.

Nell's death left her forever young and perfect in the public imagination, a beautiful testimony to the grief of child mortality. Mary's death left an equally potent impression upon Dickens. His appropriation of Mary's death as a key point of grief, both in his own life and subsequently in his portrayal of Nell's death, is somewhat opportunistic, but it is the standard tool of an author to translate their own experience into fiction. Mary's death left her, like Nell, frozen in time: an impossible ideal for other women to be measured against. Catherine, and Maria Beadnell, would grow older, and come to fall out of favour with Dickens. His admiration of these women in their youth would prove an unattainable standard which their older selves would suffer against.

Notes

1 Dickens, 'Letter to John Forster', March 1855, in Graham Storey, Kathleen Tillotson and Angus Easson (eds.), *The Letters of Charles Dickens*, Volume Seven 1853–1855 (Oxford: Clarendon Press, 1993), pp. 556–557 (pp. 556–557).

2 Charles Dickens, Acrostic, in the Autograph Album of Maria Beadnell, held in the Charles Dickens Museum, London. The verse can be read both as transcript and facsimile online at *Dickens Search* https://dickenssearch.com/verse/1830-31_Autograph_Album_of_Maria_Beadnell_Acrostic.

3 John Forster, *The Life of Charles Dickens*, Volume One (London: Chapman and Hall, 1872), p. 72.

4 Dickens, 'Letter to Maria Beadnell', 18 March 1833, in Madeline House and Graham Storey (eds.), *The Letters of Charles Dickens*, Volume One 1820–1839 (Oxford: Clarendon Press, 1974), pp. 16–17 (p. 17).

5 Michael Slater, *Charles Dickens* (New Haven: Yale, 2011), p. 37

6 Dickens, Letter to Maria Beadnell, 18 March 1833 in *Letters*, Vol. 1, pp. 16–17 (p. 17).

7 Dickens, Letter to Catherine, May 1835, in *Letters*, Vol. 1, pp. 60–61 (pp. 61).

8 Dickens, Letter to Catherine, May 1835, in *Letters*, Vol. 1, pp. 60–61 (pp. 60–61).

9 Dickens, Letter to Catherine, Late May 1835, in *Letters*, Vol. 1, pp. 61–62 (p. 61).

10 Dickens, Letter to Catherine, Late May 1835, in *Letters*, Vol. 1, pp. 61–62 (p. 61).

11 Dickens, Letter to Catherine, Late May 1835, in *Letters*, Vol. 1, pp. 61–62 (p. 61).

12 Slater, p. 48.

13 Lilian Nayder, *The Other Dickens: A Life of Catherine Hogarth* (London: Cornell University Press, 2011), p. 51.

14 Dickens, Letter to Thomas Barrow, 31 March 1836, in *Letters*, Vol. 1, pp. 144–4 (p. 144).

15 Dickens, Letter to Catherine, 19 November 1835, in *Letters*, Vol. 1, p. 95 (p. 95).

16 Dickens, Letter to Catherine, 21 February 1836, in *Letters*, Vol. 1, pp. 133–134 (p. 133).

17 Henry Burnett in *Dickens: Interviews and Recollections*, Vol. 1, ed. by Philip Collins (London: Macmillan, 1981), p. 22.

18 Nayder, p. 67.

19 Charles Dickens, *Dombey and Son* ed. by Alan Horsman (Oxford: OUP, 2008), Ch. 2, p. 18.

20 Mary Hogarth, Letter to Georgina Hogarth, 26 January 1837, cited in Nayder, p. 73.

21 Nayder, p. 73.

22 Mary Hogarth, Letter to Georgina Hogarth 15 May, cited in Slater p. 68.

23 Nayder, p. 79.

24 Dickens, Letter to Edward Chapman, 7 May 1837, in *Letters*, Vol 1, p. 256 (p.256).

25 Dickens, Letter to George Thomson, 8 May 1837, in *Letters*, Vol. 1, pp. 256–257 (p. 256).

26 Dickens, Letter to William Harrison Ainsworth, 8 May 1837, in *Letters*, Vol. 1, p. 257 (p. 257).

27 Dickens, Letter to Richard Bentley, 8 May 1837, in *Letters*, Vol. 1, pp. 257–258 (257).

28 Dickens, Letter to George Cox, 8 May 1837, in *Letters*, Vol. 1, p. 258 (p. 258).

29 Dickens, Letter to Thomas Beard, 17 May 1837, in *Letters*, Vol. 1, pp. 259–260 (p. 259).

30 Dickens, Letter to Forster, 26 April 1842, in Madeline House, Graham Storey and Kathleen Tillotson (eds.), *The Letters of Charles Dickens*, Volume Three 1842–1843 (Oxford: Clarendon Press, 1974), pp. 208–211 (p. 211).

31 Dickens, Letter to Thomas Beard, 17 May 1837, in *Letters*, Vol. 1, pp. 259–260 (p. 259).

32 Oscar Wilde cited by Marcia Mulder Eaton, 'Laughing at the Death of Little Nell: Sentimental Art and Sentimental People', *American Philosophical Quarterly*, Vol. 26, No. 4 (October 1989), pp. 269–282 (p. 269).

33 For more on pathos in *The Old Curiosity Shop*, see Paul Schlicke, 'A "Discipline of Feeling": Macready's *Lear* and *The Old Curiosity Shop*', *Dickensian*, Vol. 76, No. 391 (Summer 1980), pp. 78–90.

34 Charles Dickens, *The Old Curiosity Shop*, ed. by Elizabeth M. Brennan (Oxford: OUP, 1997), Ch. 71, p. 557.

35 *The Old Curiosity Shop*, Ch. 71, p. 557.

36 *The Old Curiosity Shop*, Ch. 71, p. 556.

37 Dickens, Letter to John Forster, 12 January 1842, in *Letters*, Vol. 2, pp. 181–182 (p. 182).

38 Dickens, Letter to John Forster, 12 January 1842, in *Letters*, Vol. 2, pp. 181–182 (p. 181).

39 *The Old Curiosity Shop*, Ch. 71, p. 558.

40 Schlicke, 'A "Discipline of Feeling"'.

41 Dickens, Letter to W. C. Macready, in Madeline House and Graham Storey (eds.), *The Letters of Charles Dickens*, Volume Two 1840–1841 (Oxford: Clarendon Press, 1969), p. 180 (p. 180).

42 Entry for 22 January 1841 in *Diaries of William Charles Macready*, ed. by William Toynbee, Vol. 2 (London: Chapman and Hall, 1912), p. 116.

43 *The Old Curiosity Shop*, Ch. 72. p. 563.

4

Dickens and Theatre

Focal Point: 1836–1838

Case Study: Nicholas Nickleby

Dickens's Early Involvement in Theatre

Theatre plays a prominent part throughout Charles Dickens's life. One of his earliest surviving works of fiction is an amateur dramatic work *O'Thello* (1833) which he also acted in; Dickens would go on to write several more, including for the professional stage, while also continuing to act in amateur theatre as well. But the greatest influence theatre had upon Dickens was as an audience member: he attended the theatre regularly throughout his life, sometimes on a nightly basis, and as a result his enthusiasm for the stage shows throughout the breadth of his prose writing. This chapter will focus primarily on his brief playwriting career in the late 1830s, but will also extend beyond that to show Dickens's perpetual fascination with the stage. Dickens's performative nature and aspirations can be seen to manifest themselves in his childhood; Forster recounts how the young Dickens 'told a story offhand so well, and sang small comic songs so especially well, that he used to be elevated on chairs and tables, both at home and abroad, for more effective display of these talents'.[1] Dickens would thus accompany his father to the pub and perform monologues there: which is a telling insight into both father and son, one proudly showing off his boy's artistic pursuits, and the other hungry for the opportunity and audience. The young Dickens would perform monologues in the style of the celebrated comic actor Charles Matthews, who was famous for his 'monopolylogues' – feats of virtuosity in which he would perform several different characters in a one-man show – and this adoption of multiple personas as a style of acting is one which we will see Dickens emulate throughout his career both on and off the stage. At the age of twenty, while still a reporter, Dickens applied for an audition in front of Matthews at Covent Garden Theatre. Recalling the event several years later he explained he missed the audition on account of 'a terrible bad cold and an inflammation of the face'; yet he never attempted to secure

The Life of the Author: Charles Dickens, First Edition. Pete Orford.
© 2023 John Wiley & Sons Ltd. Published 2023 by John Wiley & Sons Ltd.

a second audition.[2] There is therefore some uncertainty whether Dickens missed the audition because of a cold, or cold feet. As an older man looking back fondly on the moment, he wonders on what might have been: 'See how near I may have been to another sort of life?'[3] That sense of 'what might have been' is a recurring one in Dickens's fascination with the stage; time and again he would relish the praise of his friend and actor William Charles Macready, and build upon this sense that he could be a great actor if he so chose to pursue it. The idea of excelling in another field is a peculiar habit of Dickens's and a somewhat unflattering insight into his ego. Dickens frequently flattered himself whenever he dabbled in another sphere – be it acting, mesmerism, stage-magic, or public readings – that he could, should he choose, be great in it.

His juvenile work *O'Thello*, is a burlesque reworking of Shakespeare's tragedy produced for an amateur performance by Dickens and his family. The surviving pages we have are only a fragment of the whole play; his father John sold parts of his script piecemeal later in life as a way of trading off his son's literary success. His inscription at the top betrays its repurposing as opportunistic memorabilia:

> This Page is from an unpublished Travestie written by Mr Charles Dickens for private performance in his own family (1833) and is in his own handwriting. The Great Unpaid was your humble servant John Dickens.[4]

The few pages we have come from John Dickens's cue-script (a cue-script being a script with only one actor's lines on it, and just the preceding line of other actors' speeches to cue them in); so we are limited in how much we can extrapolate from it. John Dickens was playing the part of the Duke of Venice, and the dialogue is silly stuff:

> When in death I shall calm recline
> Oh take me home to my 'Missus' dear
> Tell her I've taken a little more wine
> Than I could carry, or very well bear
> Bid her not scold me on the morrow
> For staying out drinking all night
> But several bottles of Soda borrow
> To cool my coppers and set me right.[5]

Interestingly, when Dickens was writing *Sketches by Boz* one of them, 'Mrs. Joseph Porter', tells of a disastrous amateur dramatic performance by the Gattleton family of *Othello* (Shakespeare's tragedy, rather than Dickens's comedy, though the performance is so bad that it unintentionally becomes comedy). Dickens's description of the staging and event, while not being an exact retelling of his own performance, nonetheless provides insight into a typical amateur performance at this time, with family and neighbours invited to the entertainment.

> The whole family was infected with the mania for Private Theatricals; the house, usually so clean and tidy, was, to use Mr. Gattleton's expressive description 'regularly turned out o' windows;' the large dining-room, dismantled of it's furniture and ornaments, presented a strange jumble of flats, flies, wings, lamps, bridges, clouds, thunder and lightning, festoons and flowers, daggers and foil, and all the other messes which in theatrical slang are included under the comprehensive name of 'properties.' The bed-rooms were crowded with scenery, the kitchen was occupied by carpenters. Rehearsals took place every other night in the drawing-room, and every sofa in the house was more or less damaged by the perseverance and spirit with which Mr. Sempronius Gattleton, and Miss Lucina, rehearsed the smothering scene in 'Othello'—it having been determined that that tragedy should form the first portion of the evening's entertainments.[6]

These early encounters – the childhood monologues, the missed audition, and the writing of *O'Thello* – all occur before Dickens commenced his writing career. They happen at a time when Dickens does not yet know what career he will pursue; there is clearly a creative talent there, but without a definite direction to follow. While we can be inclined, with full knowledge of Dickens's career path, to look upon this as a brief dalliance, at the time it could reasonably be seen as a credible beginning to an early dramatic career. This is important to note as it helps to explain what happens next.

Dickens the Playwright

The standard narrative of Dickens's biographies is that the publishing of *The Pickwick Papers* launches Dickens's status as a novelist and confirms his career. This is both true and untrue. Looking back, it is clear this is a seminal moment, and a successful life as a novelist does indeed follow – but Dickens didn't know that at the time. When we look at his actions in the immediate trail of *Pickwick*, we see a man who is still investigating his options and negotiating different avenues. Between 1836 and 1838 Dickens wrote four works for the public stage, three of which were performed. He did this while simultaneously writing *Pickwick*, *Oliver Twist* and *Nicholas Nickleby*. These are not the actions of an assured novelist confident in the security of his career, but of a starting novelist who is exploring every option and saying yes to every offer that comes along. The plays were written for the St James Theatre, and the first three plays – *The Strange Gentleman, The Village Coquettes* and *Is She His Wife* – were sent for the attention of John Pritt Harley. Harley was a comic actor known for a particular type of role – the cheeky cockney. Harley was already performing as Sam Weller in an adaptation of *Pickwick* (like so many adaptations, this was not written by Dickens himself, copyright law at the time making no restrictions on adapting other people's novels for the stage). In *The Strange Gentleman* and *Is She His Wife?*, we can see Dickens writing with Harley in mind; Harley's eponymous character in *The Strange Gentleman* is described as 'a wonderful man to talk' who 'keeps on like a steam engine', and the character Mr Tapkins in *Is She His Wife?* is clearly cut from the same cloth:[7]

> TAPKINS: Ha, ha! How are you both? – Here's a morning! But my heart alive, *what* a morning! I've been gardening ever since five o'clock, and the flowers have been actually growing before my very eyes! The London Pride is sweeping everything before it, and the stalks are half as high again as they were yesterday. They're all run up like so many tailors' bills, after that heavy dew of last night broke down half my rose-buds with the weight of its own moisture, – something like a dew that! – reg'lar *doo*, eh? – come, that's not so bad for a before-dinner one.[8]

Both plays are short comic pieces, likely to last no longer than an hour, featuring a lovable and loquacious rascal for Harley to play. Jim Davis notes that 'Harley was not noted for his depths of characterisation and was often accused of always playing himself', and in these plays we can see Dickens catering for that same character type for which Harley was both celebrated and criticised, which is clear to see from the playbills where Harley's name is on an equal scale to Boz's [see Figure 4.1].[9] Both these short pieces are typical for the Victorian stage, but are often treated with disappointment today for not meeting our expectations of Dickens. Actually, the evidence suggests the plays were not so removed from the sketches he had been penning as Boz. *The Strange Gentleman* appears in *Sketches by Boz* as 'The Great Winglebury Duel'. This sketch was originally planned for publication in December 1835, but instead appeared later in the collected volume of 1836; it is possible the delay was influenced by Dickens's adaption of it for the stage, which premiered in the interim; Dickens wrote in 1835 that 'I have a little story by me which I have not yet published, which I think would dramatize well'.[10] Similarly, Dickens's 1838 script for *The Lamplighter* was adapted by him into print three years later as 'The Lamplighter's Story', so clearly he felt it entirely plausible for the drama and prose to be interchangeable. *The Village Coquettes* is once again built around

St.James's Theatre.

Mr. HARLEY,

STAGE-MANAGER,

Has the honor to announce that

HIS BENEFIT

Is appointed for

This Evening, MONDAY, March 13th, 1837,

On which occasion will be performed

an original Comic Burletta, in One Act, Written by BOZ, called

IS SHE HIS WIFE ?

Or, SOMETHING SINGULAR !

Alfred Lovetown, Esq. Mr FORESTER,   Mr Peter Limbury, Mr GARDNER,

Felix Tapkins, Esq. (*formerly of the India House Leadenhall Street,*) Mr HARLEY.
(*and now of Rustic Lodge near Reading,*)

Mrs Lovetown, Miss ALLISON,   Mrs Peter Limbury, Madame SALA.

Mr HARLEY

Will be the Character of

MR. PICKWICK

Make his First Visit

TO THE ST. JAMES'S THEATRE,

And relate, to a Scotch Air, his

EXPERIENCES

OF

"A White Bait Dinner at Blackwall."

EDITED EXPRESSLY FOR HIM BY HIS BIOGRAPHER

"BOZ!"

The whole to conclude with,(by Particular Desire)for the **58th&Last Night thisSeason**

THE STRANGE
Gentleman.

Mr.OwenOvetion(*Mayor of a Small Town on the Road to Gretna,& useful at the St. James's Arms*)MrHOLLINGSWORTH,

John Johnson   (*Detained at the St. James's Arms*)   Mr. SIDNEY,

The Strange Gentleman............(*Just Arrived at the St. James's Arms*)...........Mr. HARLEY.

Charles Tomkins.........(*Incognito at the St. James's Arms*)...........Mr. FORESTER,

Tom Sparks.. .... (a One Eyed " Boots." at the St. James's Arms) .... Mr. GARDNER,

John......{   {....Mr. WILLIAMSON,

Tom......}   *Waiters at the St. James's Arms*   {....Mr. MAY,

Will......{   {....Mr. COULSON,

Julia Dobbs   (*Looking for a Husband at the St. James's Arms*)   Madame SALA,

Fanny Wilson.........(*With an Appointment at the St. James's Arms*)...........Miss SMITH,

Mary Wilson ....(her Sister awkwardly situated at the St. James's Arms)...........Miss JULIA SMITH

Mrs. Noakes.......... ..... (the Landlady at the St. James's Arms)...........Mrs PENSON,

Chambermaid, (at the St. James's Arms) Miss STUART.

Duet—"I know a Bank,".... .....Miss SMITH and Miss JULIA SMITH.

TICKETS, BOXES. and PRIVATE BOXES. may be obtained of Mr HARLEY, 14, Upper Gower Street, Bedford Square; and of Mr W. WARNE, at the Box-Office, at the Theatre, from Eleven until Six o'clock daily.

Boxes 5s.--Second Price 3s.   Pit 3s.--Second Price 2s.
Gallery 1s, 6d--Second Price 1s.

VIVANT REX ET REGINA   By Messrs Howard   S. & J. Thomas, Printers &, Bazaar Street, Strand

Figure 4.1   Playbill for *Is She His Wife?*, 13 March 1837.

Harley's role but is a notable departure, being a comic operetta: Dickens with music!

> Autumn leaves, autumn leaves, lie strewn around me here;
> Autumn leaves, autumn leaves, how sad, how cold, how drear!
> How like the hopes of childhood's day,
> Thick clustering on the bough!
> How like those hopes is their decay,–
> How faded are they now!
> Autumn leaves, autumn leaves, lie strewn around me here;
> Autumn leaves, autumn leaves, how sad, how cold, how drear![11]

Well. There it is. The music was provided by John Hullah. Dickens showed great embarrassment about the opera in subsequent years, saying as much to Hullah in 1866:

> I am not proud of my share in *The Village Coquettes*, and would rather let the songs (the words of the songs, I mean) die quietly, than revive them with the name of their respected parent attached. But if you like to republish them as compositions of yours, making no mention whatever of the ingenious author's name, but leaving him to blush anonymously, you are at perfect liberty to do so.[12]

Dickens is perhaps being too hard on himself here, though subsequent critics have agreed with him, and it is unlikely to see 'Autumn Leaves' trending on Spotify anytime soon. But before we tear it to pieces, it is best to remember that the play is emphatically not a Dickens novel, but a comic operetta written by Dickens; therefore it is best understood if compared to other comic operettas rather than other Dickens's works.

The key thing to note is that these plays were successful – but *Pickwick* was more successful. John Glavin suggests that Dickens's exploration of play-writing, just as his novel-writing career was beginning, shows that Dickens 'was in effect starting two parallel careers [...] testing both himself and the marketplace to see which would reward him'.[13] The box-office numbers were good, but *Pickwick* sales were better, so of the two careers, it was the novel-writing one that offered most promise – and also the most praise for Dickens's ego, which in contrast was about to receive a knock from the rejection of his fourth play, *The Lamplighter*. The play follows the same style of *The Strange Gentleman* and *Is She His Wife?*, with another role written for Harley (Tom Grigg, the lamplighter himself). Dickens was pitching it not just to Harley, but to Harley's fellow actor (and Dickens's friend) William Charles Macready. The pair had first met on 16 June 1837 via Forster, as Macready's diary records: 'Forster came into my room with a gentleman, whom he introduced as Dickens, alias Boz – I was glad to see him.'[14] Dickens was clearly a little starstruck by Macready; his reviews of his acting are complimentary in a way that extends beyond the polite support of friends into a thoughtful and critical defence of his work. In 1849 he would write of 'the many great impersonations with which Mr. Macready is associated', judging that 'his Lear is the finest':

> The deep and subtle consideration he has given to the whole noble play, is visible in all he says and does. From his rash renunciation of the gentle daughter who can only love him and be silent, to his falling dead beside her, unbound from the rack of this tough world, a more affecting, truthful and awful picture never surely was presented on stage.[15]

Back in 1838, it was Macready who was the greater success and established talent, and therefore it was Dickens who stood to gain by having Macready approve his new farce. Dickens's letters to Macready recognise this as well as betraying Dickens's own eagerness for writing plays:

> Believe me that I only feel gratified and flattered by your enquiry after the farce, and that if I had as much time as I have inclination, I would write on and on, farce after farce, and comedy after comedy, until I wrote you something that would run.[16]

But it was not to be. Dickens performed two readings for Macready; the first seems to be Dickens reading to Macready alone, the second with a slightly larger audience. Interestingly, the first left Macready feeling more positive; 'The dialogue is very good, full of point' felt Macready, and while he was 'not sure about the meagreness of the plot' he was nonetheless impressed with Dickens himself, who 'reads as well as an experienced actor would – he is a surprising man'.[17] This is as much a testament to Dickens's own acting skills and energy, as much as an understanding of how his own comedy works, which perhaps explains why the second reading did not go well – 'it went flatly, a few ready laughs, but generally an even smile' – and Macready chose to reject the play.[18]

Dickens's reply takes this rejection in good stead – 'I perfectly concur in all you say, and thank you most heartily and cordially for your kind and manly conduct which is only what I should have expected from you' – but there are signs that this is not entirely truthful.[19] Foremost is the sheer effort Dickens put into writing the play at a time when he was already very busy, then copying it into neat hand and performing it to Macready twice. Then there is the earlier letter to Macready where he suggests he could write many such comedies and insists – a little too emphatically – that the play is really just a small trifle. This is a stark contrast to what happens after the rejection, when Dickens does *not* write another play, despite previously saying how easy it was to do. Whether he was becoming more absorbed in his role as an author or, as I suspect, did not handle the rejection as well as he professed, he would not write another solo work for the public stage again.

Dickens in the Audience

So far the chapter has focused on Dickens's direct involvement in theatre as a creative, either as actor or writer. But ultimately, Dickens's primary and most significant interaction with the theatre was an audience member. He attended several plays and the influence upon his writing is evident. Discussion of Shakespeare's influence on Dickens is divided as to how much Dickens is referencing the texts, or the performances of the texts. The theatre held a fascination for him, to be sure. *Sketches by Boz* includes three pieces discussing dramatic productions and venues ('Private Theatres', 'Mrs. Joseph Porter' and 'Astleys'), and a number of his characters attend the theatre in his novels, most notably in the extended discussion in *Great Expectations* of Mr Wopsle's disastrous performance of *Hamlet*. In all of these Dickens writes from the perspective of audience member and in so doing captures the experience and emotion of attending the theatre. Victorian Theatre is understudied today compared to other dramatic periods, though the tide is changing. Much as Dickens's dramatic works are criticised, so too, Victorian Theatre as a whole has long been considered as lacking; often the plays written in this time are focussed more on entertainment than enrichment, which makes them fascinating to watch at the time, but leaves little critical meat for academics to subsequently pick apart. In Dickens's lifetime theatre was the popular medium: those who could not read could find entertainment here, so a number of novels found new audiences through their dramatic adaptations. The lack of copyright meant that numerous adaptations of the same book were often staged at the same time; shortly after Dickens wrote his Christmas book *The Cricket on the Hearth* in 1845, there were eighteen theatres in London staging their adaptations of it. The technical capacity of the Victorian stage was unprecedented; gone were the bare stages that Shakespeare had to contend with, and instead there was a drive towards showing and displaying everything, a phenomenon subsequently dubbed 'Victorian Pictorialism'. In the instance of Shakespeare, actors such as Charles Kean put on lavish productions of the history plays with fully researched authentic historical dress, and hundreds of extras on stage (not to mention horses) to present scenes such as Richard II's walk through the London crowds which were only described in Shakespeare's plays. New plays produced in this time catered to this mania for visualisation, with ever more outlandish feats presented on stage: for Dion Boucicault's 1860 play *The Colleen Bawn* the stage was flooded with water to represent the cavern where the heroine is almost drowned, only to be saved by the dashing hero who swings down from a rope above. The spectacle on offer through the increasingly sophisticated visual effects was matched by the ever-growing spectacle of the plot. Melodrama was one of the most popular theatrical genres of the day: incredible plots of coincidence, heightened drama, twists, thrills and spills. The theatre thus presented what many worried was a dumbed-down entertainment compared to novels. Dickens explores the phenomenon in his 1850 essay 'The Amusements of the People':

> Joe Whelks, of the New Cut, Lambeth, is not much of a reader, has no great store of books, no very commodious room to read in, no very decided inclination to read, and no power at all of presenting vividly before his mind's eye what he reads about. But put Joe in the gallery of the Victoria Theatre; show him doors and windows in the scene that will open and shut, and that people can get in an out of; tell him a story with these aids, and by the help of live men and women dressed up, confiding to him their innermost secrets, in voices audible half a mile off; and Joe will unravel a story through all its entanglements, and sit there as long after midnight as you have anything left to show him.[20]

What is apparent from Dickens's description here, and corroborated through the article, is his love and admiration for how theatre can capture its audience's attention and inspire them. As much as he ridicules the hyperbole of these melodramatic plots, he recognises and applauds the joy they bring and the power they hold. Though the piece satirises many plays, Dickens's enthusiasm for them despite their absurdity – arguably *because* of their absurdity – shines through. But Dickens also enjoyed more serious drama too. A review of his friend Macready in the role of Benedict in *Much Ado about Nothing* praises him specifically for understanding what Shakespeare's character is meant to be, rather than pandering to theatrical convention and cliché, to present 'Shakespeare's Benedick – the real Benedick of the book, not the conventional Benedick of the boards'.[21] Dickens was not just an indiscriminate fan of the theatre but a discerning viewer able to identify what worked and what did not. It is notable that among his later charity work, one of the endeavours he supported was the General Theatrical Fund, which provided a pension for older actors as their careers came to an end, and in one of his many speeches for the fund he offers a stirring and heartfelt defence of the theatre that reveals his own feelings:

> I fearlessly add these words – if there be any creature here knowing a theatre well who knows any kind of place, no matter what, cathedral, church, chapel, tabernacle, high cross, market, change, where there is

a more sacred bond of charitable brotherhood, where there is a more certain reliance to be placed on sympathy with affliction, where there is a greater generosity in ready giving, where there is a higher and more sacred respect for family ties, where there is habitually a more cheerful, voluntary bearing of burdens on already heavily burdened backs, then let him take his money out to that place, to me unknown, and not produce it here.[22]

If Dickens was enthralled by the stage as a participant, he was yet more in awe of its power as a spectator. Whether as diversion, amusement for the masses, or source of education and hope, he championed the theatre and aspired to it.

Amateur Dramatics: What Dickens Did Next

Given his love of the stage, it is unsurprising that the stifling of his professional playwriting would not end Dickens's involvement in theatre. Even as his literary career progressed, he maintained an interest and enthusiasm in acting; this manifested in amateur dramatics, such as those he had taken part in when living with his parents. Now as the man of the house the dynamics had shifted, but the principles were the same. The appeal of amateur dramatics is explained by a curious perception of the time: professional acting was still, despite the success of Macready, Harley and others, seen as a somewhat lowly profession unbecoming of a gentleman. Macready noted how 'whilst the law, the church, the army and navy give a man the rank of gentleman, on the stage that designation must be obtained in society [...] by the individual'.[23] It was not impossible to be an actor and a gentleman, but it was certainly not the norm. Amateur dramatics, on the other hand, in which the players were not reliant upon the endeavour for financial support, were seen with more acceptance as a droll and entirely suitable pursuit for gentlemen to enjoy. In terms of production value, Dickens invested heavily in each, and presented them to a paying public, so that the distinction between professional and amateur was not always clear. Ultimately, acting in an 'amateur' capacity meant Dickens could have his cake and eat it: he could act on a stage without relying upon it for income, meaning he could indulge fantasies of being an actor while maintaining his new position as a gentleman. Each endeavour could be excused as a necessary act to raise funds for a good cause, but clearly Dickens was having a whale of a time while doing it.

In 1845 Dickens staged and acted in Shakespeare's *The Merry Wives of Windsor*, and Ben Jonson's *Every Man in His Humour*. The cause was raising funds for a curator for Shakespeare's birthplace, but the result was Dickens taking the opportunity to play comic roles in two celebrated plays. In both works he did not play the main role, but instead took an overly comic role: Justice Shallow in *Merry Wives* and Captain Bobadil in *Every Man*, both a good opportunity to steal the stage during the time he was on it. Five years later he was involved in another amateur performance, but this time he was writing again as well as acting. In addition to performing in Bulwer Lytton's *Not So Bad as We Seem*, Dickens and his friends also performed a short comic farce *Mr. Nightingale's Diary* in 1851. This was originally written by Dickens's friend Mark Lemon, who as the editor of *Punch* was no stranger to comic writing; but Dickens made extensive revisions to the piece so that he was now considered co-author of the piece. Whatever dent in his confidence the rejection of *The Lamplighter* had made, clearly he now felt able and willing to revise his friend's work ready for performance. The plot of the play is relatively slim, with the notable point for our consideration being Dickens's part, Mr Gabblewig, who adopts various disguises and personas during the course of the farce. This allowed Dickens to provide a virtuoso performance exactly like that of his childhood hero Charles Matthews – the skill of the piece was in the number of different characters assumed, so that it was the energy of Dickens's performance which wowed the audience.

The most infamous of Dickens's amateur dramatic productions is *The Frozen Deep*, for reasons that extend far beyond the performance itself, as this was the means in which he first met his mistress Ellen Ternan. The play was written by Dickens's friend and author Wilkie Collins, and in a departure from Dickens's previous comic forays, is a melodrama in which Dickens played the tragic hero Richard Wardour, who goes on a polar expedition which ends in disaster. The two survivors are Wardour and his rival in love; but faced with the opportunity to dispose of his competitor (which everyone fears he will do), Wardour instead saves him, and dies at the end of the play a noble and selfless hero who has ensured the happiness of the woman he loves with the man she loves. Like *Mr. Nightingale's Diary*, Dickens made numerous revisions to the text while preparing it for the stage, so that once again there is contention over whether Dickens should be considered as co-author of Collins's play. It was originally performed as a purely amateur production alongside the comic piece *Uncle John* by John Baldwin Buckstone, and when first performed it was staged in Dickens's home in Tavistock House with the female roles played by his daughters Katey and Mamie, and his sister-in-law Georgina. The play was a success so that Dickens decided to launch it to a public audience – still as a charitable endeavour, of course, and therefore still maintaining a sense of decorum. However, social etiquette being the fickle thing it is, while it was acceptable for Dickens and his male peers to act the play still to a wider public, it was not felt appropriate for the ladies of the family to be on stage, so they were replaced by professional actresses, including Ellen Ternen, who would become Dickens's lover. Discussion of *The*

Frozen Deep therefore frequently turns to this as an ominous moment, predominately due to its afterlife; Dickens wrote *A Tale of Two Cities* shortly afterwards and openly admitted it was inspired by Collins's drama, and both here and in later fiction Ellen Ternan can be seen in the heroines of the stories.

Dickens would write one more play, once again a collaboration, and with Collins. But the circumstances are somewhat different from before. *No Thoroughfare* was originally a special number of *All the Year Round* co-authored by Dickens and Collins, the work of which appears to have been evenly split between the two, before they then being adapted for the stage. Collins had shown far more interest in adapting his works for the stage than Dickens had; as a younger author he was part of a generation that perhaps viewed the theatre in a different manner without the hang-ups of appropriate/inappropriate professions for gentlemen. It is likely therefore that the adaptation of *No Thoroughfare* was driven by Collins rather than Dickens, but that is not to say Dickens did not take a healthy interest in the adaptation, despite being abroad at the time and in the inevitable limitations that introduced to his interaction with Collins. In one letter written from America he speaks of plans to see 'the most speculative of dramatic men' in New York to 'ascertain what terms he will make for the Play', with the strong belief that he will get 'a very handsome addition to our gains.'[24] Paul Lewis has done excellent work piecing together the correspondence and internal evidence to theorise the likely split, concluding that it was actually relatively equal.[25] However, Dickens's distance from London certainly complicated issues and limited his involvement with final decisions. One letter from Dickens shows the urgent, brief and hurried nature of these edits that queries quite how much Dickens was involved:

> I am obliged to write very hastily, to catch the Mail over at New York. The Play is done *with great pains and skill*. But I fear it is too long. It's fate will have been decided before you get this letter, but I greatly doubt its success.
>
> Your points follow in their order.
>
> 1) Whatever is most dramatic in such a complicated thing as the Clock Lock, I think the best for the stage – without reference to the nicety of the real mechanism.
> 2) I would keep Vendale and Marguerite on the state. And I would end with Obenreizer's exit.
> 3) Madame D'Or's speaking, unquestionably better out. She herself unquestionably better out. I have not the least doubt of it.
>
> But my dear boy, what do you mean by the whole being left 'at my sole discretion'? Is not the play coming out, the day after tomorrow???[26]

The bullet point response to Collins's previous queries is reminiscent of a PhD supervisor's reply to their student; calling Collins 'my dear boy' further emphasises the dynamic of senior and junior partner. But the amusement at Collins's assurance that any decisions are at Dickens's discretion, when in reality the play was shortly to go onstage and possibly after Collins would have even received Dickens's letter, betrays the extent to which Collins, though theoretically the sidekick, was actually taking control of the work. Nonetheless, it was hailed as Dickens's and Collins's joint work, and it was a return to the public stage; had Dickens lived longer it could have been the first of more such ventures.

I have mentioned Dickens's ego a number of times in this chapter; it is worth thinking about it one more time in relation to the public readings. These will be discussed in more detail in Chapter 11, but they obviously draw on the same enthusiasm for the stage that has been discussed here. They also offer Dickens the opportunity once more to indulge his admiration of Charles Matthews and his monopolylogues, with Dickens playing all the parts. This too brings us back to the ego of the man, and his sense of control. In many respects a one-man show better suited Dickens's temperament. This can be extended to his novel-writing career too; as an author, Dickens had complete control over his narrative and characters in a way that acting on the stage did not allow. When reading a Dickens novel, the narrator is a dominating voice with his own opinions and interjections to make. Dickens literally controls the story and the way in which it is told; therefore when considering that parallel dimension where the twenty-year-old Dickens did go to the audition, and did pursue an acting career, once cannot help wonder how he would have fared, and whether he would have proved to be a difficult and frustrating actor to work with in his constant suggestions and reworkings. The fact that he revised both Lemon's and Collins's plays is an indication of this. His appreciation of praise, and the almost addictive behaviour he shows towards the public readings despite the concerns of his friends and doctor, show a need, an insatiable desire, to hold the audience's attention.

Case Study: *Nicholas Nickleby* and Melodramatic Conventions

Dickens dedicated his third novel *Nicholas Nickleby* to Macready, a fitting choice given that *Nickleby* is one of Dickens's most explicitly theatrical novels, for the sheer presence of Vincent Crummles, actor–manager extraordinaire, and his troupe of players. Nicholas meets Crummles while trying to find a new living, and he and his friend Smike soon find a home as actors in Crummles's company. Crummles and his troupe deserve consideration here, but I will also show how theatre emerges in subtler ways in this and other novels. But, to begin with Crummles, the reader's first encounter with him reveals him to be a typical actor–manager of the time:

> I am in the theatrical profession myself, my wife is in the theatrical profession, my children are in the theatrical profession. I had a dog that lived and died in it from a puppy; and my chaise-pony goes on, in Timour the Tartar.[27]

Before the evolution of the theatre director as a distinct role and profession, British theatres and playing companies would be run by an actor, the head of the troupe. This actor–manager would choose plays and assign roles; unsurprisingly then, they would play the main role themselves, with the female lead usually assigned to their wife. The system helped establish a celebrity system in theatre: Thomas Betterton and his wife were respected actors of their time, followed (and outshined) in turn by David Garrick. In Dickens's lifetime the stage would see the likes of Macready, of course, but also other leading stars such as Edmund Kean, and his son Charles Kean, both actor–managers, the latter working with his wife. In *Nickleby*, Dickens takes such nepotism further and has Crummles assign role to his daughter, dog and pony too. We meet said daughter in the next chapter, where the enthusiasm of Crummles for her talents is checked by the cold reality of Dickens's narrative voice:

> 'May I ask how old she is?' inquired Nicholas.
> 'You may, sir,' replied Mr. Crummles, looking steadily in his questioner's face, as some men do when they have doubts about being implicitly believed in what they are going to say. 'She is ten years of age, sir.'
> 'Not more!'
> 'Not a day.'
> 'Dear me!' said Nicholas, 'it's extraordinary.'
> It was; for the infant phenomenon, though of short stature, had a comparatively aged countenance, and had moreover been precisely the same age – not perhaps to the full extent of the memory of the oldest inhabitant, but certainly for five good years. But she had been kept up late every night, and put upon an unlimited allowance of gin-and-water from infancy, to prevent her growing tall, and perhaps this system of training had produced in the infant phenomenon these additional phenomena.[28]

Crummles is clearly being mocked by Dickens here; the Infant Phenomenon has been proclaimed as ten years old for five years; has been kept up late to perform in plays, and imbibed copious amounts of gin to stunt her height. The father has done everything he can to perpetuate her career as child-actress, often at odds with what might be best for her health and well-being. Mr Folair, a fellow actor in the company, makes the nepotism of Crummles's casting choices more explicit when he tells Nicholas 'She may thank her stars she was born a manager's daughter'; the implication in his subsequent explanation being that Crummles's pride as a father dictates his decisions as a director:

> Isn't it enough to make a man crusty to see that little sprawler put up in the best business every night, and actually keeping money out of the house, by being forced down the people's throats, while other people are passed over? Isn't it extraordinary to see a man's confounded family conceit blinding him, even to his own interest? Why I *know* of fifteen and sixpence that came to Southampton one night last month, to see me dance the Highland Fling; and what's the consequence? I've never been put up in it since—never once—while the "infant phenomenon" has been grinning through artificial flowers at five people and a baby in the pit, and two boys in the gallery, every night.[29]

There is of course a personal motivation in Folair's criticism, namely that the Infant Phenomenon's continued presence on stage leaves less time and opportunity for Folair to enjoy the spotlight. The company and its internal politics are used for comic effect, contrasting the high aspirations of the theatre with the more earthly considerations of who gets a bigger role and how much money can be made. Crummles is not the successful actor that Macready was, but a provincial actor, touring the country and dreaming of London, and thus mixing the self-importance of the stereotypical actor-manager with the pragmatism (sometimes desperation) of a touring company in the sticks. He is therefore quick to recommend Nicholas to the stage as a natural:

> 'There's genteel comedy in your walk and manner, juvenile tragedy in your eye, and touch-and-go farce in your laugh,' said Mr. Vincent Crummles. 'You'll do as well as if you had thought of nothing else but the lamps, from your birth downwards.'[30]

This is either remarkable astuteness on Crummles's part in spotting Nicholas's innate talent to immediately, purely upon an initial meeting, or it is the eagerness of a man looking to recruit more people to his company and flattering a newcomer into signing up. At either rate, what is important to note here, and throughout Crummles's role in the novel, is that there is nothing malicious either in Crummles's behaviour nor in Dickens's portrayal of him. If Crummles is ridiculous, we are invited to laugh kindly, and his actions are ultimately benevolent: Nicholas and Smike need a job, and Crummles happily takes them both in.

Once again, however much Dickens enjoys pointing out the absurdity of theatre and those who work in it, it is always done with affection and sympathy.

Crummles's subsequent offer to Nicholas to write for the company as well is yet a further nod to Dickens's own dual role as playwright and amateur actor, in addition to an insight into theatrical practice of the time and the manner in which spectacle often dictated the plots of the plays:

> 'We'll have a new show-piece out directly,' said the manager. 'Let me see
> – peculiar resources of this establishment – new and splendid scenery
> – you must manage to introduce a real pump and two washing-tubs.'
> 'Into the piece?' said Nicholas.
> 'Yes,' replied the manager. 'I bought 'em cheap, at a sale the other day,
> and they'll come in admirably. That's the London plan. They look up
> some dresses, and properties, and have a piece written to fit 'em. Most
> of the theatres keep an author on purpose.'
> 'Indeed!' cried Nicholas.
> 'Oh, yes,' said the manager; 'a common thing. It'll look very well in the
> bills in separate lines – Real pump! – Splendid tubs! – Great attraction!
> You don't happen to be anything of an artist, do you?'[31]

Just like Crummles's employment of this man he has just met, so too in his use of props and spectacle there is an element of opportunism and simply using the resources that are available to him, even down to asking Nicholas if he is an artist, in addition to employing him on the spot as an actor and writer. There is also that admiration and imitation of 'the London plan'; like many provincial actors, Crummles enjoys the celebrity status on tour while dreaming of hitting the big time in the capital. This is particularly ironic given that Nicholas meets Crummles in Portsmouth, Dickens's home town. The chapter introducing Crummles was published in the seventh monthly number of *Nickleby* in September 1838, and is likely to have been written no more than three months before that. This coincides with Dickens's involvement with the St James Theatre; his first three plays had been performed already, while he would offer *The Lamplighter* to Macready in December of that year. In other words, it was at a time when the potential of being a playwright as well as a novelist was still a possibility in Dickens's mind, and so the discussion of the theatre and how it works here has the air of an insider, especially in the reference above to authors being kept 'on purpose' by theatres to write pieces around the props they had. Dickens is using his position as an industry insider to inform and inspire his novel. This is evident in Nicholas and Smike's contrasting response to their first sight of the stage of the Portsmouth Theatre:

> It was not very light, but Nicholas found himself close to the first entrance
> on the prompt side, among bare walls, dusty scenes, mildewed clouds,

heavily daubed draperies, and dirty floors. He looked about him; ceiling, pit, boxes, gallery, orchestra, fittings, and decorations of every kind,—all looked coarse, cold, gloomy, and wretched.

'Is this a theatre?' whispered Smike, in amazement; 'I thought it was a blaze of light and finery.'

'Why, so it is,' replied Nicholas, hardly less surprised; 'but not by day, Smike—not by day.'[32]

The juxtaposition of the 'coarse, cold, gloomy, and wretched' surroundings with the expectations of 'a blaze of light and finery' expose the reality behind the illusion and gives Dickens's readers a peek behind the scenes – literally. Smike and Nicholas could almost be seen to represent the dual nature of Dickens as audience and playwright, the naivety and enthusiasm of the former tempered by the experience and coolness of the latter. In this, and the gleeful exposure of company politics, Dickens is not presenting a revelation to his audience, but rather confirming and exaggerating their suspicions of how a theatre works, and balancing his own enthusiasm for the stage with a frank acknowledgement of its more pompous and ridiculous aspects.

The Crummles family and their antics are an explicit theatrical reference in *Nickleby*, but the influence of the stage pervades Dickens's writing style in a subtler and more prevalent way. If Crummles is a conscious actor, the other characters in the tale are unconscious actors in Dickens's melodrama, filling the standard roles and providing scenes of spectacle such as might be seen on the stage. Dickens's descriptive writing frequently paints a scene precisely as it would be portrayed on a stage, directing his character into certain positions and poses to create a visual effect. Consider, as one example, the case of Mr Mantalini, the extravagant tailor whose wife employs Nicholas's sister Kate. Mantalini is not his real name, but a fake Italian name he has adopted for the sake of reputation and business; he is really not so different from Crummles. His extravagant spending and associated debts makes for a turbulent relationship with his wife who is trying to run the business, leading to several moments of comic outbursts and heightened drama. At one point, the ever-dramatic and hyperbolic Mantalini attempts to kill himself for the seventh time, in a remarkably over-the-top sign of despair deliberately designed to engender sympathy from his wife and stop any real damage from occurring. Dickens describes the scene of Mantalini, his wife, and the various women who work for her all swarming around the apparently desperate Mantalini in much the same way as a modern director would assemble his cast on the stage:

There were all the young-lady workers, some with bonnets and some without, in various attitudes expressive of alarm and consternation; some gathered round Madame Mantalini, who was in tears upon one chair; and others round Miss Knag, who was in opposition tears upon another; and others round Mr Mantalini, who was perhaps the most striking figure in the whole group, for Mr. Mantalini's legs were extended at full length upon the floor, and his head and shoulders were supported by a very tall footman, who didn't seem to know what to do with them, and Mr. Mantalini's eyes were closed, and his face was pale and his hair was comparatively straight, and his whiskers and moustache were limp, and his teeth were clenched, and he had a little bottle in his right hand, and a little tea-spoon in his left; and his hands, arms, legs, and shoulders, were all stiff and powerless. And yet Madame Mantalini was not weeping upon the body, but was scolding violently upon her chair; and all this amidst a clamour of tongues perfectly deafening, and which really appeared to have driven the unfortunate footman to the utmost verge of distraction.[33]

Dickens prefaces this as a 'confused and inexplicable scene', and a scene it is. The description of the characters focuses on their visual appearance rather than their internal thoughts: we are told what they are *doing*, not what they are *feeling*. We are invited to look upon the characters and deduce their emotions from how they are arranged. Madame Mantalini is not described as angry, but rather 'scolding violently upon her chair'; Mr Mantalini is highlighted as 'the most striking figure in the whole group' followed by a detailed description of his pose and attitude. This is exactly the manner of melodramatic theatre of the time, with actors adopting poses associated with certain emotions, which an audience could deduce and understand in much the same way that cinema audiences instinctively know the inner thoughts of a character by the style of music being played on the soundtrack at that moment. This emphasis upon the character's actions rather than their inner thoughts has led some to criticise Dickens for creating caricatures as though this is a failing on his part; in actuality he is drawing upon the popular medium of theatre to provide an energy and immediacy to his writing and engage the imagination of his reader. The passage above actively demands the reader to visualise the scene in their head, to 'see' the scene rather than passively reading and having all the inner-dialogue of the characters fed to them. It encourages greater interaction and engagement with the text as well as providing striking visual moments that stay on the memory. This is further enabled by the illustrations that accompanied Dickens's novels, especially those by Hablot Knight Browne, or Phiz, who worked with Dickens more times than any other illustrator. The scene above is illustrated by Phiz to further cement and capture the moment of the scene in much the same way as painters and illustrators of the age would depict key tableaux from famous theatrical productions [see Figure 4.2]. The illustration, like those paintings, becomes both commemoration of the moment and invitation to it; readers can experience Dickens's description first before looking upon Phiz's rendering, or

MR. MANTALINI POISONS HIMSELF FOR THE SEVENTH TIME.

Figure 4.2   Phiz, 'Mr Mantalini poisons himself for the seventh time', April 1839.

else see the illustration when they first open the number and anticipate seeing that moment emerge as they peruse the plot. Elsewhere I have compared the serialised fiction of Dickens to boxsets and tv series, but ultimately the prescient and more timely comparison for Dickens's work is the stage: he lived it, breathed it, and utilised its conventions and style into his novelistic writing.

Notes

1 John Forster, *The Life of Charles Dickens*, Volume One (London: Chapman and Hall, 1872), p. 10.
2 Dickens in John Forster, *The Life of Charles Dickens*, Volume Two (London: Chapman and Hall, 1873), p. 180.

3 Dickens in Forster, Vol. 2, p. 180.

4 John Dickens, Inscription on Charles Dickens, *O'Thello*, in Charles Dickens, *The Bill of Fare, O'Thello & Other Early Works*, ed. by Christine Alexander with Donna Courto and Kate Summer (Sydney: Juvenilia Press, 2012), pp. 48–59 (p. 49).

5 *O'Thello*, p. 57.

6 Charles Dickens, 'Mrs. Joseph Porter', in Paul Schlicke and David Hewitt (eds.), *Sketches by Boz* (Oxford: OUP, 2020), pp. 11–20 (p. 11).

7 Charles Dickens, *The Strange Gentleman*, in Richard Herne Shepherd (ed.), *The Plays and Poems of Charles Dickens*, Volume One (London: W H Allen, 1885), pp. 97–171 (p. 104).

8 Charles Dickens, *Is She His Wife?*, in Shepherd, pp. 275–300 (p. 283–284).

9 Jim Davis, 'John Pritt Harley as Low Comedian and Dickensian Actor', *Dickensian* Vol. 117, No. 514 (Summer 2021), pp. 132–145 (p. 138).

10 Dickens, Letter to John Hullah, 29 December 1835, in Madeline House and Graham Storey (eds.), *The Letters of Charles Dickens*, Volume One 1820–1839 (Oxford: Clarendon Press, 1974), pp. 113–114 (p. 113).

11 Charles Dickens, *The Village Coquettes*, in Shepherd, pp. 172–273 (p. 197).

12 Dickens, Letter to John Hullah, 8 May 1866, in Graham Storey (ed.), *The Letters of Charles Dickens*, Volume Eleven, 1865–1867 (Oxford: Clarendon Press, 1999), p. 197 (p. 197).

13 John Glavin, 'Dickens and Theatre', in John O. Jordan (ed.), *The Cambridge Companion to Charles Dickens* (Cambridge: CUP, 2001), pp. 189–203 (p. 191).

14 Entry for 16 June 1837 in *Diaries of William Charles Macready*, ed. by William Toynbee, Volume One (London: Chapman and Hall, 1912), p. 399.

15 Charles Dickens, 'Theatre Review', *The Examiner*, 27 October 1849.

16 Dickens, Letter to W. C. Macready, 19 November 1838, in *Letters*, Volume One, pp. 456–457 (pp. 456–457).

17 Entry for 5 December 1838 in *Diaries of William Charles Macready*, ed. by William Toynbee, Vol. 1 (London: Chapman and Hall, 1912), p. 480.

18 Entry for 10 December 1838, *Diaries of Macready*, Vol 1, p. 481.

19 Dickens, Letter to W. C. Macready, 13 December 1838, in House and Storey, Vol. One, p. 468 (p. 468).

20 Charles Dickens, 'The Amusements of the People', *Household Words*, 30 March 1850, pp. 13–15 (p. 13), available via *Dickens Journals Online* at www.djo.org.uk.

21 Theatre Review, *The Examiner*, 4 March 1843.

22 Speech to the General Theatrical Fund, 4 April 1863.

23 W. C. Macready cited in Malcolm Andrews, *Charles Dickens and his Performing Selves* (Oxford: OUP, 2006), p. 33.

24 Dickens, 'Letter to Wilkie Collins', 28 November 1867, in Graham Storey (ed.), *The Letters of Charles Dickens* Volume Eleven, 1865–1867 (Oxford: Clarendon Press, 1999), pp. 491–492 (pp. 491–492).

25 I am indebted to Paul Lewis for his keen insights, first discussed during his guest seminar 'Who Wrote No Thoroughfare' for the Dickens MA Seminar Series, held on 28 May 2020. Lewis is currently writing up his research for publication in the *Dickensian*; for further information on Dickens and Collins see also Lewis's site *The Wilkie Collins Pages* http://www.web40571.clarahost. co.uk/index.htm, and Lillian Nayder, *Unequal Partners: Charles Dickens, Wilkie Collins and Victorian Authorship* (Ithaca: Cornell University Press, 2002), especially pp. 129–162 which discuss *No Thoroughfare*.

26 Dickens, Letter to Wilkie Collins, 24 December 1867, in *Letters*, Vol. 11, pp. 520–521 (p. 520).

27 Charles Dickens, *Nicholas Nickleby*, ed. by Paul Schlicke (Oxford: OUP, 2008), Ch. 22, p. 283.

28 *Nicholas Nickleby*, Ch. 23, p. 290.

29 *Nicholas Nickleby*, Ch. 23, p. 291.

30 *Nicholas Nickleby*, Ch. 22, p. 283.

31 *Nicholas Nickleby*, Ch. 22, p. 284.

32 *Nicholas Nickleby*, Ch. 23, pp. 287–288.

33 *Nicholas Nickleby*, Ch. 44, p. 577.

5

Dickens Abroad

Focal Point: 1842–1846

Case Study: Little Dorrit

Dickens's first trip abroad had been in July 1837, when he travelled to France and Belgium for a week, accompanied by his wife Catherine and his illustrator H. K. Browne (who signed his illustrations as Phiz). Browne's biographer suggests it was he who proposed the trip in the aftermath of Mary Hogarth's death, as 'a change of scene might do Charles, Catherine, and himself some good.'[1] Dickens's brief letters from this week tell us he suffered from 'the dismal extremity of qualmishness into which I am accustomed to sink when I have "the blues above and the blue below"' (i.e. seasickness) but he nonetheless shows a giddy excitement at the novelty of being abroad:[2]

> A gentleman in a blue surtout and silken Berlins accompanied us from the Hotel, and acted as Curator. He even waltzed with a very smart lady (just to show us, condescendingly, how it ought to be done) and waltzed elegantly too. We rang for slippers after we came back, and it turned out that this gentleman was the 'Boots'. Isn't this French?[3]

In time, excitement would prove to champion over and above any misgivings, and Dickens would return abroad many more times in his life. For an author who is so frequently championed specifically as an English author, especially grounded in London and the south east, it is eye-opening to realise just how international Dickens really was. Not only would he visit France several more times, but would also make repeat trips to Italy, Switzerland and America. He was fluent in French and Italian, and proud of it. In a letter to Emile de la Rue he boasted 'I read French as easily as English', and a surviving letter to his sister-in-law Georgina dated 25 October 1853 switches between English and these two other languages as Dickens records his conversations abroad.[4] This chapter will consider Dickens's interaction with other countries and cultures to show their influence upon him, as well as his reaction to them.

The Life of the Author: Charles Dickens, First Edition. Pete Orford.
© 2023 John Wiley & Sons Ltd. Published 2023 by John Wiley & Sons Ltd.

America

After that first brief trip across the English Channel, Dickens's next major voyage was a major one indeed: America. The year was 1842 and Dickens's prospects had continued to grow. The success of *Pickwick* and *Oliver* had been followed by *Nicholas Nickleby*, and while his journal *Master Humphrey's Clock* had experienced an uneven start, its subsequent publication of *The Old Curiosity Shop* had once more confirmed Dickens's popularity and skill, not only in his own country but abroad as well. The publication of his works in a serial format allowed for the wider dissemination of his writing, with ships and passengers taking instalments across the Atlantic, leading to the infamous anecdote of the crowds at New York harbour waiting for the boats to come in with news of Little Nell's fate. Dickens stood on the precipice of international fame. There was still some wrestling as to under which name he was famous: his own, or his pseudonym Boz (in fact, William Long and Paul Schlicke have noted the name is still used in advertisements for Dickens's works as late as 1848, long after Dickens had ceased to use it himself), so the fame of his writing was not necessarily matched by the fame of the man.[5] However, a portrait of the author by his friend and artist Daniel Maclise had been reproduced as an engraving by William Finden in the 1839 volume edition of *Nicholas Nickleby*, which allowed the wider world their first glimpse of this new and successful author, who turned out to be but a young man [see Figure 5.1].[6] Now, in 1842, Dickens took the opportunity to cross the Atlantic and meet his American fans face to face. Slater notes how newspaper articles captured the excitement of America on the imminent arrival of the author, this 'young stranger, about whose path we crowd with so warm and eager a homage of our hearts ... whom we are so anxious to clasp hand to hand, and to meet in that silent sympathy which passes between men like the transit of an electric spark when their eyes meet'.[7]

A warm welcome was promised to Dickens, but there was a secondary motive in his heading to America: money. Dickens's popularity came at a price – or rather, the absence of a fee, with others seeking to profit from his work without paying a dime to him. In England, there were several pirated editions of his works that had appeared, unauthorised sequels and clear imitations such as *Oliver Twiss, Nicholas Nickleberry* and *Pickwick Abroad* (this latter book, by Dickens's long-term rival G. W. Reynolds, was a huge hit and enjoyed alongside the original in much the same way as fans today will gladly watch a movie sequel continuing their favourite character irrespective of whether the original creative team is behind it). These works were, ultimately, new works, and therefore able to evade the copyright laws of the time (as did the various dramatic adaptations of Dickens's works that sprung up at this time, from

Figure 5.1 Daniel Maclise, 'Charles Dickens', engraved by William Finden, 1839.

which he received no royalties). The one thing they were *not* allowed to do was to replicate his work in its original state, so while there was a wave of imitations and adaptations, ultimately the only way to read the original in the UK was to buy an authorised copy. However, as loose as these copyright laws may seem to us, international copyright law was even looser. There was no restriction on reprinting foreign literature, meaning that Dickens's works were reproduced and published around the world without the need for Dickens's permission, and without any payment to him either. Eventually Dickens would find ways around this, by sending advance copies of proofs to selected publishers, for a fee, so that they could get the jump on their competitors and Dickens could at least share in some of the profits. But the situation rankled him.

Thus America offered both opportunity and grievance to Dickens: opportunity to enjoy his popularity and fame, and a grievance to air over international copyright law (or the lack of) and the way in which American publishers were freely profiting from his labour. Initially however, it was the opportunity that held most sway in his decision, and Dickens's plans to go abroad are full of excitement at seeing the New World, as in this letter to an American editor:

> Our stay will be six months; during which times, I must see as much as can be seen in such a space, of the country and the people.
>
> You make me very proud and happy by anticipation, in thinking of the number of friends I shall find; but I cannot describe to you the glow into which I rise, when I think of the wonders that await us, and all the interest I am sure I shall have in your mighty land.[8]

He had completed his fifth novel, *Barnaby Rudge*, in late 1841 and so the time had come for a sabbatical. He would be accompanied by Catherine once again, but no Phiz this time; and no children either. This was a sticking point. He told his brother Fred that 'We must, I grieve to say (for everyone advises me to do so) leave the darlings behind us, which will be a very severe trial', which would give the impression that Dickens was equally sad to leave them behind, were it not for his earlier letters.[9] Just twelve days before he was writing to William Hall, his publisher, that 'I can't persuade Mrs. Dickens to go, and leave the children at home; or to let me go alone.'[10] There are two solutions to the discrepancy; either Dickens was really rather keen to go, but presenting the impression of being sorry to leave the children behind; or he truly was grieving to miss them but did not want to admit to his publisher that which he was happy to tell his brother. This may be giving him too much credit; ultimately, sad or not, he did go to America, he did leave the children behind.

There were now four Dickens children: Charley, Mary, Katey and Walter, all aged five and under, and they were all left behind in London, with Dickens's friend William Charles Macready and his family while Dickens and his wife toured America. Just as Daniel Maclise had provided the portrait of Dickens which would announce him to the wider world, so now, at Catherine's request, he painted a portrait of the Dickens children for her to take to America. The decision not to take them was a practical one, but no less heart-breaking. Instead the couple would be accompanied by Catherine's maid, Anne Brown.

They set sail on 4 January 1842 from Liverpool on the S. S. *Britannia*, a paddle steamer. In an age of steam, transport was becoming both faster and more readily available, though it still had some way to go: the trip across the Atlantic would take eighteen days, and it was not smooth sailing. Dickens recalled a particularly treacherous part of the crossing:

It is the third morning. I am awakened out of my sleep by a dismal shriek from my wife, who demands to know whether there's any danger. I rouse myself, and look out of bed. The water-jug is plunging and leaping like a lively dolphin: all the smaller articles are afloat, except my shoes, which are stranded on a carpet-bag, high and dry, like a couple of coal-barges. Suddenly I see them spring into the air, and behold the looking-glass, which is nailed to the wall, sticking fast upon the ceiling. At the same time the door entirely disappears, and a new one is opened in the floor. Then I begin to comprehend that the state-room is standing on its head.[11]

They arrived at Boston Harbour on 22 January 1842. The United States was still a fledgling nation, having achieved independence less than sixty years earlier. It was seen as a place of innovation and potential; for Dickens, who so regularly criticised the more archaic aspects of English law and society, he hoped to see a land of progress. The Americans in turn saw him as a champion of such progress, campaigning against the old ways and ready to meet his spiritual home in the New World. He was inundated with invitations and surrounded by crowds. Slater notes that 'Young ladies wrote to Dickens soliciting a lock of his flowing hair, everyone who was anyone in Boston society paid him a visit, and the local papers loudly celebrated the arrival of this writer'.[12] Over the next few months, Dickens would visit (among other places) New York, Philadelphia, Washington, Baltimore, Pittsburgh, travelling as far west as St Louis in Illinois, then heading north into Canada before returning to New York, and then home. The enthusiasm of the Americans (and Canadians) for Dickens remained, but his enthusiasm in return began to wane. The novelty of celebrity faded and the constant interruptions on his time became less flattering and more annoying. He was also seeing a side to America he was less enthralled by, be it the physical disgust he felt from the 'odious practices of chewing and expectorating' tobacco, or 'the revolting evidences of the state of society which exists in and about the slave districts of America' which made him aware that here in the New World too, there was a gap between the promises made and the promises realised.[13] He began to speak more vocally to his American hosts about the copyright laws, which caused consternation and offence. Equally, Dickens was visiting unusual places alongside the normal tourist attractions: he visited hospitals, asylums and even prisons to really get an insight into how America worked, and inevitably it did not – could not – live up to his previously optimistic expectations.

On his return to England Dickens published his experiences as a travelogue *American Notes* – he would also use the experience to provide adventures for the protagonist in *Martin Chuzzlewit*. In both instances Dickens applied the same sharp tools of criticism and observation to explore the faults in American society that he had long practiced on his native society; but while it is one thing to identify the faults in your own country, it is quite another to note them in someone else's country. The Americans did not take kindly to what they saw as unfair criticism, which Dickens began to anticipate even as he was completing the book:

> I have now arrived at the close of this book. I have little reason to believe, from certain warnings I have had since I returned to England, that it will be tenderly or favourably received by the American people; and as I have written the Truth in relation to the mass of those who form their judgments and express their opinions, it will be seen that I have no desire to court, by any adventitious means, the popular audience.[14]

The trip had backfired for both Dickens and the Americans, but nor was it a complete disaster. Dickens made many friends in America, among them the author Washington Irving (who Dickens called '*a great* fellow'), and the publisher James Fields, whose company became the authorised publisher of Dickens's novels in America.[15]

Italy

The trip to America was supposed to confirm Dickens's reputation on the world stage. But actually there were signs that his career was in trouble. The disappointing early sales of *Master Humphrey's Clock* and the lukewarm reviews of *Barnaby Rudge* were now followed by dwindling sales for *Martin Chuzzlewit*. He did produce what is now his most famous work, *A Christmas Carol*, in this time, but even that proved financially disappointing (at first at least), not due to lack of sale but rather the enormous cost of each individual book which Dickens had lavishly insisted should include colour illustrations. Dickens was concerned about finances, and moreover was facing signs that he may have peaked too soon with *Pickwick*. Before *Chuzzlewit* was finished, he was already contemplating a second sabbatical abroad.

> If I had made money, I should unquestionably fade away from the public eye for a year, and enlarge my stock of description and observation by seeing countries new to me; which it is most necessary that I should see, and which with an increasing family can scarcely hope to see at all, unless I see them now. Already for some time I have had this hope and intention before me; and though not having made money yet, I find or fancy that I can put myself in the position to accomplish it.[16]

But this one would be very different from the first. If America offered the new world, Italy offered an old one; what's more, if America offered a world of celebrity and adoration, Italy offered a retreat of seclusion. Though Dickens once again offered a travel narrative as incentive to his publishers, ultimately going to Italy was more about getting away, not to mention the potential financial benefits. Renting in Italy was cheaper than renting in London, so by subletting his London home he could actually make money while abroad (as well as escaping London society and the associated costs). This time it would be a family trip, with all four children, his sister-in-law Georgina, and several servants accompanying Dickens and Catherine. Also in attendance was Louis Roche, repeatedly referred to by Dickens as 'The Brave Courier' or simply 'The Brave'. Roche would be Dickens's guide, as well as arguably a servant, but ultimately a trusted friend. Dickens bought a carriage for the family and they set forth on 2 July 1845 to spend the next year abroad. They travelled through France by carriage, crossing the sea from Nice to Genoa, which would be their base of operations. From there they would make smaller trips across Italy, visiting Verona, Venice, Pisa, Carrara and Rome, travelling as far south as Naples, with a return trip through the Alps and Switzerland. In doing this, Dickens was emulating the Grand Tour which lords and ladies had been doing for centuries, with all the associated status and credibility that presented, but he was also joining an ever growing number of travellers in what was becoming a burgeoning tourist industry. Publishers like Murray and Baedeker were producing guidebooks for travel that not only told people where to go, but how to get there. Thus while America was about the undiscovered, Italy promised a familiar heritage, and Dickens's writing about Italy is steeped as much in the history and culture of the land as its geography. The Coliseum in Rome had a particularly striking impact (Dickens claimed to have visited it once a day during his stay in the city):

> It is no fiction, but plain, sober, honest Truth, to say: so suggestive and distinct is it at this hour: that, for a moment – actually in passing in – they who will, may have the whole great pile before them, as it used to be, with thousands of eager faces staring down into the arena, and such a whirl of strife, and blood, and dust, going on there, as no language can describe. Its solitude, its awful beauty, and its utter desolation, strike upon the stranger, the next moment, like a softened sorrow; and never in his life, perhaps, will he be so moved and overcome by any sight, not immediately connected with his own affections and afflictions.[17]

In contrast, there was also the disappointment of seeing long-anticipated sights, familiar through their fame and artistic reproductions, in the flesh. Of the Tower of Pisa, Dickens wrote '[l]ike most things connected in their first associations with school-books and school-times, it was too small.'[18] Elsewhere, his own enthusiasm shone, especially when visiting Verona:

> I had been half afraid to go to Verona, lest it should at all put me out of conceit with Romeo and Juliet. But, I was no sooner come into the old Marketplace, than the misgiving vanished. It is so fanciful, quaint, and picturesque a place, formed by such an extraordinary and rich variety of fantastic buildings, that there could be nothing better at the core of even this romantic town: scene of one of the most romantic and beautiful of stories.[19]

It is comforting, considering how many fans of Dickens now pursue literary trails to see the 'real-life' settings of his books, to see Dickens himself indulging in similar fantasies.

Dickens and his family initially stayed at the Villa Bagnerello in Genoa; this place had been chosen by his friend Angus Fletcher who was already in Genoa at the time, and Dickens was not fully impressed with it, dubbing it 'the pink jail' (on account of its colour) and bemoaning the temperature, which alternated between too hot in the day and too cold in the night. After a few months they moved into the first floor of the Palazzo Peschiere, a beautiful palace up on a hillside looking over Genoa with high ceilings and remarkable fresco paintings, a magnificent abode showing that Dickens's decision to move to Italy for cheaper rent by no means entailed any drop in living standards. While it offered a retreat compared to the intense social schedule of the American visit, nonetheless Dickens attended various events and cultivated a number of friendships in Italy. He was especially interested in Emile de la Rue and his wife Augusta; Mme de la Rue was of a nervous disposition and so Dickens began experimenting in mesmerism to seek the source of her condition through dreams and visions. As will be discussed in Chapter 10, it sounds remarkable, but it was an endeavour which Dickens was deeply interested in and enthusiastic about, much to the concern of Catherine who worried her husband was spending rather too much time in Mme de la Rue's company. However, nothing survives to suggest anything untoward occurred; with Dickens showing more enthusiasm for mesmerism itself than the young woman he was mesmerising.

Just as he had explored the less-travelled parts of America, so too Dickens took an interest in looking beyond the tourist spots of Italy. In his subsequent writing about the country, Dickens takes care to note the deprivations of the poor as much as the beauty of the art:

> But, lovers and hunters of the picturesque, let us not keep too studiously out of view, the miserable depravity, degradation, and wretchedness,

with which this gay Neapolitan life is inseparably associated! It is not well to find Saint Giles's so repulsive, and the Porta Capuana so attractive. A pair of naked legs and a ragged red scarf, do not make *all* the difference between what is interesting and what is coarse and odious? Painting and poetising for ever, if you will, the beauties of this most beautiful and lovely spot of earth, let us, as our duty, try to associate a new picturesque with some faint recognition of man's destiny and capabilities; more hopeful, I believe, among the ice and snow of the North Pole, than in the sun and bloom of Naples.[20]

Once again, Dickens is extending the same critical eye he used in England, treating Italy in exactly the same way; in fact, his insistence above that 'it is not well to find Saint Giles's [a slum area of London] so repulsive, and the Porta Capuana so attractive' actively argues that we should not allow ourselves to view foreign sites through a romantic lens, but rather view them honestly as we would our own land. Dickens does not write about the poor to attack Italy, but to expose the inequality of riches and plead on the behalf of the poor just as his writing in England does.

What angered Dickens most in Italy was the Catholic Church. Dickens was Christian, but had misgivings over the established church; if he felt that way about the Church of England, then the glamour and extravagance of the Catholic faith were bound to sit ill with him. There are mutterings against it in the early pages of *Pictures*, but it is when he reaches Rome, and the Vatican, that his disgust for all the pomp and splendour comes pouring out. Watching the Pope being born aloft on a chair during the Easter celebrations, Dickens is savage in his condemnation of the spectacle of the moment:

I must say, that I never saw anything, out of November, so like the popular English commemoration of the fifth of that month. A bundle of matches and a lantern, would have made it perfect. Nor did the Pope, himself, at all mar the resemblance, though he has a pleasant and venerable face; for, as this part of the ceremony makes him giddy and sick, he shuts his eyes when it is performed: and having his eyes shut, and a great mitre on his head, and his head itself wagging to and fro as they shook him in carrying, he looked as if his mask were going to tumble off.[21]

Balanced against this high adoration of one man which Dickens witnesses is the constant sight of the people of Italy prostrating themselves in traditional ceremonies. Watching a host of people climbing upstairs upon their knees as an act of contrition, he writes 'I never, in my life, saw anything at once so ridiculous, and so unpleasant, as this sight – ridiculous in the absurd incidents

inseparable from it; and unpleasant in its senseless and unmeaning degradation.'[22] These attacks on the Catholic Church did not go unnoticed; Dickens's
friend and artist Clarkson Stanfield, a staunch Catholic himself, who was
intended to illustrate *Pictures from Italy*, stepped away from the project as the
book's writings clearly presented a conflict of interests for him. *The Dublin
Review*, a staunchly pro-Catholic paper, was damning of Dickens's attacks:

> We have met with books more flippant, more insolent, more blasphe-
> mous; with as much false colouring and childish reasoning. We knew
> their authors, however, and from them hoped for nothing better [...]
> But that a production like this, exhibiting, from beginning to end, such
> extreme narrowness, littleness, one-sidedness of mind; so much cock-
> ney trifling and sneering on topics regarded by a hundred and fifty
> millions of Christians as of a solemn and sacred character – that such
> a production should have come to us, under the sanction of a name so
> honoured by us, and, as we fondly thought, so deserving of honour, has
> confounded and shocked us more than we can express.[23]

It might be assumed from the above that Dickens did not like Italy; nothing
could be further from the truth. Religious concerns aside, he was enthralled by
it, and lapped up the culture. He took great delight in the theatre, the history
and the sights as well as the people. For a man taken out of school and put into
work in a factory, this trip abroad offered an opportunity to re-establish his
education and cultural pedigree. He hired an Italian tutor, Antonio Gallenga,
to teach him the language. Equally there are still signs of Dickens's insecurity:
he attempts to avoid discussing art in his writing, which would have been an
area he was not as knowledgeable or educated in as many of his university-
trained peers were. Instead, Dickens often adapts an attitude of 'I don't know
much about art, but I know what I like', praising great works but also pointing
out those that received perhaps too much praise, such as Da Vinci's *Last
Supper*. Being in Italy afforded Dickens the life of a gentleman indeed; it also
provided the necessary break for him to take stock of his career and plan his
next steps. On his return to England he wrote back to Mme de la Rue, fondly
remembering life in Italy and longing to go back. He was only in England for a
year before he travelled abroad *again*; this time to Switzerland. It was here he
would write his fourth Christmas book, *The Battle of Life*, and more significantly his next novel, *Dombey and Son*, which has often been hailed as a
turning point for Dickens. Given his previous awkwardness about writing *The
Chimes* in Genoa, it is notable to see that he learns from the experience and
welcomes the trip abroad as a writing retreat. Switzerland would appear in
David Copperfield's narrative as a retreat for its hero as it had been for its

author, where 'All at once, in this serenity, great Nature spoke to me'.[24] The Dickens family left for Switzerland on 31 May 1846, accompanied once again by the brave courier Roche. They spent nearly a year there and in Paris, before returning to England in April 1846.

Future Trips Abroad

On 10 October 1853, Dickens set out abroad to revisit past destinations; his route would take him through Paris, Lausanne, Milan and Genoa. But this was not an exact replica of previous holidays; this time his travelling party was not family but friends: Augustus Egg and Wilkie Collins accompanied him along with a new courier Edward Kaub. Louis Roche, that faithful brave courier, had tragically died in 1848 – Dickens mourned the loss of 'one of the gentlest and most genial natures in the world'.[25] Both Egg and Collins were younger men than Dickens, and most of their time was spent in entertainment: 'We go to the Opera wherever there is one, see sights, eat and drink, sleep in a natural manner two or three nights, and move on again.'[26] This would be his last trip to Switzerland and Italy, but France would remain a constant destination. Its proximity to England was obviously a factor here, with Dickens making a number of shorter trips across to Paris on the ever improving transport system. He writes of the dizzying speed with which the trains propel him across England and France as he looks out of the window and sees, rushing past, 'Fields, windmills, low grounds, pollard-trees, windmills, fields, fortifications, Abbeville, soldiering and drumming'.[27] For the Victorians, the ever-increasing speed which the ever-developing transport was allowing meant in turn for an ever-decreasing world where Paris was now on a Londoner's doorstep, where one can wake up in England and go to bed in France:

> So, I pass to my hotel, enchanted; sup, enchanted; go to bed, enchant-
> ed; pushing back this morning (if it really were this morning) into the
> remoteness of time, blessing the South Eastern Company for realising
> the Arabian Nights in these prose days, murmuring, as I wing my idle
> flight into the land of dreams, 'No hurry, ladies and gentlemen, going to
> Paris in eleven hours. It is so well done, that there really is no hurry!'[28]

This proximity would later allow Dickens an opportunity to lead two lives after he met Ellen Ternan and separated from his wife; he provided Ternan a home in France which he would then regularly commute to. France afforded a place of seclusion for Dickens in later life just as Italy once had, somewhere he could retreat from the knowing gaze of his fellow Londoners to enjoy time alone with Ternan.

One final trip abroad awaited Dickens: America again. This may seem a surprising decision given the results of his last trip there, but three things had occurred to encourage a fresh perspective. The American Civil War had given a blow to slavery, something Dickens had especially abhorred on his past visit. Also Dickens was now enjoying more of a share in the American sales of his works; this was thanks to publishers like James Fields to whom Dickens was sending advance copies. A number of Dickens's serial works were published almost simultaneously in America now, in magazines such as *Harper's*. Finally, and most decidedly, Dickens had been conducting a public reading tour throughout the UK for several years which was proving most profitable; the opportunity to extend this tour to America promised even more riches for him. Money talks, and it was telling Dickens to go back to the States. But if France and Italy offered seclusion, America had already proved itself to be a place where Dickens was constantly under the gaze of the public, so there was much deliberation therefore whether Ellen should or should not accompany him. Eventually Dickens went on alone to assess the situation, promising to send word to Ellen either to join him or stay put: in the end, the message was the latter, and Dickens travelled America without wife, children or mistress. The second American tour was a great success and an opportunity to heal the rift. Dickens offered a public apology for his previous attacks on the country, and promised that all subsequent editions of *American Notes* would carry a transcript of that apology in the postscript of the book:

> But what I have intended [...] is, on my return to England, in my own person, in my own Journal, to bear, for the behoof of my countrymen, such testimony to the gigantic changes in this country as I have hinted at tonight. Also, to record that wherever I have been, in the smallest places equally with the largest, I have been received with unsurpassable politeness, delicacy, sweet temper, hospitality, consideration, and with unsurpassable respect for the privacy daily enforced upon me by the nature of my avocation here and the state of my health.[29]

The American tour may have been a success financially, but as the close of the passage above implies, it carried a heavy toll on Dickens's physical well-being. So much travelling was proving exhausting. Dickens had hoped to travel to Australia as well, where his sons Alfred and Edward (Plorn) lived, to do another reading tour to a whole new audience on the other side of the world; but ultimately it was not to be. After the second tour of America, Dickens's international travelling days were done.

Case Study: *Little Dorrit*, and Losing/Finding Yourself Abroad

Little Dorrit first appeared in print in monthly numbers published from December 1855 to June 1857, by which point Dickens had visited Italy twice, once with his family, and again with his friends. The book was dedicated to Dickens's friend Clarkson Stanfield – the same Clarkson Stanfield who had decided *not* to illustrate *Pictures from Italy* on the grounds of its anti-Catholicism. There is a sense in the timing of the novel, and the recognition of Stanfield, of a general reflection not only on the more recent trip to Italy, but also the first. The country, and Dickens's interpretation of it, weaves its way into the narrative of the Dorrit family, who experience a change of fortunes. The father, William Dorrit, has spent most of his life in the debtor's prison, with his uncomplaining child Amy (the eponymous Little Dorrit) and his rather-more complaining children Fanny and Tip. After it is discovered that William Dorrit is heir to a great fortune, the family not only leave debtor's prison, but England, to find a new life for themselves on the continent as a great family. For the Dorrits, Italy and the Grand Tour offer the same dual benefits Dickens had enjoyed of cultural respectability and social retreat, where they can renew themselves and their reputation. We can see throughout the narrative how Dickens draws on his own memories and impressions of the country to provide a background for his characters' experiences. The description of Venice echoes Dickens's first impressions of it as a magical, ethereal place. The Dorrits are said to be 'descending into the sea again after dinner, and ascending out of it at the Opera staircase, preceded by one of their gondoliers, like an attendant Merman, with a great linen lantern', much as Dickens himself wrote about travelling along each 'phantom street' with 'dark mysterious doors that opened straight upon the water'.[30] In Rome the Dorrits encounter the same oppressive sense of history weighing down upon the contemporary, 'in a city where everything seemed to be trying to stand still for ever on the ruins of something else'.[31]

Both of the travelogues began as letters sent home; Dickens would write letters to Forster primarily and ask him to keep them, so that on his return he could use them as source material. Just as Dickens wrote letters home, so too does Little Dorrit, and in those letters we see too not only that desire for escape, but also the futility of it:

> It is the same with all these new countries and wonderful sights. They are very beautiful, and they astonish me, but I am not collected enough – not familiar enough with myself, if you can quite understand what I mean – to have all the pleasure in them that I might have.[32]

While her family swiftly and wilfully forget their humble beginnings, she cannot. Her awareness of who she is, and what they are running from, infiltrates and obstructs her appreciation of life abroad. Her father reprimands her for her inability to forget the past and embrace the illusion of their life abroad, telling her that there is 'a painful topic, a series of events which I wish – ha – altogether to obliterate'.[33] But Little Dorrit cannot obliterate that topic; her past informs who she is, so that the geographical distance is rendered null by temporal proximity.

There is an insecurity at the heart of Little Dorrit's reaction to living abroad, that her experiences abroad are hindered by who she is and the subsequent lack of education or culture which that entails. Like Dickens, she is conscious that she is retreading familiar steps abroad, and not discovering so much as reviewing sights that others have already seen and discussed many times before. She writes to Clennam:

> If you should ever get so far in this long letter, you will perhaps say, Surely Little Dorrit will not leave off without telling me something about her travels, and surely it is time she did. I think it is indeed, but I don't know what to tell you. Since we left Venice we have been in a great many wonderful places, Genoa and Florence among them, and have seen so many wonderful sights, that I am almost giddy when I think what a crowd they make. But you could tell me so much more about them than I can tell you, that why should I tire you with my accounts and descriptions?[34]

This echoes Dickens's own self-deprecating preface to *Pictures from Italy* in which he repeatedly points out all the topics which have already been covered authoritatively before him; '[m]any books have been written upon Italy' he notes, covering the history and politics of the country, and also the art:

> There is, probably, not a famous Picture or Statue in all Italy, but could be easily buried under a mountain of printed paper devoted to dissertations on it. I do not, therefore, though an earnest admirer of Painting and Sculpture, expatiate at any length on famous Pictures and Statues.[35]

Both Dickens and Little Dorrit exhibit the same awareness of their limitations. In Dickens's case this is slightly ironic as he then proceeds to say a great deal about the paintings and sculptures that he has seen, usually to counter the critics who have raved about it. There's something defensive in this; Leonee Ormond notes how Dickens's interrupted childhood would have left him with 'comparatively little experience of Italian art' which many of his better educated adult peers would have.[36] There is also a sense of insecurity about travel as much as culture; that awareness in this growing age of tourism of not being explorers, but followers. Dickens and Little Dorrit are not reporting on anything new.

Little Dorrit's father has employed the tyrannically pragmatic Mrs General, who seeks to raise the younger Dorrits up in elocution and appreciation of fact over fancy. Mrs General becomes a spokesperson for all those many authorities that Dickens references in *Pictures from Italy*; those many books and mountains of paper to which he owes a debt. In *Little Dorrit*, the oppressive nature of this backlog of opinions is made strikingly clear:

> Nobody said what anything was, but everybody said what the Mrs. Generals, Mr. Eustace, or somebody else said it was. The whole body of travellers seemed to be a collection of voluntary human sacrifices, bound hand and foot, and delivered over to Mr. Eustace and his attendants, to have the entrails of their intellects arranged according to the taste of their sacred priesthood. Through the rugged remains of temples and tombs and palaces and senate halls and theatres and amphitheatres of ancient days, hosts of tongue-tied and blindfolded moderns were carefully feeling their way, incessantly repeating Prunes and Prism, in the endeavour to set their lips according to the received form. Mrs. General was in her pure element. Nobody had an opinion.[37]

Eustace's popular travel book *A Classical Tour through Italy* (1813) was one used by Dickens, so it is unsurprising to see it referenced in the Dorrit's expedition. But what is clear in this passage is how these travel books can cross a line between instruction and command. This new generation of tourists are not only following the geographical directions of the guidebooks, but the cultural directions too. They tread the same path, seeing the same sights, and responding as the guidebook instructs them to. The 'moderns' are 'tongue-tied and blindfolded' because they are not able to look upon these sights and make their own judgements, or pronounce their own ideas upon them. Travel, intended to broaden the mind, becomes indoctrination, where the traveller merely follows a set route with set outcomes. In Dickens's hands, the trip abroad becomes just as constricting for the Dorrit family as the prison from which they have escaped, and one from which they must ultimately break free if they are to find any genuine closure on their past. *Little Dorrit* is not a travel book, but in the novel we can see how Dickens shows the limitations of travel and offers honest criticism on the emotional baggage we take with us wherever we attempt to escape to. Utilising his own experience of Italy, the location is used to highlight both the wonders and riches of travel abroad, while simultaneously attacking some of the snobbery, expectations and restrictions travellers placed upon themselves by treating the experience as a tick-box exercise. True exploration lay in investigating the unfamiliar, and enlightenment awaited in recognising that familiar problems persisted even in the most exotic of locations.

Notes

1 Valerie Browne Lester, *Phiz: The Man Who Drew Dickens* (London: Pimlico, 2006), p. 55.

2 Dickens, Letter to John Forster, 2 July 1837, in Madeline House and Graham Storey (eds.), *The Letters of Charles Dickens*, Volume. One 1820–1839 (Oxford: Clarendon Press, 197), pp. 280–281 (p. 280).

3 Dickens, Letter to John Forster, 2 July 1837, in *Letters*, Vol. 1, p. 281.

4 Dickens, Letter to Emile de la Rue, 23 and 25 February 1845, in Kathleen Tillotson (ed.), *The Letters of Charles Dickens*, Volume. Four 1844–1846 (Oxford: Clarendon Press, 1977), pp. 272–274 (p. 273); Dickens, Letter to Georgina Hogarth, 25 October 1853, in Graham Story, Kathleen Tillotson and Angus Easson (eds.), *The Letters of Charles Dickens*, Volume. Seven 1853–1855 (Oxford: Clarendon Press, 1993), pp. 175–176.

5 William F Long and Paul Schlicke, 'Positively the Last Appearance: "BOZ" in Advertisements for *Dombey and Son*', *Dickens Quarterly*, Vol. 35, No. 2 (2018), pp. 101–109.

6 For more on the Finden engraving and its reception, see William F Long, 'An Irreverent Contemporary Comment on the Impact of the *Nickleby* Portrait', *Dickensian*, Vol. 112, No. 498 (Spring 2016), pp. 46–54.

7 *The United States Magazine and Democratic Review*, April 1842, cited in Michael Slater, *America and the Americans* (Hassocks: Harvester Press, 1979), p. 8.

8 Dickens, Letter to Lewis Gaylord Clark, December 1841, in Madeline House and Graham Storey (eds.), *The Letters of Charles Dickens*, Volume Two, 1840–1841 (Oxford: Clarendon Press, 1969), p. 445 (p. 445).

9 Dickens to Frederick Dickens, 26 September 1841, in *Letters*, Vol. 2, pp. 391–392 (p. 392).

10 Dickens to William Hall, 14 September 1841, in *Letters*, Vol. 2, p. 383 (p. 383).

11 Charles Dickens, *American Notes and Pictures from Italy*, ed. by F S Schwarzbach and Leonee Ormond (London: Everyman, 1997), Ch. Two, p. 28.

12 Michael Slater, *Charles Dickens* (New Haven: Yale, 2011), p. 180.

13 *American Notes*, Ch. 8, p. 113; Ch. 17, p. 241.

14 *American Notes*, Postscript, p. 252.

15 Dickens, Letter to John Forster, 28 February 1842, in Madeline House, Graham Storey and Kathleen Tillotson (eds.), *The Letters of Charles Dickens*, Volume Three 1842–1843 (Oxford: Clarendon Press, 1974), pp. 95–96 (p. 96).

16 Charles Dickens, Letter to John Forster, 1 November 1843, in *Letters*, Vol. 3, pp. 587–588 (p. 587).

17 Charles Dickens, *Pictures from Italy*, ed. by Pete Orford (Oxford: OUP, 2023), p. 107.

18 *Pictures from Italy*, p. 98.

19 *Pictures from Italy*, p. 78.

20 *Pictures from Italy*, p. 152.

21 *Pictures from Italy*, p. 110.

22 *Pictures from Italy*, p. 143.

23 Anon. '*Pictures from Italy*. By Charles Dickens. London: 1846', *Dublin Review*, Sep 1846, pp. 184–201 (pp. 184–185).

24 Charles Dickens, *David Copperfield*, ed. by Nina Burgis (Oxford: OUP, 1981), Ch. 58, p. 698.

25 Charles Dickens, Letter to John Elliotson, 10 June 1848, in Leon Litvack, Emily Bell, Lydia Craig and Jeremy Parrot (eds.), *Charles Dickens Letters Project* (London: Dickens Fellowship), https://dickensletters.com/letters/john-elliotson-10-jun-1848.

26 Charles Dickens, Letter to Georgina Hogarth, 25 November 1853, in Graham Story, Kathleen Tillotson and Angus Easson (eds.), *The Letters of Charles Dickens*, Volume Seven 1853–1855 (Oxford: Clarendon Press, 1993), pp. 209–212 (p. 210).

27 Charles Dickens, 'A Flight', *Household Words* (30 August 1851), pp. 529–533 (p. 532).

28 'A Flight', p. 533.

29 *American Notes*, Postscript, p. 254.

30 Charles Dickens, *Little Dorrit*, ed. by Harvey Peter Sucksmith (Oxford: OUP, 1979), Book II Chapter 6, p. 488; *Pictures from Italy*, p. 71.

31 *Little Dorrit* Book II Chapter 7, p. 497.

32 *Little Dorrit*, Book II Chapter 4, p. 456.

33 *Little Dorrit* Book II Chapter 5, p. 464.

34 *Little Dorrit* Book II Chapter 11 p. 537.

35 *Pictures from Italy*, p. 3.

36 Leonee Ormond, 'Dickens and Italian Art', in Charles Dickens, *American Notes and Pictures from Italy*, ed. by F S Schwarzbach and Leonee Ormond (London: Everyman, 1997), pp. 499–503 (p. 499).

37 *Little Dorrit* Book II Chapter 7, p. 498.

6

Boz to Man

Dickens, Serialisation and 'The Turning Point'

Focal Point: 1846–1848

Case Study: Dombey and Son

Dickens's trip to Italy was described by his friend John Forster as 'the turning-point in his career'.[1] This has both inspired, and been subsequently endorsed by, the perception of a change in Dickens's novels that separates his career as an author into two parts: the early comic novels from *The Pickwick Papers* through to *Nicholas Nickleby*, and the later, more serious socio-political novels from *Dombey and Son* through to *The Mystery of Edwin Drood*. Like all theoretical models, the idea seems to have been contested as often as it has been commended. Splitting Dickens's writings into early and later novels has in turn led to controversy over the superiority of either half; Dickens's contemporaries wrote in constant favour of his first works, especially *Pickwick*, and the joy they afforded, whereas twentieth-century critics applauded the greater ambition and purpose of the later novels; this in turn has then been challenged by a reappraisal of the earlier works and their own complexity. Questions that arise from this are whether we can confidently mark a point at which Dickens's writing changes, or whether it is truer to chart a steady evolution across his works; others have suggested that there is a turning point, but questioned the timing (most recently Robert Douglas-Fairhurst has proposed 1851, and the writing of *Bleak House*, as the real moment of change in Dickens's career).[2] This chapter will consider Dickens's career in the late 1840s when Forster presumed the 'turning point' occurred, to look at the changes which Dickens consciously adopted in this period, as well as considering the counterarguments and nuances surrounding the attempt to identify a schism in Dickens's career.

If we are to talk about how (if at all) things changed from *Dombey* onwards, it is helpful, before proceeding, to consider the pattern of publishing which Dickens

The Life of the Author: Charles Dickens, First Edition. Pete Orford.
© 2023 John Wiley & Sons Ltd. Published 2023 by John Wiley & Sons Ltd.

had adopted by this stage, in order that we can better appreciate what has come before, prior to considering what comes next. By 1846, the year he started writing *Dombey*, all of Dickens's novels had been published in serial instalments; in the case of *Pickwick*, *Nickleby* and *Chuzzlewit*, these were monthly publications, each instalment being its own individual publication, with a green wrapper that would become synonymous with Dickens, and accompanying illustrations (after an initial variation in the first two numbers of *Pickwick*, this had now settled at two illustrations per number). *Oliver Twist* had also been released in monthly instalments, but was published within the pages of *Bentley's Miscellany*; thus the story was enveloped and accompanied by other articles too. *The Old Curiosity Shop* and *Barnaby Rudge* were similar, in that they both appeared within another publication, *Master Humphrey's Clock*; however, in this instance the *Clock* essentially included nothing but Dickens's novel. The other significant difference with these two is that they were published weekly, not monthly: Dickens would later produce three more weekly publications in his career: *Hard Times, A Tale of Two Cities* and *Great Expectations*, but the majority of his novels would be monthlies. With the exception of *Oliver* and *The Mystery of Edwin Drood*, these monthlies were all published in twenty instalments, or numbers, with the final two numbers published together as a double bill.

On completion of the series, and not before, the entire book would be available to buy in a complete set of either three volumes, two, or sometimes just one. From a reader's perspective, we can liken this to a TV series and the ensuing boxset, where many readers would experience the story as it developed, with opportunity between numbers to share and discuss with their friends and speculate on the potential plots and fortunes of their favourite characters. This would present difficulties to Dickens as he often had to counter his readers either expressing disappointment in an ending being not what they hoped, or even worse, accurately guessing the ending ahead of time. Edgar Allan Poe correctly prophesised – and published – the solution to the murder plot in *Barnaby Rudge* as early as May 1841 (the first instalment of the story was published in February of that year), warning his readers that 'the anticipation must surpass the reality' and that they 'will surely be disappointed'.[3] Nearly twenty-five years later, a great number of readers all predicted early on that the mysterious stranger in *Our Mutual Friend*, John Rokesmith, was none other than the supposedly dead John Harmon, leading Dickens to defend the decision as something which was always supposed to be obvious:

> When I devised this story, I foresaw the likelihood that a class of readers and commentators would suppose that I was at great pains to conceal exactly what I was at great pains to suggest: namely, that Mr John Harmon was not slain, and that Mr John Rokesmith was he.

Pleasing myself with the idea that the supposition might in part arise out of some ingenuity in the story, and thinking it worth while, in the interests of art, to hint to an audience that an artist (of whatever denomination) may perhaps be trusted to know what he is about in his vocation, if they will concede him a little patience, I was not alarmed by the anticipation.[4]

The author doth protest too much, methinks. It is telling that the note is printed at the end of the novel, not the beginning, under the heading 'Postscript: in lieu of preface'. Even though Dickens was apparently happy for people to know Rokesmith's true identity, he nonetheless did not want it in print at the start of the story. At other times anticipations of Dickens's novels proved woefully wrong; a dramatic adaptation of *The Old Curiosity Shop* appeared on stage while Dickens was still writing it, and therefore the adaptors had no recourse but to guess the ending, in which Little Nell lived happily ever after with Kit. There were thus two pressures on Dickens: to provide a story that could not be immediately guessed by his readers, while also not disappointing readers for not providing the ending they wanted. It is a familiar woe faced by television serials today, with *Game of Thrones*, *How I Met Your Mother* and *Line of Duty* all facing a backlash from critics and fans alike for not sticking the landing. The additional pressure on Dickens in the early days of his career is that he was frequently starting stories without a clear sense of where they were going to end. The initial concept for *Pickwick* was an open-ended series of monthly adventures for four sporting gentlemen; it was only as the series developed that Dickens began to include the underlying plot (if it can be called that) of Pickwick's unfortunate misunderstanding with Mrs Bardell and the subsequent trial, imprisonment and liberation of the hero.

When we look back on these early works we can see telltale, almost laughable signs of Dickens's lack of foresight. The final chapters of *Oliver Twist* contain painful contortions of exposition as Dickens attempts to rewrite the earlier narrative of his hero to account for all the loose ends he has written for himself. The worst offender is *The Old Curiosity Shop*, which begins in the first-person narrative only for Dickens to realise this is unsustainable, and thus leads to a painful U-turn at the end of chapter three:

And now that I have carried this history so far in my own character and introduced these personages to the reader, I shall for the convenience of the narrative detach myself from its further course, and leave those who have prominent and necessary parts in it to speak and act for themselves.[5]

Similarly, characters such as Little Nell's brother, who features prominently in the early chapters, disappears completely from the narrative without further mention until the final pages where we learn he 'rioted abroad' before drowning.[6] Considered like this, it is understandable how twentieth-century critics would prefer the structure and organisation of Dickens's later novels, but it is equally important to note the sheer energy of these early works, and their comic interludes, which in turn explains their immense popularity with Dickens's contemporary audience. The predominant reason for *Dombey* being identified as a transitional novel is our awareness of an overarching plan behind it; a collection of notes written by Dickens in which he sketched out the potential plot points for each monthly instalment ahead of writing the first one. While this does not inherently constitute an improvement, it does show an advancement in Dickens's ability and confidence as a writer of grand narratives, and from the perspective of a literary critic it allows for more foreshadowing, self-referencing and general cohesion across the novel. Separate to this is the perception that Dickens's novels from *Dombey* onwards also show greater interest in reflecting upon the political moment, or have a grander commentary to offer on society than can be seen in the earlier comic novels. This is a topic that is more contentious and open to debate: *Oliver Twist*, for all of its sensationalism, melodrama and sheer lack of planning, nonetheless can be said to engage just as significantly with the plights of the poor as Dickens's later works do. Sophistication of plot structure does not automatically equate to greater depth of social criticism, and the strength of Dickens's early works can be said to rest in that very popularism which would prompt later critics to deride them. The impact of a work like *Oliver* is immediately made greater by the wider readership it enjoyed. The question of whether this 'turning point' is an improvement, a deterioration, or not even a change at all, remains open to interpretation, and is something which will be considered as I discuss the writing of *Dombey*.

'The Story I Have in Mind': Dickens's Early Conceptions of *Dombey*

Dickens began writing *Dombey and Son* in the middle of 1846, with the first instalment published in October of that year. However, he originally writes of it as early as November 1843, when he first proposed the idea of travelling abroad to Europe to Forster:

> At the same time I shall be able to turn over the story I have in my mind, and which I have a strong notion might be published with great advantage, *first in Paris* – but that's another matter to be talked over. And of course I have not yet settled, either, whether any book about the travel, or this, should be the first.[7]

As discussed in Chapter 5, Dickens's trip to Italy was informed as much by the dual need for a break and financial concerns, as it was for the desire to actively visit new countries, with the composition of a travel book relegated to fourth position. In his prior discussion with Forster, this is particularly evident, as Dickens is already thinking about another story, which would eventually become *Dombey*, and is uncertain which of that or the travelogue will appear first. There is no indication that any writing of *Dombey* occurred while Dickens was abroad; so the impact of the trip is less in the location than in the time it afforded for Dickens to stop and reset. Given the frantic and frenetic writing schedule he had adopted thus far, it is a notable departure to see Dickens talking about *Dombey* as early as November 1843 while proposing the Italy trip to Forster. It is hard to say which prompts which: whether the desire to plan and write the book is a primary reason for getting away, or whether writing a book is a helpful excuse for Dickens to use when justifying the holiday to his friend.

Up until this point Dickens had written with the urgency and desperation of a hungry young author attempting to establish himself. Forster suggested his friend 'had unwittingly sold himself into a quasi-bondage': the end of *Pickwick* had overlapped with the beginning of *Oliver*; the end of *Oliver* overlapped with the beginning of *Nickleby*.[8] During this time Dickens also wrote four dramatic pieces for the stage (only three of which were actually performed), as well as editing *Bentley's Miscellany*. Even then he was also seeking more work, and in May 1836 he signed a contract with John Macrone to produce 'the first Edition of a Work of Fiction (in Three Volumes of the usual size) [...] entitled *Gabriel Vardon, the Locksmith of London*'.[9] Eventually this emerged instead as *Barnaby Rudge*, which in turn had followed immediately on from *The Old Curiosity Shop*, which had been borne out of the ashes of *Master Humphrey's Clock* that had followed hard upon *Nickleby*. *Rudge* was followed by a supposed sabbatical in America which instead turned out to an exhausting and invasive tour where Dickens was constantly on display and at the mercy of the crowds, and his return to England was quickly taken up by the writing of *American Notes* and *Martin Chuzzlewit*, which in turn also enveloped the writing of *A Christmas Carol* which involved him 'working from morning until night'.[10]

In short, for the past ten years Dickens had been working at a hectic pace, and ultimately an unsustainable one. Far too frequently he was starting projects without a clear sense of how they would end, or taking on new projects while still enmeshed in other ones and therefore not affording time to think and plan before proceeding. Writing *The Old Curiosity Shop* and *Barnaby Rudge* in weekly instalments added an additional challenge; when Dickens returned to that format in 1854 for *Hard Times* he wrote about the challenges of writing not only to such a limiting deadline but also such limited space:

> The difficulty of the space is CRUSHING. Nobody can have an idea of it who has not had an experience of patient fiction-writing with some elbow-room always, and open places in perspective. In this form, with any kind of regard to the current number, there is absolutely no such thing.[11]

Dickens would have hated Twitter. The situation was simply not sustainable, and it was inevitable that he would be looking for an opportunity to slow down and adopt a more manageable pace of working. He justified his trip to Italy to Forster precisely as an escape: 'I am afraid of putting myself before the town as writing tooth and nail for bread, headlong, after the close of a book taking so much out of one as *Chuzzlewit*.'[12]

Dickens was thinking about taking control of the process; being less responsive in agreeing to every possible contract, and planning ahead to produce works with a planned conclusion. The trip to Italy afforded Dickens an opportunity to pause, reflect and anticipate. When he returned from Italy in July 1845 however, it seems as though he had not immediately learned his lesson; in addition to writing *The Cricket on the Hearth* and *Pictures from Italy* he agreed to be editor of the *Daily News*, a new paper being launched by his publishers Bradbury and Evans in the beginning of 1846. Being a newspaper editor had its appeal, it would elevate Dickens's status as a man of letters, as well as offering a steady income, but given his previous complaints about meeting weekly deadlines, the pressure of meeting daily ones proved, unsurprisingly, to be too much, and between this and disagreements with the publishers, Dickens departed as editor on 9 February, only eighteen days after the first issue had been published. Freed from the 'daily noose' as he called it, Dickens could now return to his original ambition of writing the longer work with a clearer roadmap ahead of him.[13] A week after his resignation, he wrote to Emile de la Rue to explain the benefits of this new freedom:

> I am again a gentleman. I have handed over the Editing of the Paper (very laborious work indeed) to Forster; and am contemplating a New Book – most probably in Numbers.[14]

The connection of the 'New Book' and once more being 'a gentleman' are not coincidental. Novel-writing was often seen as a pursuit rather than a profession at this time, which would usually be a source of irritation for Dickens, but here at least there is a recognition of the agency which writing a novel in monthly numbers allowed him compared to editing the daily writings of others; instead of being beholden to the whims of other people, writing a novel afforded him more mastery over the narrative, quite literally. In terms of self-fashioning, it is also worth noting that by this stage Dickens was publishing in his own name. His earlier works had all continued the pseudonym of Boz, trading on the success of the sketches, then *Pickwick*, then *Oliver* – Dickens had trapped himself, gaining his reputation under the name of Boz which meant he simultaneously had and had not a famous name, eventually transitioning to his own name with *Nicholas Nickleby* and its accompanying portrait by Maclise, so by the time he went to America, he went as Charles Dickens, not Boz. Dickens had begun with this frantic energy born from insecurity, writing each new book with the fear it might be his last, and clinging to that pseudonym he had adopted early on as the one which his audience recognised. But from this moment, Dickens was stepping into his role and fame and claiming it for himself.

After his resignation from the *Daily News*, the new book began to dominate more and more of Dickens's imagination: even while finalising details for *Pictures from Italy* he was planning ahead for the next project, as is clear from a letter to Bradbury and Evans in which he aims that *Pictures* 'certainly must be published in May' for no other reason than to clear the path for *Dombey*:

> I want to know, when you have had time to think of it, how soon after June, you think we might, safely, and with real effect, begin a story in Monthly Numbers - so that it should not commence at a dead time of the year.[15]

Of equal consideration to when was *where*: Dickens's entanglement with the *Daily News* had made him wistful to go abroad yet again, to rekindle that sense of peace and calm he had experienced in Italy. He wrote to Mme de la Rue on 17 April and told her of his plans 'to produce a new story in twenty monthly parts,' and explained he 'could write it more comfortably and easily, abroad, than at home.' This is a very different perspective from that he exhibited while trying to write *The Chimes* in Genoa in 1844, where he missed his old London walks and the inspiration they afforded. Now, more than anything, Dickens wanted space and time; a retreat in which to write. The days of writing reactively were to be put behind him, in favour of a more dignified and composed manner of authorship. He made plans to travel to Switzerland, so that the middle of 1846 was split between completing *Pictures*, planning the trip abroad and planning the new book. When *Pictures* was published on 19 May 1846, it carried an advertisement promising the new work:

A NEW ENGLISH STORY,

BY MR DICKENS,

in *Twenty Monthly Parts, price One Shilling each, uniform with*

"MARTIN CHUZZLEWIT," &c.

IS NOW IN PREPARATION.

No I. will be published on the First of October.[16]

Moreover, in the preface to *Pictures*, called 'The Reader's Passport', he addresses the errors of the past (presumably his decision to edit *The Daily News*) and promises his readers a return to the glory days of his monthly numbers:

> For I need not hesitate to avow, that, bent on correcting a brief mistake I made, not long ago, in disturbing the old relations between myself and my readers, and departing for a moment from my old pursuits, I am about to resume them, joyfully, in Switzerland: where, during another year of absence, I can at once work out the themes I have now in my mind, without interruption...[17]

Thus we see a moment of reflection and anticipation: Dickens aims to 'resume' his old relations and old pursuits, but equally the moment ahead promised something new. Dickens and his family left for Switzerland on 31 May 1846, accompanied again by Louis Roche. The family would be based in Lausanne until September, when they moved to Geneva, then Paris. But it was not only the trip abroad, and the distance from the daily distractions and pressures of London life which it afforded, that offered something new in Dickens's life, but also the detailed planning and preparation which he would make for this novel and which would become a staple of his future literary endeavours.

Planning Ahead

In comparison to the scrappy second-guessing and retconning which can be seen in earlier works like *Oliver Twist* and *The Old Curiosity Shop*, *Dombey and Son* shows several signs of a grand overarching plan. This is immediately noticeable in Hablot Knight Browne's cover illustration for the monthly numbers [see Figure 6.1]. Dombey himself sits at the top of the picture, his proud profile unmistakeable, with a familiar selection of allegorical motifs around him that are not dissimilar to previous cover illustrations. The tumbling of financial books and playing cards, which form the two pillars upon which Dombey's throne rests, is a clear indication of the fragility of his fortunes, but

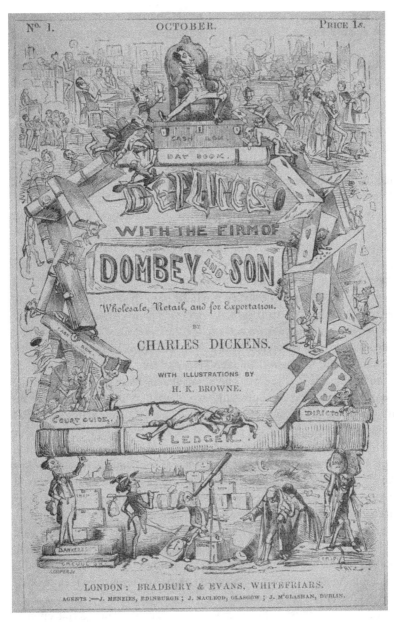

Figure 6.1 Hablot Knight Browne, Cover Illustration for *Dombey and Son*, 1846.

thus far any indications are suggestive rather than absolute. When Dickens first saw the cover he worried about the amount of information presented:

> Browne is certainly interesting himself, and taking pains. I think the cover very good: perhaps with a little too much in it, but that is an ungrateful objection.[18]

The cover is no less detailed than previous covers; so Dickens's objection to it having too much is purely about the veracity of those details. Surrounding Dombey are illustrations of various specific scenes yet to come: to the right of the picture we see Dombey's marriage to Edith Grainger, an event which would not occur until the tenth number; moreover, at the bottom of the illustration we see the older Dombey supported in his dotage by his daughter Florence, a scene which will not occur until the end of the novel. The cover illustration is similar to the strategy adopted by many modern-day movie posters that display a myriad of different scenes and moment from the film in a montage; far from spoiling the plot it provides anticipation and promise of what is to come. Given that *Dombey* would be published over the duration of October 1846 through to April 1848, this afforded plenty of time and opportunity for his readers to gaze upon and explore the cover illustration. As the plot unfolded they would recognise scenes from the latest instalment upon the cover, and in doing so might reasonably peruse the rest of the cover for clues of what might come next. The cover's blending of allegorical figures and specific plot scenes allows a certain ambiguity, where readers might suspect certain events, but would not be able to authoritatively expect their coming. The aged Dombey and his daughter at the bottom of the illustration stands among four unidentified figures who are respectively gazing through a telescope, marching forth on an expedition, and holding the pillars of books and card aloft: looked at with hindsight we can confidently identify Dombey, but without that benefit we might well mistake him for one more allegorical character. The cover thus provides evidence of Dickens's forward planning in a way that would not be immediately obvious or decipherable to his readers. This ambiguity is seen most clearly in the cacophony of attempts to interpret the cover for his final, unfinished, novel *The Mystery of Edwin Drood*, where critics will each confidently claim the figure at the bottom of the page to be Edwin/ Helena /Neville /Datchery/ [enter own suggestion here].

Beyond the cover illustration, there is Dickens's memoranda: a collection of notes laid out per number, in which he proposes chapter titles and potential plot points. This is the strategy he would then adopt for every novel afterwards, and is the greatest indication of his forward planning and overarching structure. However, it is not necessarily the first time he has made notes like this, just the first time when those notes have survived. In the preface to *Martin Chuzzlewit* Dickens proudly talks about how he has 'put a strong constraint' on his imagination, and has endeavoured 'to resist the temptation of the current Monthly Number, and to keep a steadier eye upon the general purpose and design.'[19] But without the notes to support this claim, Dickens's promise of a steadier eye is open to our interpretation. *Dombey* attracts our notice not because Dickens is planning, but because he is planning on paper, and those notes have endured. It allows us opportunity to unpick Dickens's writing process from start to finish. Furthermore, in a letter to Forster on 25 July 1846, Dickens gives his friend a complete, and highly detailed, plan for what will follow in the novel:

> I will now go on to give you an outline of my immediate intentions in reference to *Dombey*. I design to show Mr. D. with that one idea of the Son taking firmer and firmer possession of him, and swelling and bloating his pride to a prodigious extent. As the boy begins to grow up, I shall show him quite impatient for his getting on, and urging his masters to set him great tasks, and the like. But the natural affection of the boy will turn towards the despised sister; and I purpose showing her learning all sorts of things, of her own application and determination, to assist him in his lessons: and helping him always. When the boy is about ten years old (in the fourth number), he will be taken ill, and will die...[20]

It goes on for much longer, working through the central plot Dombey's personal growth through the novel. It does *not* discuss the various subplots or the fortunes of supporting characters, but rather hinges upon this central storyline. So the main plot was fixed, while still allowing some room to manoeuvre in the details. The pinning of the plot to individual numbers, as in the discussion above of young Paul Dombey taking ill 'in the fourth number' shows that Dickens is not merely imagining the narrative ahead but actively measuring it within the structuring of his monthly numbers: that process of serialisation which he had initially stumbled into, and at times resisted, was now a welcome constraint that provided order and discipline to his novels.

Case Study: The Grand Vision of *Dombey and Son*

Alexander Welsh notes 'the widely accepted conclusion that, whereas *Martin Chuzzlewit* may be superior in wit and invention, *Dombey and Son* is superior in organisation and serious depiction of society', but warns this 'should not be allowed to obscure the close relation of the two'.[21] On occasion our enthusiasm to explore the notes which survive for *Dombey* can encourage us to ignore the complexity of the earlier novels. Dickens wrote to Forster comparing his new novel, *Dombey*, to its immediate predecessor *Chuzzlewit*, saying it 'was to do with pride what its predecessor had done with Selfishness'.[22] If *Dombey* offered a novel with an overriding theme and purpose, then Dickens saw this as a continuation of the same approach adopted in his previous work. Nonetheless a distinction can be seen from *Dombey and Son* onwards in Dickens's working notes, which are presented in a uniform fashion: two columns, with notes and ideas in the left column, and chapter headings and structure in the right column. As an illustration, the plans for the first monthly number of *Dombey* is written thus (including the text Dickens crossed out):

Sketch of Dombey – Mother confined with long-expected boy. Boy born, to die, Neglected girl, Florence – a child	(Dealings with the Firm of Dombey and Son N°I)
Mrs Chick – common-minded, family humbug	Chapter I
	Dombey and Son
Wet nurse – Polly Toodle	Death of the Mother
Toodle a stoker	Chapter II
Lots of children	In which timely provision is made for an
Wooden Midshipman	emergency that will sometimes arise in the
Uncle – adventurous	best regulated families.
Nephew – Captain cuttle	Wet nurse introduced.
Miss Tox introduces 'the party'	Chapter III
Dombey and Son	In which Mr Dombey, as a Man and a Father, is seen at the head of the home Department
Mr Dombey keeps an eye upon Richards	Mr Dombey Miss Nipper
	Chapter IV
	In which some more first appearances are made on the stage of these adventures

The common view is that the left column represents Dickens's preplanning stage, written first, whereas the right hand column shows Dickens coming back to those ideas as he is writing and organising them into a set order, grouped into chapters. The deletions and emendations show that these plans were not fixed but open to adaptation. In contrast, some of the underlined sections show more conviction – 'Boy born, to die' demonstrates emphatically that Paul Dombey's tragic death in the fifth number, just a quarter of the way into the story, is entirely planned and prepared for. Planning a book is hardly revolutionary, and is of course the route most authors take, so it is only notable in this instance because of how utterly unplanned Dickens's earlier works had been up to this point. Most famously, in *Pickwick* one of the major characters,

Sam Weller, just sort of tumbles into the narrative: he first appears in the fourth number as a supporting character for one scene, only to then be introduced in the next number as Pickwick's new servant. Kathleen Tillotson and John Butt suggest Dickens may have 'noticed that [sales] began to rise in July with the introduction of Sam Weller', accounting for the long-term inclusion of an incidental character; William Jerdan had also advised Dickens to 'develop [Sam] to the utmost'.[23] Weller was not written with the intention of being Pickwick's servant, but the popularity of his interaction with Pickwick prompted Dickens to develop the character retroactively; in contrast, Paul Dombey was written to die, and his character points towards that from the beginning. We are told the newborn Paul clenches his fists 'in his feeble way', but the most striking thread running through the book is the narrative of water, and of death being a sea which we drift into.[24] When Paul's mother dies at the end of the first chapter, Dickens tells us that 'the mother drifted out upon the dark and unknown sea that rolls round all the world.'[25] The water is then referenced in the background through the succeeding chapters, especially given the introduction of Walter and his nautical family, who make a favourable impression on Paul and his sister Florence. But when Paul's death scene arrives, the intensity of references to water increases as a call back to the death of his own mother. The chapter title is 'What the waves were always saying', and in it, as Paul grows evermore ill and weak, he constantly focuses upon an imagined idea of the sea:[26]

> When the sunbeams struck into his room through the rustling blinds, and quivered on the opposite wall like golden water, he knew that evening was coming on, and that the sky was red and beautiful. As the reflection died away, and a gloom went creeping up the wall, he watched it deepen, deepen, deepen, into night. Then he thought how the long streets were dotted with lamps, and how the peaceful stars were shining overhead. His fancy had a strange tendency to wander to the river, which he knew was flowing through the great city; and now he thought how black it was, and how deep it would look, reflecting the hosts of stars–and more than all, how steadily it rolled away to meet the sea.[27]

The illusion of water, and the dream of the river, becomes a growing fixation as Paul becomes fainter and his grip on life, and reality, weakens. Dickens tells us that 'How many times the golden water danced upon the wall; how many nights the dark, dark river rolled towards the sea in spite of him; Paul never counted, never sought to know'.[28] Lying in his bed with his sister Florence at his side, Paul is feverish and believes himself to be on a boat:

'How fast the river runs, between its green banks and the rushes, Floy! But it's very near the sea. I hear the waves! They always said so!'

Presently he told her the motion of the boat upon the stream was lulling him to rest. How green the banks were now, how bright the flowers growing on them, and how tall the rushes! Now the boat was out at sea, but gliding smoothly on. And now there was a shore before him. Who stood on the bank–! He put his hands together, as he had been used to do at his prayers. He did not remove his arms to do it; but they saw him fold them so, behind her neck.

'Mama is like you, Floy. I know her by the face! But tell them that the print upon the stairs at school is not divine enough. The light about the head is shining on me as I go!'

The golden ripple on the wall came back again, and nothing else stirred in the room. The old, old fashion! The fashion that came in with our first garments, and will last unchanged until our race has run its course, and the wide firmament is rolled up like a scroll. The old, old fashion–Death! Oh thank GOD, all who see it, for that older fashion yet, of Immortality! And look upon us, angels of young children, with regards not quite estranged, when the swift river bears us to the ocean![29]

In retrospect, the frequent references to water and golden ripple are a clear sign of foreshadowing. Many readers will already have suspected that a tragic event was approaching, and Dickens's own foreknowledge of the event allowed him to prepare his readers for its coming – whereas Little Nell's death in *The Old Curiosity Shop* was dreaded, but not confirmed in many reader's expectations, in *Dombey* Paul's death seems much more certain. The same imagery of water is called back to again in the closing lines of the novel: 'Never from the mighty sea may voices rise too late, to come between us and the unseen region on the other shore! Better, far better, that they whispered of that region in our childish ears, and the swift river hurried us away!'[30] It is interesting to return to Dickens's working notes here, as the plan for the final number states 'End with the sea – carrying through, what the waves were always saying, and the invisible country far away.' What we do not know with any certainty is *when* Dickens wrote that note. Did he plan everything in advance, or was he planning a few months in advance only? Did he write the early notes in the left-hand column for each number first, then return to the right-hand column each month as an early drafting stage? It is an interesting question because it affects whether we see that very first mention of the sea in Chapter 1 as a knowing nod to how Dickens planned to end the novel, or whether Dickens decided later to close the novel on this same idea which had closed the first chapter. Either way, what it does emphatically show is how much more reflective and self-referential Dickens's novels had become, to use and reuse this motif throughout the narrative. Pickwick could easily have gone on to have more adventures – in fact he did, both in Reynold's spin-off tale *Pickwick Abroad*, and in Dickens's own *Master Humphrey's Clock* where both Pickwick and Sam Weller join Master Humphrey's circle of storytellers. His adventures are linear, with no sense of completion or closure; but *Dombey* ends precisely where it is meant to, and the reader is left with the satisfaction of a complete and enclosed narrative. In *Pickwick* Dickens is writing as a reporter still, responding to scenes as they unfold; with *Dombey* he offers commentary instead, and larger reflections on the state of the world.

It is certainly true then, to say that *Dombey* does indeed mark a key development point in Dickens's writing. After *Dombey*, Dickens proceeded to write further grand narratives: his next novel, *David Copperfield*, would involve a reappraisal of, and reconciliation with, his own childhood, while its successor *Bleak House* is now widely recognised in critical circles as one of his finest works. In each and every novel that follows, that sense of an overarching plan continues to thrive; whether this marks a turning point or simply an evolutionary step forward, Dickens was looking ahead, rather than backwards. As he proclaimed during the writing of *Copperfield*, 'the world would not take another Pickwick from me now': that same character who had made his name, and for whom his readers were always clamouring, was now a figure of the past, and Dickens was intentionally striving to move away from that early prototype towards more complicated and nuanced plots and characters.[31]

But, if I may play devil's advocate, does an increase in forward-planning and closure necessarily mean an improvement in writing – is *Dombey* better than *Pickwick*? There is much that can be said in favour of Dickens's earlier work, not despite their lack of planning, but because of it. As already noted, it allowed Dickens to respond to his readers and their tastes, developing the character of Sam Weller who would otherwise have been just a one-scene character. The capacity for reader-responsive writing which serialisation allowed can be considered as one of the key reasons for Dickens's early popularity, and certainly the success of *Pickwick*. In contrast, having a fixed idea for the plot of a novel, and then having to pursue that while his readers speculated could often lead to frustration, as in the case of *Our Mutual Friend* where Dickens urges that he always meant for readers to guess the 'twist' halfway through the novel. The younger, earlier Dickens, might have been inclined to shift course and change the twist; equally the younger Dickens's own ignorance of where his own story was heading prevented him from making the anticipatory remarks which readers could pick up on to predict the plot. In a tale like *Pickwick*, no-one knew what was going to happen next (including the author), which can create a far more energetic and involving work. On a technical level, we are inclined to favour *Dombey* because we conflate planning and organisation with skill and craft; but there is much to be said for Dickens's improvisation skill in the early novels, and that sense of responsiveness and reactive creativity. There is a flair in the white heat of his early writing pace, a flair which proved unsustainable for Dickens, but nonetheless produced the works which would prove most popular in his own lifetime.

This is not intended as an attack on *Dombey*. Speaking personally for a moment, *Pickwick* and *Dombey* are my two favourite Dickens novels, and my judgement on which is number one differs from day to day. *Dombey* certainly exhibits a maturity, and a greater sense of purpose. Dickens is no longer writing comic narratives to divert his reader, but attempting to make important grand narratives to *inspire* his reader. *Pickwick* offered readers an escape from reality, but *Dombey* and its successors challenge us to confront reality, and Dickens's later novels all take opportunity to highlight and expose the issues in his society with an underlying message that change was required. Therefore, while the early novels offer the most fun for a reader, it is the later novels which fulfil our more common conceptions of Literature with a capital L. There is an element of snobbery here, of course, and it can be quickly countered that some of Dickens's early works – especially *Oliver* and *A Christmas Carol* – make equally important interventions on behalf of the poor, made more potent in this case by the popularity of each work which allowed that message to reach (and continue to reach) a wider audience. But there is also then a reverse snobbery which would denounce the later works as boring and pretentious, which I certainly do not believe. The later novels maintain those same Dickensian characters and vibrancy of portrayal that made the first books so successful. As late as *Edwin Drood*, Dickens's last novel, reviewers were noting the familiarity of writing and the recycling of characters, with one parody piece ironically saying that Mr Sapsea 'is not Pecksniff, as you might imagine'.[32] Dickens may have believed he had evolved, but his readers were still seeing the old works in his new ones. Perhaps then, the idea of Dickens writing in two stages is a fallacy after all; instead we can see his career not as one of two opposites – the social commentary and the humour – but of a scale, with each work containing a mix of both.

Notes

1 John Forster, *The Life of Charles Dickens*, Volume Two (London: Chapman and Hall, 1873), p. 51.

2 Robert Douglas-Fairhurst, *The Turning Point: A Year that Changed Dickens and the World* (London: Vintage, 2021).

3 Edgar Allan Poe, 'Original Review', *Philadelphia Saturday Evening Post*, 1 May 1841.

4 Charles Dickens, *Our Mutual Friend*, ed. by Michael Cotsell (Oxford, OUP, 2008), Postscript: In Lieu of preface, p. 821.

5 Charles Dickens, *The Old Curiosity Shop*, ed. by Elizabeth M. Brennan (Oxford: OUP, 1997), Ch. 3, p. 33.

6 *The Old Curiosity Shop*, Ch. 73, p. 572.

7 Dickens, Letter to John Forster, 1 November 1843, in Madeline House, Graham Storey and Kathleen Tillotson (eds.), *The Letters of Charles Dickens*, Volume Three 1842–1843 (Oxford: Clarendon Press, 1974), pp. 587–588 (p. 588).

8 John Forster, *The Life of Charles Dickens* Volume One (London: Chapman and Hall, 1870), p. 100.

9 Charles Dickens, Letter to John Macrone, 9 May 1836, in Madeline House and Graham Storey (eds.), *The Letters of Charles Dickens*, Volume One 1820–1839 (Oxford: Clarendon Press, 1974), p. 150 (p. 150).

10 Dickens, Letter to Marion Ely, 29 November 1843, in House, Storey and Tillotson, Volume Three, p. 602 (p. 602).

11 Dickens, Letter to John Forster, February 1854, in Graham Story, Kathleen Tillotson and Angus Easson (eds.), *The Letters of Charles Dickens*, Volume Seven 1853–1855 (Oxford: Clarendon Press, 1993), p. 282 (p. 282).

12 Dickens, Letter to John Forster, 1 November 1843, in *Letters*. Vol. 3, pp. 587–588 (p. 587).

13 Dickens, Letter to Forster, 26–29 October 1846, in Kathleen Tillotson, *The Letters of Charles Dickens*, Volume Four 1844–1846 (Oxford: Clarendon Press, 1977), pp. 647–650 (p. 649).

14 Dickens, Letter to Emile De La Rue, 16 February 1846, in *Letters*, Vol. 4, pp. 497–499 (p. 498).

15 Dickens, Letter to Bradbury and Evans, 16 March 1846, in *Letters*, Vol. 4, pp. 520–522 (pp. 520–521).

16 Advertisement, in Charles Dickens, *Pictures from Italy* (London: Bradbury & Evans, 1846).

17 Charles Dickens, *Pictures from Italy*, ed. by Pete Orford (Oxford: OUP, 2023), p. 4.

18 Dickens, Letter to John Forster, 6 September 1846, in *Letters*, Vol. 4, pp. 618–620 (p. 620).

19 Charles Dickens, *Martin Chuzzlewit*, ed. by Margaret Cardwell (Oxford: OUP, 1982), Preface.

20 Dickens, Letter to John Forster, 25–26 July 1846, in *Letters*, Vol. 4, pp. 589–593 (p. 589).

21 Alexander Welsh, *From Copyright to Copperfield* (Cambridge, Massachusetts: Harvard UP, 1987), p. 75.

22 Forster, Vol. 2, p. 309.

23 William Jerden, cited in John Butt and Kathleen Tillotson, *Dickens at Work* (London: Methuen, 1968), p. 66.

24 Charles Dickens, *Dombey and Son*, ed. by Alan Horsman (Oxford: OUP, 1974), Ch. 1, p. 1.

25 *Dombey and Son*, Ch 1, p. 11.

26 *Dombey and Son*, Ch. 16, p. 220.

27 *Dombey and Son*, Ch 16, pp. 220–221.

28 *Dombey and Son*, Ch 16, p. 222.

29 *Dombey and Son*, Ch.16, pp. 224–225.

30 *Dombey and Son*, Ch. 62, p. 833N.

31 Dickens, Letter to Dudley Costello, 25 April 1849, in Graham Storey and K. J. Fielding, *The Letters of Charles Dickens*, Volume Five 1847–1849, p. 527 (p. 527).

32 Anon., 'The Mystery of Rude Dedwin', *Judy*, 13 April 1870, p. 240.

7

Dickens and Charity

Focal Point: 1847

Case Study: Bleak House

As a young writer Dickens chased contracts and opportunities to secure and further his career; but it is important to note that Dickens's restless spirit did not focus solely on his own progression and needs. In life he proved himself to be a great social campaigner, and his words had power to help and inspire real change. Dickens's works certainly had some form of impact; Joanna Hofer-Robinson has noted how 'the social improvements promised by advocates of Field Lane's redevelopment were repeatedly articulated and conceptualised through references to *Oliver Twist* as a consequence of Dickens choosing Field Lane as the location for Fagin's den.[1] This shows how Dickens's words could translate into the actions of others, but there is little to suggest that such change was intentional or anticipated by Dickens at the time. In contrast, Dickens boldly claimed in 1843 that he was going to write a piece which would prove a 'sledgehammer' for the poor; that work eventually emerges as *A Christmas Carol*, although some would argue the real sledgehammer is *The Chimes* which followed the year after.[2] Equally, in his journalism he raised and tackled issues of inequality; in 1849 he wrote a series of articles for *The Examiner* attacking Bartholomew Drouet's Infant Pauper Asylum in Tooting, where several children died of cholera due to the despicable conditions.[3]

Subsequent generations have come to praise Dickens for his great social campaigning and his championing of those in need because of his prolonged discussion and exploration of the poor in his novels. But writing alone is not enough. Today the world is awash with celebrities tweeting sad messages of support for those in need, but doing little beyond that; the simple act of raising awareness is often as much as they will get involved, rather than taking more direct action and being more deeply engaged in raising funds to help others in need. It is to Dickens's credit then that he tends more towards the latter, even though it's the former we remember him for today. This is understandable: the popularity and presence of his writing means his words have lasted and can

The Life of the Author: Charles Dickens, First Edition. Pete Orford.
© 2023 John Wiley & Sons Ltd. Published 2023 by John Wiley & Sons Ltd.

still inspire today, but it is equally important to consider the work he was doing in his own lifetime, helping people in his own society. These actions do not have the same range of impact and legacy that his writings do, but arguably did more real good and made a more significant difference to those people that he helped. This chapter will look at Dickens's deeds as well as his words, to see what Dickens himself did to try and improve the lives of others through his charitable work and campaigning, to get a better sense of his position on these political and social matters.

The General Theatrical Fund

Interestingly, one of Dickens's earliest charitable engagements was with the arts. In 1839 a General Theatrical Fund was established to help actors. The ambition of the fund was to provide a pension and income for actors no longer able to work, either through illness or old age. At the time, actors were reliant on each performance to make money, so they would continue to work for as long as they were able. The reputation of actors at this time was still contentious; for all of the celebrated actors like Macready or Kean, there were many more dismissed as hacks or mere entertainers. It was a precarious form of employment for many, and difficult to attract sympathy for those who had now left the stage and were struggling. Laugh and the world laughs with you, but once the performances stopped these actors found little support. The General Theatrical Fund was consequently a very humane foundation to help those in need, and to gain funds it needed to appeal to those who enjoyed the theatre, to show how they profited from the experience and so encourage a sense of moral debt that might prompt patrons to help those who had entertained them. Dickens gave many speeches for the fund in which he built on this sense of what the arts do for us, and unsurprisingly we see Dickens's own enthusiasm for theatre spill out.

But the enthusiasm of Dickens's speeches is tempered by an awareness of the limitations of charity. In his 1846 speech for the fund he noted the existence of two other funds run by 'Covent Garden and Drury Lane – both of long standing, both richly endowed', and with both of which Dickens had 'had the honour of being connected at different periods of [his] life': this was not Dickens's first engagement with such fundraising societies then, but the GTF notes a significant change in the sense of purpose.[4] The problem, as Dickens notes, with the existing two funds is how exclusionary there were: 'it was essential in order to become a member of the Drury Lane Society that the applicant, either he or she, should have been engaged for three consecutive seasons as a performer', while Covent Garden asked for 'a period of two years'.[5]

Covent Garden and Drury Lane were the two great theatres of the age; both places to aspire to, but Covent Garden was in decline and Drury Lane was 'devoted to foreign ballets and foreign operas'.[6] Consequently both funds, charitable as they appeared, were excluding many actors from eligibility: 'How can the profession generally hope to qualify for the Drury Lane or Covent Garden institutions, when the oldest and most distinguished members have been driven from the boards on which they earned their reputations, to delight the towns to which the General Theatrical Fund alone extends?'[7] The GTF thus offered support to actors outside those two institutions, recognising actors at all theatres and treating them with equal status and eligibility. Dickens's recognition of the failings in the first two funds, and his engagement with the GTF, shows a better understanding on his part, and a distinction between charities and what they actually do: Dickens wanted to help *every* actor, not just those at the great theatres. His description of the GTF in his 1851 speech highlights the fund's inclusivity in contrast to those funds which proclaim great benevolence when not actually offering it:

> [This fund] is not a rich old gentleman, with the gout in his vitals, brushed up and got up once a year to look as vigorous as possible, and taken out for a public airing by the few survivors of a large family of nephews and nieces, who keep him laid up in lavender all the rest of the year as a mighty delicate old gentleman: then ask his poor relations, whom they lock out with a double turn of the street door key, why they don't come in and enjoy his money? [...] No, gentlemen, if there be any such funds, this Fund is not of that kind. This Fund is a theatrical association, addressed to the means, and adapted to the wants – and sore and dire those often are – of the whole theatrical profession throughout England.[8]

Dickens's enthusiastic support for *all* actors attacks the hierarchy of the profession and the institutions which profess to help all while excluding many. But at the heart of the speech is a horror that those who work to entertain and enrich our lives can be so casually forgotten and dismissed. A similar realisation motivated Dickens's involvement with the Shakespeare Birthplace. The house where Shakespeare was born and raised in Stratford-upon-Avon is now a treasured heritage site, but this was only established as such in the Victorian age when the building was in danger of demolition. A movement was made to save Shakespeare's home and Dickens was called upon for his support, which he duly gave. Much like his work for the GTF, what appears to be an interest in the arts on the surface is informed by more humane considerations underneath. Dickens organised a charitable performance of *The Merry Wives of*

Windsor and *Every Man in his Humour*, supposedly to raise funds for the birthplace, but the letters make it clear that Dickens was interested primarily in raising money for its curator. This curator would be James Sheridan Knowles, a playwright himself who, much like the actors the GTF was trying to help, was now in desperate financial need despite his earlier success as the writer of *Virginius*. For Dickens, preserving Shakespeare's home was important, of course, but helping Knowles was even more important:

> We do not play to purchase the house (which may be positively considered as paid for) but towards endowing a perpetual curatorship of it, for some eminent literary veteran. And I think you will recognise in this, even a higher and more generous object than the securing, even, of the debt incurred for the house itself.[9]

Dickens's work for the GTF and the Shakespeare birthplace indicates this growing awareness of the distinction between large proclamations of help that are heard by many, and the more direct action of providing genuine support to people. It is notable that Dickens was approached about becoming a politician on several occasions, and each time refused:

> I beg to assure you that I thoroughly satisfied myself long ago, that I can be far more useful and far more independent, in my own calling than in the House of Commons[.][10]

Dickens's response recognises the greater reach he had as a novelist, but it also champions the idea of independent projects doing more good, and being more use, than could ever be achieved within the ranks of a larger organisation. One of Dickens's major charitable projects, Urania Cottage, would continue this idea of making a significant change to a small number of people, rather than a small change to a large number of people.

The House of Fallen Women

Dickens established Urania Cottage in 1847 as a Home for 'fallen women' where they could be offered a fresh start, education and improvement ending in a new life working abroad. The key figure in this was Dickens's friend Angela Burdett-Coutts, who provided the necessary financial support for the project. Burdett-Coutts was one of the richest women in England; her father Sir Francis Burdett was an MP, and her maternal grandfather Thomas Coutts, who had died in 1822, had established Coutts's bank – when his wife (Burdett-Coutts's step-grandmother) died in 1837, her share of the fortune went to Burdett-Coutts, who was just 23 years old at the time. Unsurprisingly, this incredibly rich young woman became the centre of attention for various marriage proposals, all rejected – in 1847 she was instead interested in the Duke of Wellington, who politely refused *her* offer of marriage on account of his advanced age (in the end, she got married when aged 67 to her 29-year-old secretary). Burdett-Coutts is remembered today for her philanthropy, and her involvement with Urania Cottage was one of her earliest endeavours.

The plan for Urania Cottage had begun in 1846, before Dickens left for Switzerland. He and Burdett-Coutts had visited a ragged school two years prior, and Burdett-Coutts was now planning to endow a school in Westminster. At this moment, Dickens wrote a long letter to her detailing plans for a home for fallen women:

> A woman or girl coming to the Asylum, it is explained to her that she has come there for *useful* repentance and reform, and because her past way of life has been dreadful in its nature and consequences and full of affliction, misery and despair to *herself*. Never mind Society while she is at that pass. Society has used her ill and turned away from her, and she cannot be expected to take much heed of its rights or wrongs. It is destructive to *herself*, and there is no hope in it, or in her, as long as she pursues it. It is explained to her that she is degraded and fallen, but not lost, having this shelter; and that the means of Return to Happiness are now about to be put into her own hands, and trusted to her own keeping.[11]

Note how Dickens is at pains to gain the trust of these women and acknowledge their own mistrust of the society which has failed them. Like the theatrical funds, Dickens is painfully aware of organisations which aim to help but do not, and the subsequent challenge of convincing others that this, unlike those, could make a real difference. Note also the description of the intended addressee. A 'fallen woman' could refer to any number of cases: prostitutes, thieves, women in prison – the one thing they had in common was the belief held in wider society that they were now lost for ever, and Dickens's own belief that these women were not to blame for this misfortunes. Dickens hoped to rehabilitate these women so they could start their lives anew. He wrote a letter which was printed and distributed to prisons; in it he takes great pains to appeal to the better side of these women and, in turn, offer them hope instead of condemnation:

> You will see, on beginning to read this letter, that it is not addressed to you by name. But I address it to a woman – a very young woman still – who was born to be happy, and has lived miserably; who has no

prospect before her but sorrow, or behind her but a wasted youth; who, if she has ever been a mother, has felt shame, instead of pride, in her own unhappy child.[12]

It was vital for Dickens that this opportunity be offered to the right people. His letter continues: 'You are such a person, or this letter would not be put into your hands'; by sending this letter to prisons the appeal was for the governors to select appropriate recipients, people who were not wholly lost, but who regretted their choices and wanted to find a better tomorrow. This was not a charitable endeavour that aimed to blindly bestow fortune upon all, but one that sought out those who wanted to change: those women who wanted redemption had to show themselves willing to work for it. Dickens's letter does not mention his own name, signing it off instead as 'your friend'; instead he puts the emphasis on Burdett-Coutts, who equally remains nameless but none-theless becomes an active agent in the narrative of the letter.

> There is a lady in this town, who, from the windows of her house, has seen such as you going past at night, and has felt her heart bleed at the sight. She is what is called a great lady; but she has looked after you with compassion, as being of her own sex and nature; and the thought of such fallen women has troubled her in her bed. She has resolved to open, at her own expense, a place of refuge very near London, for a small number of females, who, without such help, are lost for ever: and to make it A HOME for them.[13]

What is extraordinary in this passage is the extent to which Dickens erases himself from the narrative. Reading this letter, you would assume it was all Burdett-Coutts's idea, and that it was not Dickens who had initiated the plan. Dickens was hardly a shy person, and in other areas of life was more than happy to soak in praise and recognition, but in this instance he writes himself as a side-character or, more accurately, the narrator. The writing style of the letter could easily fit into any number of his novels – it has the same appeal to our sentiments, and the evocative description of Burdett-Coutts watching these women from her windows creates a narrative that draws us in. In many respects all of this is redundant; Dickens could have simply written a much shorter letter of a paragraph or two offering a place. But that misses the point. Firstly, Dickens did not just want to offer this to anyone, but someone who he felt deserved it (this raises questions in itself of what qualifies a deserving recipient); secondly the style of the letter shows Dickens getting rather carried away with the emotion of the moment; as much as he centres Burdett-Coutts in the narrative, his presence is everywhere in the letter. The more Dickens emphasises the destitution of the fallen woman's current condition, and the promise of the better life that is being offered, there grows a sense of pleasure, almost self-congratulation, from the thought of doing good to others. The concluding paragraph of the letter does not hold back:

> In case there should be anything you wish to know, or any question you would like to ask, about this Home, you have only to say so, and every information shall be given to you. Whether you accept it or reject it, think about it. If you awake in the silence and solitude of night, think of it then. If any remembrance ever comes into your mind of any time when you were innocent and very different, think of it then. If you should be softened by a moment's recollection of any tenderness or affection you have ever felt, or that has ever been shown to you, or of any kind word that has ever been spoken to you, think of it then. If ever your poor heart is moved to feel, truly, what you might have been, and what you are, oh think of it then, and consider what you may be yet![14]

It is curious to see a charitable organisation making such an impassioned plea to those it is supposed to be helping. The tone of the letter above is such that one would expect instead in a message to potential donors. But that insistence of the letter reveals the fundamental belief that these women had to want to save themselves. Dickens did not see the poor as automatically virtuous and pure any more than he saw the rich as automatically wise and benevolent. Malignancy thrived across all sectors of society; Dickens wanted to help those who wanted to be helped, or who showed signs of effort to deserve that help. The extreme of this can be seen in 'The Begging-Letter Writer', a short piece in which Dickens complained of the many people who regularly contacted him asking for free handouts without deserving it:

> He has besieged my door, at all hours of the day and night; he has fought my servant; he has lain in ambush for me, going out and coming in; he has followed me out of town into the country; he has appeared at provincial hotels, where I have been staying for only a few hours; he has written to me from immense distances, when I have been out of England. He has fallen sick; he has died, and been buried; he has come to life again, and again departed from this transitory scene; he has been his own son, his own mother, his own baby, his idiot brother, his uncle, his aunt, his aged grandfather. He has wanted a great coat, to go to India in; a pound, to set him up in life for ever; a pair of boots, to take him to the coast of China; a hat, to get him into a permanent situation under Government.[15]

The distant, scathing tone of this article seems at complete odds with the passionate and imploring tone of the Urania Cottage letter, but the distinction lies in that judgement of who is worthy. For Dickens, there are those who deserve charity through an awareness of their flaws and most importantly, a willingness to change. It is interesting to note that Dickens's engagement in charity frequently involved him offering his time or endorsement, rather than a direct cash donation. He would readily organise funds or encourage ways to raise money, but did not show the same eagerness to donate himself.

Dickens does not judge the poor as one entity but as a collection of individuals, some of whom are capable of redemption and some who are not. One of the most cherished and famous scenes in *A Christmas Carol* is the Cratchit family's dinner: the entire tone of the piece moves towards celebration over and above pity. Indeed, at various points the narrator actively defies the reader to feel pity, implying that it would be an insult to do so. When the pudding is brought in, we are told that 'Everyone had something to say about it, but nobody said or thought it was at all a small pudding for a large family'; moreover Dickens states 'It would have been flat heresy to do so. Any Cratchit would have blushed to hint at such a thing.'[16] Dickens is not writing poverty tourism here; he is not emphasising their destitution to elicit tears, but rather is celebrating their industriousness and the homeliness of the scene. The Cratchits work hard, and earn their Christmas dinner. If more can be done then so be it, but in this instance the family evoke not sympathy but almost envy at the warmth of the moment:

> There was nothing of high mark in this. They were not a handsome family; they were not well dressed; their shoes were far from being waterproof; their clothes were scanty; and Peter might have known, and very likely did, the inside of a pawnbroker's. But, they were happy, grateful, pleased with one another, and contented with the time[.][17]

Of course, in the *Carol* the Cratchit family are helped; Scrooge's transformation into a benevolent soul means that Tiny Tim's death is averted. But Scrooge does not simply give a donation to the family but instead raises Bob Cratchit's wages: Bob Cratchit continues to work, to earn a better life for his family. The Cratchit's are not suddenly treated to a life of relaxation and idleness, but instead given fair recognition for the work they are doing and the effort they are making. They show themselves deserving of Scrooge's help.

Urania Cottage thus represents much of what Dickens considers to be a successful charity. It is local, making a direct and significant impact on a small number of people. It aimed to help those who wanted to be helped. It did not merely give them a free handout, but trained them, educated them, asked for effort and work on their part too. It attempted to avoid judgement; the naming of it as a Home, rather than Institution or Centre, emphasises the warmth and the intended welcoming nature of the building. I say 'intended': in Jenny Hartley's fascinating exploration of Urania Cottage she notes how not everyone made it through, and some either chose to leave or were asked to leave if they were not seen to be sufficiently improving or respecting the rules of the house. Martha Williamson had been at Urania Cottage for five weeks when she was accused of stealing a bonnet and gown, and Hartley notes 'Although Dickens felt sorry for her, there were no extenuating circumstances. He told her she must put on her old clothes and leave by noon tomorrow.'[18] Redemption was not a given.

On entry to the house, the women were interviewed by Dickens where their life-story would be discussed, after which they were encouraged not to speak again of their past lives. This can be seen both as an opportunity for a fresh start, but also a silent judgement on their previous behaviour. The experience at Urania Cottage was effectively promoting erasure of the past, rather than acceptance of it. Once the women had been sufficiently retrained in the necessary skills, a new life waited for them – abroad. This was a key part of Dickens's plan, that the women could then emigrate to another country to have a fresh start. Much like the request not to discuss their previous lives while in the Home, this removal to a new country can be seen as a benevolent and well-intended opportunity to start a new life in an environment where no-one would ever know their former misdemeanours, but it also implies a sense of shame and removal. As much as the women were offered a new life, it came at the cost of burying their old ones.

This is not to say that Urania Cottage was not a worthwhile endeavour. On the contrary, it was a successful charitable organisation that ran for several decades, and made an impact on the lives of several women who went on to live happy and comfortable lives abroad. Dickens and Burdett-Coutts made that happen, and their involvement in the fortunes of these women was ultimately a positive one. Dickens was doing more than he needed to; he was far more involved in the running of Urania Cottage than was Burdett-Coutts, who preferred to be more of a silent partner. Like the GTF and the Shakespeare Birthplace, Urania Cottage showed Dickens's interest and passion in helping people, in doing what could be done. He was not merely a man of words, but a man of action as well.

Hartley notes in her book that interest in Dickens and Urania cottage normally rests on a focus on 'extra-curricular Dickens, the side of him which is not writing fiction'.[19] She challenges this by showing how Dickens used the experience to inform the portrayal of women in his subsequent works. His interviews with the residents at Urania Cottage were conducted with a case book, now lost, in which he would write down their stories, and it is likely that these stories then formed the inspiration for the many fallen women who subsequently appear in his works, such as Edith Grainger in *Dombey and Son*, Little Em'ly in *David Copperfield*, or Tattycoram and Miss Wade in *Little Dorrit*. In a subsequent conversation with Hartley she told me this was the aspect of her book that had most shocked readers and generated the most discussion, with their sense being that Dickens was using these women. Hartley feels this is not the case, and that rather than seeing this as Dickens taking advantage, rather it is Dickens offering a platform to these women's stories, which would otherwise be silenced. There is no indication that any of the Urania women were identified in their lifetime as the real-life counterparts for Dickens's characters, nor any reaction from the women themselves (in contrast, say, to the complaint made against Dickens by his neighbour Mrs Jane Seymour Hill for his portrayal of her as Miss Mowcher in *David Copperfield*). Either they themselves were unaware of any fictional counterpart, or else they considered it a fair swap for a new start in life:

> For eleven years Dickens questioned, listened and wrote, as the young women disclosed to him the most intimate details of their lives. Was this the price they had to pay for their warm beds and the passage out to Australia? Or was there anything in it for them? A study conduced a few years ago in America would suggest that there was [...] What they found was that the act of shaping and telling your autobiography can be a force for good.[20]

Whatever benefit Dickens may have gained from the experience for his fiction is secondary to the benefit the women themselves gained, not only through the safe haven and new life offered, but in the closure of telling and owning their story. Equally, there is a sense of Dickens himself evolving and coming to terms with his own upbringing: once he had sat at the blacking factory waiting for a benefactor to save him; now he could be to others the benefactor he himself never had. Equally, as much as Dickens may have been inspired by the women of Urania Cottage, there is a sense of life imitating art given his earlier character of Nancy in *Oliver Twist*. If his experience at Urania deepened his understanding of these women's plight, it expanded on an area he was already interested in rather than introducing him to the idea. Dickens's fascination with these women featured in both his writing and life; his concern for them is evident in his earlier writings, and then developed further in his later writing as a consequence of meeting the women at Urania Cottage.

Case Study: Telescopic Philanthropy and a Multitude of Sins in *Bleak House*

The first instalment of *Bleak House* was published in March 1852, five years after the establishment of Urania Cottage. The novel is remarkable for its breadth of scope; there are several institutions and character types targeted and criticised within its pages. In terms of charity, the obvious candidate that usually draws our attention is the chaotic Mrs Jellyby, who we first meet in Chapter 4, titled 'Telescopic Philanthropy'. Dickens has the capacity for great subtlety in his writing – this is not one of those occasions. His depiction of Mrs Jellyby is so extreme as to be absurd: depicting a woman utterly fixated on helping the lives of those abroad with complete disregard for the lives of those closer to home. When the book's heroine Esther Summerson arrives with her friends Richard and Ada at Mrs Jellyby's house, she finds a disturbance outside, the cause being that 'One of the young Jellybys been and got his head through the area railings'.[21] Esther reports passing 'several more children on the way up, whom it was difficult to avoid treading on in the dark; and as we came into Mrs. Jellyby's presence, one of the poor little things fell downstairs – down a whole flight (as it sounded to me), with a great noise'.[22] Upon meeting Mrs Jellyby herself, it soon becomes apparent that the welfare of her children is not an immediate concern to her; Esther's narrative recalls that she 'received us with perfect equanimity' even while 'the dear child's head recorded its passage with a bump on every stair.'[23] It transpires that Mrs Jellyby can 'see nothing nearer than Africa', hence the idea of 'telescopic philanthropy' hinted at in the chapter's title: Mrs Jellyby is so concerned with helping those abroad that she ignores the plight of those at home – even her own home, in the case of her children.[24] Her constant ignorance of her children often turns into a flat refusal to hear them:

> Peepy (so self-named) was the unfortunate child who had fallen down-stairs, who now interrupted the correspondence by presenting himself, with a strip of plaster on his forehead, to exhibit his wounded knees, in which Ada and I did not know which to pity most – the bruises or the dirt. Mrs. Jellyby merely added, with the serene composure with which she said everything, 'Go along, you naughty Peepy!' and fixed her fine eyes on Africa again.[25]

It is not a subtle portrayal, and the reader is left in little doubt but that they are meant to scorn Mrs Jellyby's misdirected efforts. Dickens portrays her as failing in her duties as a mother, and as a woman too: we are told for example that Esther's friend Richard, finding the house to be in disarray, 'had washed his hands in a pie-dish' and 'found the kettle on his dressing-table'; we are told also that 'Mrs. Jellyby had very good hair but was too much occupied with her African duties to brush it.'[26] Interestingly, some have subsequently examined Mrs Jellyby in a more flattering light as a progressive challenge to gender norms. Holly Furneaux explores 'an available, though not Dickens-endorsed reading' of Mrs Jellyby as 'a threatening, intriguing and perhaps even inspiring character', one who 'offers an alternative value system to that of modern capitalism which posits financial success, marriage, and reproduction as goals essential to happiness.'[27] It is worth noting that however much Dickens stresses the concerns of Esther, Ada and Richard, he also shows how Mrs Jellyby is championed by wider society. She is spoken of entirely positively by the general population for virtue of her charitable work, as

> ...a lady of very remarkable strength of character who devotes herself entirely to the public. She has devoted herself to an extensive variety of public subjects at various times and is at present (until something else attracts her) devoted to the subject of Africa, with a view to the general cultivation of the coffee berry – AND the natives – and the happy settlement, on the banks of the African rivers, of our superabundant home population.[28]

The introduction seems flattering, but the hints of disquiet are already apparent (although given how explicit Dickens is in his condemnation later in the chapter, the subtlety of the attack here can be missed). The mention of whatever 'attracts her' suggests in turn a very superficial view on her part; she is responding to the latest tragedy or trending topic rather than thinking deeply about how to help others, as Dickens liked to think he did. Likewise, the focus on the 'general cultivation of the coffee berry' hints at more economical concerns: Africa is important to Mrs Jellyby because of the produce Britain can take from it – the interpolation 'AND the natives' suggests their welfare is an afterthought next to this. So too, the plan for 'the happy settlement ... of our superabundant home population' in Africa suggests that the project is as much concerned with getting rid of the crowds from England as much as helping those in Africa. This is surprisingly close to Dickens's own project, and his keenness to send the fallen women abroad. Is such a venture for their own good, or just an opportunity to remove problematic members of society and relocate these issues to someone else? Mrs Jellyby tells Esther:

The African project at present employs my whole time. It involves me in correspondence with public bodies and with private individuals anxious for the welfare of their species all over the country. I am happy to say it is advancing. We hope by this time next year to have from a hundred and fifty to two hundred healthy families cultivating coffee and educating the natives of Borrioboola-Gha, on the left bank of the Niger.[29]

The reference to 'their species' is toe-curling. The issue of racism in Dickens's work is a difficult one to unpick, and one I will touch upon more in the final chapter, but Laura Peters is accurate when she notes that Dickens's 'perception of race tended to veer between the celebrated exotic and the demonised savage'.[30] In *Bleak House* we are left to question whether the ideas being expressed belong to Dickens or Mrs Jellyby: is he speaking of other races condescendingly, or writing ironically to mock her for speaking of other races condescendingly? What is particularly remarkable is that this bizarre character is based on a real-life person. In 1850 Dickens had met Caroline Chisholm, who ran the Family Colonisation Loan Society which helped poor families to emigrate abroad; Dickens wrote privately to Burdett-Coutts about the terrible condition of Chisholm's home and children:

> I dream of Mrs Chisholm, and her housekeeping. The dirty faces of her children are my continued companions. I forgot to tell you that she asked me if it were true that the girls at Shepherd's Bush 'had pianos'. I shall always regret that I didn't answer yes – each girl a grand, down stairs – and a cottage in her bedroom – besides a small guitar in the wash-house.[31]

The second point about pianos betrays either a naivety or prejudice on Chisholm's part, and no less a prejudice on Dickens's part for sneering against such naivety. Dickens's concern about Chisholm's housekeeping could be said to reflect worse on him and his ideas of what a woman should be, but equally there is a validity in his concern that Chisholm, and Jellyby, are misfocused. Dickens is not advising against overseas aid, but rather is criticising those who fetishize the idea of helping those abroad – what would nowadays be referred to as white saviour syndrome – rather than helping those who do not so readily fit our image of a charitable case. This is the same exoticism of the poor abroad compared to the poor at home that he had attacked in *Pictures from Italy*, when he said 'It is not well to find Saint Giles's so repulsive, and the Porta Capuana so attractive. A pair of naked legs and a ragged red scarf, do not make *all* the difference between what is interesting and what is coarse and odious'.[32] As

Grace Moore writes, Dickens was suggesting that '[t]he civilized nation was only interested in the novelty of the African, and the only way the urban poor could compel the eye of the telescopic philanthropist to fall upon them was through deception.'[33] Helping the poor natives of an African country carries a romanticism lacking in the idea of helping just an ordinary beggar who lives on your own street. In contrast, as we have seen from Dickens's involvement in Urania Cottage, that idea of making a demonstrable difference to the individual, of helping those close by rather than investing in grand projects, is one which he absolutely subscribed to. Mrs Jellyby is doing good by sending money, and families, abroad, but what could she also be doing with those same resources in her own community?

Mrs Jellyby dominates discussions of charity in *Bleak House*, but an equally illuminating character is Mrs Pardiggle, who first appears in Chapter 9, the evocative title for which is 'Covering a multitude of sins'. Like Mrs Jellyby, Mrs Pardiggle appears to be as concerned with her reputation and the appearance of doing good, as much as actually considering what might be genuinely helpful. The character sees her own position as distinct from Mrs Jellyby's:

> Mrs. Jellyby is a benefactor to society and deserves a helping hand. My boys have contributed to the African project – Egbert, one and six, being the entire allowance of nine weeks; Oswald, one and a penny halfpenny, being the same; the rest, according to their little means. Nevertheless, I do not go with Mrs. Jellyby in all things. I do not go with Mrs. Jellyby in her treatment of her young family. It has been noticed. It has been observed that her young family are excluded from participation in the objects to which she is devoted. She may be right, she may be wrong; but, right or wrong, this is not my course with my young family. I take them everywhere.[34]

If Mrs Jellyby ignores her children, Mrs Pardiggle wilfully insists on her children's involvement in her work, donating their pocket money to charitable causes. She fails to recognise the needs of her children, but for a supposedly good and valid reason. Logically, her actions are right, but instinctively we know them to be wrong. Whether selfish or not, the children are right to spend the money as they wish; it is theirs after all, and in insisting they spend it on others she is failing to recognise their needs. The implicit criticism by Dickens is that this charitable woman is never heeding the needs and wants of her children; to be so fixated on a moral crusade as to miss her more immediate requirements as a mother. Moreover, her blind assumption that her children willingly 'expend the entire amount of their allowance in subscriptions' is an indication of Mrs Pardiggle's inability to listen to others.[35] She believes she knows what is best, and so insists upon it, ignoring the desires of those she professes to help. When she takes Esther and Ada on her charitable rounds, the disconnect between Mrs Pardiggle's perception of her own benevolence, with the actual response from those she is supposedly helping, is startling:

> Ada and I were very uncomfortable. We both felt intrusive and out of place, and we both thought that Mrs. Pardiggle would have got on infinitely better if she had not had such a mechanical way of taking possession of people. The children sulked and stared; the family took no notice of us whatever, except when the young man made the dog bark, which he usually did when Mrs. Pardiggle was most emphatic. We both felt painfully sensible that between us and these people there was an iron barrier which could not be removed by our new friend. By whom or how it could be removed, we did not know, but we knew that.[36]

The key point here is the 'iron barrier' which exists between Mrs Pardiggle and those she professes to help. She does not understand them, nor try to understand them. She visits them regularly to read the Bible to them, and sees it as obstinacy on their part that this does not automatically make their lives better. Like with her own children, Mrs Pardiggle presumes she knows what is best for others and makes decisions on their behalf either without consulting them, or ignoring their answers. While the discussion of Mrs Pardiggle's poor children verges on humour and satire, the intrusion into the house of the poor tips the episode into something far more savage and scathing, articulated through the bitter monologue of the father of the family as he rebukes her for yet another intrusion into their home:

> I wants an end of these liberties took with my place. I wants an end of being drawed like a badger. Now you're a-going to poll-pry and question according to custom – I know what you're a-going to be up to. Well! You haven't got no occasion to be up to it. I'll save you the trouble. Is my daughter a-washin? Yes, she IS a-washin. Look at the water. Smell it! That's wot we drinks. How do you like it, and what do you think of gin instead! An't my place dirty? Yes, it is dirty – it's nat'rally dirty, and it's nat'rally onwholesome; and we've had five dirty and onwholesome children, as is all dead infants, and so much the better for them, and for us besides. Have I read the little book wot you left? No, I an't read the little book wot you left. There an't nobody here as knows how to read it; and if there wos, it wouldn't be suitable to me. It's a book fit for a babby, and

I'm not a babby. If you was to leave me a doll, I shouldn't nuss it. How have I been conducting of myself? Why, I've been drunk for three days; and I'da been drunk four if I'da had the money. Don't I never mean for to go to church? No, I don't never mean for to go to church. I shouldn't be expected there, if I did; the beadle's too gen-teel for me. And how did my wife get that black eye? Why, I give it her; and if she says I didn't, she's a lie![37]

The man is aggressive in the midst of his despair: his daughter washes, but the water is dirty so it is to no effect; his children are dead, and better for not having to endure the suffering of life; the Bible is no good for him because he cannot read, and church offers no salvation to him. The man drinks, and beats his wife, and does not deny it. Mrs Pardiggle assumes that the Bible will save them, that washing and presenting themselves neatly will save them, but has wholly missed the point of the underlying conditions affecting these people's lives, and the absolute privilege that comes from assuming such people just need a more positive attitude to change their lives around. Dickens gives this man a voice, and forces the reader to listen to him. In a world where the Pardiggles and Jellybys speak loudest, over and above the subjects of their pity, Dickens provides a platform to those in dire circumstances, not to express their gratitude, but their anger.

The complete disaster of Mrs Pardiggle's charitable efforts, contrasted with her own perception that they are an absolute triumph, demonstrates the worst kind of charity to which Dickens was opposed. Mrs Pardiggle, like Mrs Jellyby, is doing charity out of conceit rather than concern. She does not understand the people she is helping; she simply assumes she knows better. She demands that they make changes without providing the necessary resources or support to make those changes. As much as Dickens asks that the people he helps are willing to change, he does not ignore the fact that real support is needed to help them change. More importantly, Dickens gets to know the people he is helping; he interviews the girls in Urania Cottage, and he would regularly walk the streets of London to see the poor up close. Like his description of the Cratchits, Dickens avoid patronising the poor and instead focuses on what they need, rather than what he might presume they need. Mrs Jellyby's telescopic philanthropy and Mrs Pardiggle's mechanical efforts show the danger of not knowing the people you are helping, of assuming that there is a set type of person needing charity, and a set type of charity to bestow on them. In his own charitable endeavours, Dickens showed a far greater appreciation for the realities of those who needed help, and the practicalities of what help might be better appreciated.

Notes

1 Joanna Hofer-Robinson, *Dickens and Demolition: Literary Afterlives and Mid-Nineteenth-Century Urban Development* (Edinburg: EUP, 2020), p. 93.

2 Dickens, Letter to Dr Southwood Smith, 10 March 1843, in Madeline House, Graham Storey and Kathleen Tillotson (eds.), *The Letters of Charles Dickens*, Volume Three 1842–1843 (Oxford: Clarendon Press, 1974), p. 461 (p. 461).

3 In total Dickens wrote four articles for *The Examiner* on the Tooting scandal: 'The Paradise at Tooting' (20 January 1849), 'The Tooting Farm' (27 January 1849), 'A Recorder's Charge' (3 March 1849) and 'The Verdict against Drouet' (23 April 1849).

4 Charles Dickens, Speech to the General Theatrical Fund, 6 April 1846, cited in K.J. Fielding (ed.), *The Speeches of Charles Dickens* (Oxford: OUP, 1960), pp. 73–77 (p. 74).

5 Dickens, Speech to GTF, 6 April 1846 in Fielding, p. 74.

6 Dickens, Speech to GTF, 6 April 1846 in Fielding, p. 74.

7 Dickens, Speech to GTF, 6 April 1846 in Fielding, p. 74.

8 Dickens, Speech to the General Theatrical Fund, 14 April 1851, cited in Fielding, pp. 118–127 (pp. 120–121).

9 Dickens, Letter to Mrs Cowden Clarke, 14 April 1848, in Graham Storey and K. J. Fielding (eds), *The Letters of Charles Dickens*, Volume Five 1847–1849 (Oxford: Clarendon Press, 1981), pp. 277–279 (278–279).

10 Dickens, Letter to Charles de la Pryme, 14 March 1857, in *Letters*, Volume Eight, p. 300 (p. 300).

11 Dickens, Letter to Angela Burdett Coutts, 26 May 1846, in Kathleen Tillotson (ed.), *The Letters of Charles Dickens*, Volume Four 1844–1846 (Oxford: Clarendon Press, 1977), pp. 552–556 (p. 553).

12 Dickens, 'An Appeal to Fallen Women', in *Letters*, Vol. 5, pp. 698–699 (p. 698).

13 'An Appeal to Fallen Women', p. 698.

14 'An Appeal to Fallen Women', p. 699.

15 Charles Dickens, 'The Begging-Letter Writer', *Household Words*, 18 May 1850, pp. 169–172.

16 Charles Dickens, *A Christmas Carol*, in *A Christmas Carol and other Christmas Books*, ed. by Robert Douglas-Fairhurst (Oxford: OUP, 2008), Stave 3, p. 51.

17 *A Christmas Carol*, Stave 3, p. 54.

18 Jenny Hartley, *Charles Dickens and the House of Fallen Women* (London: Methuen, 2008), p. 112.

19 Hartley, p. 3.

20 Hartley, p. 154.

21 Charles Dickens, *Bleak House*, ed. by Stephen Gill (Oxford: OUP, 2008), Ch. 4, p. 46.

22 *Bleak House*, Ch. 4, p. 46.

23 *Bleak House*, Ch. 4, p. 46.

24 *Bleak House*, Ch. 4, p. 47.

25 *Bleak House*, Ch. 4, pp. 48–49.

26 *Bleak House*, Ch. 4, p. 50; p. 47.

27 Holly Furneaux, 'Domesticity and Queer Theory' in Robert L. Patten, John O. Jordan and Catherine Waters (eds.), *The Oxford Handbook of Charles Dickens* (Oxford: OUP, 2018), pp. 372–387 (pp. 375–376).

28 *Bleak House*, Ch. 4, p. 44.

29 *Bleak House*, Ch. 4, pp. 47–48.

30 Laura Peters, *Dickens and Race* (Manchester: MUP, 2013), p. 5.

31 Dickens, Letter to Angela Burdett-Coutts, 4 March 1850, in Graham Storey, Kathleen Tillotson and Nina Burgis (eds.), *The Letters of Charles Dickens*, Volume Six 1850–1852 (Oxford: Clarendon Press, 1988), pp. 52–53 (p. 53).

32 Charles Dickens, *Pictures from Italy*, ed. by Pete Orford (Oxford: OUP, 2023), p. 153.

33 Grace Moore, *Dickens and Empire* (Aldershot: Ashgate, 2004), p. 68.

34 *Bleak House*, Ch. 8, p. 114.

35 *Bleak House*, Ch. 8, p. 115.

36 *Bleak House*, Ch. 8, p. 122.

37 *Bleak House*, Ch. 8, pp. 121–122.

8

Dickens and Money

Focal Point: 1851–1856

Case Study: Great Expectations

As Dickens approached his forties, we can see how he had matured from the young, hungry man eager to secure contracts and establish his reputation, to become a confident and established writer, with ambitions to see the world and do good in it. In this chapter I wish to consider his own sense of status, in particular thinking about his finances and associated insecurities. The days of the young writer trying to make his name were behind him, and he was now establishing himself as a celebrated author, and a gentleman to boot. In 1851 he would move to Tavistock House, and just five years later he would buy the grand property of Gad's Hill, just outside Rochester. To all appearances then, Dickens had made it. But as this chapter will show, Dickens's life was plagued and informed by financial anxiety, both informed and uninformed. The shadow of his father's debts, and his own aspirations to move beyond that, created a hydra of insecurity, and a constant awareness of how much money was coming in and going out.

Being a Gentleman: Dickens's Spending

When Dickens created the character of Micawber, widely considered to be a fictional portrait of his father, Dickens had the careless debtor offer good advice on expenses which he would have been wise to follow:

> Annual income twenty pounds, annual expenditure nineteen and six, result happiness. Annual income twenty pounds, annual expenditure twenty pounds ought and six, result misery.[1]

You might reasonably think that Dickens's childhood experiences of his father's constant debts, culminating in John Dickens's imprisonment in the

The Life of the Author: Charles Dickens, First Edition. Pete Orford.
© 2023 John Wiley & Sons Ltd. Published 2023 by John Wiley & Sons Ltd.

Marshalsea, might well have made Dickens somewhat wary of overspending himself. However, as was discussed in Chapter 1, Dickens's primary emotional response to this time is shame; and so as Dickens became an adult and in charge of his own fortunes, we see his habits tend not towards prudence and care, but aspiration and expenditure. His choice of potential brides, Maria Beadnell and Catherine Hogarth, were both daughters of prosperous and respectable men. His subsequent marriage to Catherine, and the coincidental timing of *Pickwick*'s publication, saw Dickens adopting respectability and presenting the exterior of a young gentleman to London society. The young couple had moved to Doughty Street in 1837, a fine property which came with its own expenses. Ground-breaking research is currently being undertaken into Dickens's finances by Warren Weiss, an accountant himself who states that while diaries and letters can be subjective, the accounts never lie. Weiss's research into Dickens's personal account held at Coutts's bank has identified some startling revelations about Dickens's expenses. For one thing, Dickens was regularly spending around large sums on wine; over the course of 1838 he spent £248 and two shillings, which in modern terms equates to around £28,000.[2] This was not for personal consumption, I hasten to add, but rather a consequence of Dickens's regular entertainments put on for friends and family. It could be argued that there is a shrewd business advantage being pursued here, as Dickens networked with influential figures who might further his standing and career; but equally the amount spent on these entertainments speaks of a man keen to display his wealth. Appearances could be everything, and by holding these dinners and events in his house, Dickens was proclaiming his success and prosperity to all of London society. The pattern of Dickens's finances in his early career is one of high expenditure and no saving, with each new book contract being almost a necessity to cover the escalating costs Dickens was incurring while presenting himself as a gentleman to the world. Robert Patten refutes the idea that Dickens writing for money is any slight on his artistic creativity, but rather a reality of life:

> Of course Dickens wrote for money. He had to. Gissing's *New Grub Street* provides a grim reminder of the fate reserved for writers who, like Dickens, had no prospect of inheriting or marrying wealth. Dickens's writing was his means of livelihood [...] Those who failed were legion, and their ends sordid: Laman Blanchard cut his throat, Leigh Hunt sponged, the dramatist John Poole shivered in a Parisian garret.[3]

Dickens's eagerness to help impoverished actors with the General Theatrical Fund, or arrange a position for James Knowles at the Shakespeare Birthplace, is both a sign of benevolence but also a recognition of the precariousness of fortune for those working in the creative industry. Dickens helped these older artists for whom their income had stopped, but in so doing must have been aware that their fate could equally be his own one day if the work stopped. He told Angela Burdett-Coutts that 'few have known such suffering and bitterness at one time or other, as those who have been bound to Pens.'[4]

Rather than learning from his father's debts and spending carefully, Dickens was enjoying the comforts of wealth and spending more. Dickens's avoidance of the sort of debt his father had incurred is not a result of careful spending, but a frantic rate of work which ensured a steady stream of income to match his spending. As mentioned in Chapter 6, there is a hunger in the young Dickens's career choices. No sooner is he writing *Pickwick* but he is courting publishers for other contracts, including *Gabriel Varden*, a planned novel which eventually became *Barnaby Rudge* instead, and of course *Oliver Twist*, with *Nicholas Nickleby* following soon after, alongside several short pieces written for the stage AND the editing of *Bentley's Miscellany*. Dickens was not idle, but eagerly and feverishly pursuing new avenues for writing and publication to keep the money coming in. Patten, and others following him, have suggested that while there was a cleverness in Dickens's acquisition of new contracts and the manner in which he was able to sign profitable deals with his publishers, it benefitted the publishers too. Each deal was a lock upon the young Dickens, securing him in to produce several instalments of fiction for his publishers over the coming months. As a young man, Dickens would have been enthralled by this influx of money, but ultimately it was a leash, tying him down to a punishing schedule of writing deadlines coming at a frantic pace.

The Sins of the Father: John Dickens

Of course, the influence of John Dickens upon his son was not limited to Dickens's childhood. As Dickens's fortunes rose, so the father began to rely and capitalise on the success of his son, much to Dickens's distress. The father and son had both been working in the same circle; John had been the first to learn shorthand and work as a reporter, with his son following in his footsteps and ultimately overtaking him. As a consequence, John Dickens was known to the people Dickens worked with, and indeed often worked with his son too. But the older Dickens was proving to be both an embarrassment and liability to the younger Dickens. John was applying to Dickens for financial support (as were Dickens's siblings) – 'directly I build up a hundred pounds' complained Dickens, 'one of my dear relations comes and knocks it down again'.[5] Such applications were a drain on Dickens's resources, but were at least contained; but John Dickens was also sending letters of appeal to Dickens's publishers Chapman and Hall. Dickens's father was no longer a threat just to Dickens's finances, but to his reputation as well. The solution was to send his parents away; Slater suggests generously that Dickens may have done this to remove his parents 'from metropolitan temptation',[6] which could certainly be true, but equally sending his parents away benefitted Dickens as much as, if not more than, his parents. In March 1839 he found a cottage in Alphington, just outside of Exeter, which he rented and furnished as a home for his parents to live in – away from London, and him. The new home for his parents was around 200 miles away from Doughty Street, and given the transportation of the time, would have required a journey of two or three days: not the sort of location to which Dickens could easily pop to for a weekend, nor one from which he could expect regular visits from his parents. Dickens showed great generosity in arranging a home for his parents, but it was equally a gentle form of exile.

It was not wholly successful. Dickens's father continued to borrow money regardless, and each time he did so he was using his son's name and reputation to secure credit. And he wasn't alone: Dickens's brother Augustus was also applying to him for support (and Slater suggests Dickens's other brothers may well have been doing the same).[7] This coincided with Dickens's own attempts to further his position. He had moved out of Doughty Street in 1841 and taken a twelve-year lease of Devonshire Terrace, which was a grand statement of his success, but financially put him under even more stress and pressure; additionally, he, Catherine and their growing assortment of children (four at the time they were moving to Devonshire Terrace) were taking regular holidays in Broadstairs. In addition, this is the time when Catherine's sister Georgina moved in with the family, where she would remain for the rest of Dickens's life as a constant companion for Dickens as much as the children, which in turn meant another mouth to feed. As Weiss notes from the accounts, 'the first five years at Devonshire Terrace were marked by almost constant financial stress'.[8] The applications of his parents and siblings to him for money were an attack both on his finances and reputation at precisely the time when he was trying to cultivate both. As much as Dickens complained about these family members applying to him for money, his own spending policies were not much better. Increasingly he became concerned about the costs of maintaining Devonshire Terrace, and the expenditure being laid out. Worse still, the money coming in was no longer guaranteed. *Master Humphrey's Clock* was something of a flop when it first started; the meteoric success of *Pickwick* which Dickens must have hoped was the start of many more to come, was turning out to be more of a one-off. The success of *A Christmas Carol* was marred by the high costs of production: much like his private life, the money coming in was being eaten away by the costs going out. Dickens's success as a writer, and his relentless pursuit of new work and contracts meant that ultimately there was more coming in than going out, so he was not reduced to the condition of his father, but nonetheless if there had been just a little less going out, then he would have been much more secure. There is a Catch-22 here: Dickens's anxiety about his parents' experiences of debts was both heightening his anxiety about being in debt too, while also encouraging him to spend even more to prove to the world that he was NOT his father, but a great success instead. And of course, the more he spent, the more precarious his finances, and so the anxieties became almost self-perpetuating. Little wonder then that Dickens would eventually seek to move abroad to Italy for a year, the financial benefits being threefold: rent was cheaper (and with his own lodgings in London sublet, meant he could turn a profit); his own family were removed from London and its temptations (much as he had aimed to remove his parents from it); and it removed him in turn from those who would apply to him for credit.

After the publication of *Dombey and Son*, Dickens reached a moment of self-reflection. He began to write his autobiography. In rewriting his childhood, Dickens exacerbated his pain and shame, subjecting his hero David to a far more traumatic childhood than he had ever experienced. Both David and Dickens emerge from a childhood of shame to establish themselves as young gentlemen. David's father has died before he is born; Dickens's father is reinvented instead as the hapless debtor Mr Micawber. Curiously enough, there's no evidence to suggest that Dickens's father was offended by the comparison. With publication of *Copperfield*, Dickens told Forster 'the world will not take another Pickwick from me now' – a curious proclamation, given the success of *Pickwick*, but the indication is that Dickens felt he had now moved into new territory.[9] But the timing of it coincides with a new maturity and, soon after, a new property. Dickens was about to elevate his status once more. If *Copperfield*, the autobiographical fragment and the confession to Forster had forced Dickens to confront his past, there was now a sense of moving forward.

A Gentleman's Property: Tavistock House and Gad's Hill

Shortly after *Copperfield*, Dickens's twelve-year lease on Devonshire Terrace came to an end, in 1851, and the family moved once more into even grander accommodation at Tavistock House. This large building was one of several in Bloomsbury built by James Burton in the late eighteenth and early nineteenth century. By this point, Dickens had eight children, having just lost his youngest, Dora at only eight months old. It was a large household, with servants too, but a grander one was to follow. In 1856, Dickens bought a second property, the country house of Gad's Hill, just outside of Rochester. This was a significant moment in Dickens's life for a number of reasons. The name and location of the property was especially pleasing to Dickens for its Shakespearean connections: in *Henry IV Part One*, Falstaff and Prince Hal are engaged in a comic episode of highway theft at Gad's Hill, and after buying the property Dickens put up a sign inside the house championing this connection, proudly stating 'This House Gad's Hill Place stands on the summit of Shakespeare's Gadshill ever memorable for its association in his noble fancy with Sir John Falstaff'.[10] Gad's Hill offered Dickens a literary heritage that obviously pleased him, however tenuous. Second, it is worth noting that this was now Dickens's *second* property; Tavistock House still being under lease and kept as a town house. Buying this larger property in the country, while maintaining a town house, was a clear sign of Dickens's position as a gentleman of wealth and prosperity. But finally, and most often told, is the personal connection Dickens held with the estate. As a young boy, while living in the area, he had walked past the house with his father, who told him that if he worked hard he might one day buy that property. The anecdote is recorded by Dickens in an 1860 essay under his persona of the Uncommercial Traveller:

> 'You admire that house?' said I.
>
> 'Bless you, sir,' said the very queer small boy, 'when I was not more than half as old as nine, it used to be a treat for me to be brought to look at it. And now I am nine, I come by myself to look at it. And ever since I can recollect, my father, seeing me so fond of it, has often said to me, *If you were to be very persevering and were to work hard, you might some day come to live in it.* Though that's impossible!' said the very queer small boy, drawing a low breath, and now staring at the house out of window with all his might.
>
> 'I was rather amazed to be told this by the very queer small boy; for that house happens to be my house, and I have reason to believe that what he said was true.'[11]

The extract was then repeated verbatim in Forster's biography as a true account of Dickens's own childhood, but the passages raises more questions than it answers. Firstly, there is Dickens's father, and the irony of a man who would acquire so much debt tutoring his son on the virtue of hard work and money earned. Secondly, there is the irony of Dickens remembering the story so wistfully given the several annoyances and embarrassment his father would cause in later life. Then there is the strange reimagining of the moment as an interaction between the older Dickens and his childhood self; the older man looking upon 'the very queer small boy' who likes to read and thinks it impossible that he should one day live in such a fine house. Dickens's father had died on 31 March 1851 and never got to see his son in Gad's Hill. In this reimagining of events, Dickens effectively replaces his own father in the narrative; it is he himself who looks upon his infant self while he wistfully gazes upon the house, and it is he himself who is able to reflect back on the journey from boy to man. Dickens's decision to purchase Gad's Hill can be considered then to be borne of a wistful nostalgia or of a steely determination to show his father how far he had come. Purchasing Gad's Hill was a statement, to both of them, that he had now made it, and that he had succeeded in ways his father had not.

The purchase of Gad's Hill also meant an increase in the number of servants Dickens employed. Like all respectable households of the time, Dickens had employed servants since his time in Doughty Street, but with each new property the number increased. He never went so far as to get a butler, but did employ a number of manservants at different times. He appears to have treated them fairly, and in many cases earned their respect and loyalty. Anne Brown was first employed as his wife's maid; she accompanied them to America and Italy, and even after she left their service to marry, she remained loyal to Dickens, speaking in his favour during the separation of Dickens and his wife, and receiving a payment in Dickens's will. Dickens's close relationship with his brave courier Louis Roche in Italy, and later his tour manager George Dolby on his reading tours, both resemble a similar dynamic to Pickwick and Weller; and there's a sense that Dickens almost sought this out. His decision not to get a butler shows the limitations of his aspirations, or rather his unwillingness to become the master rather than a friend. As much as Dickens sought to prove himself a gentleman, nor did he want to alienate himself from the working class either. He prided himself as a man of the people. A photograph taken by Robert Hindry Mason of Dickens's servants at Gads Hill shows a happy group; the taking of the photograph is noteworthy, and likely to coincide with the more familiar photos of Dickens and his children [see Figure 8.1].[12] Did the servants take advantage of the photographer's presence that day to request their own photo, or did Dickens himself suggest, or insist upon it? Either way, the recording of the moment signals too Dickens's position: owner of a country house with its own assortment of staff. The little boy in the blacking factory window had come a long way, no longer 'the gentleman' as a gently mocking epithet, but a gentleman indeed.

Figure 8.1   Robert Hindry Mason, Photograph of Dickens's Servants at Gad's Hill, c. 1866.

Dickens's Restless Spirit: Future Anxieties and Insecurities

One might well think this moment marks the culmination of Dickens's financial journey, and the end of his insecurities and anxieties. Not so. Bigger properties meant bigger costs, and a bigger family meant yet more people to support. Dickens's father may have died, but his place was filled by Dickens's siblings and now children as well. At the time he moved into Gad's Hill, Dickens's eldest child Charley was nineteen, and increasingly Dickens would start thinking about their futures, and their security. Quite frequently his parenting can be seen as overbearing; he demanded much of his children, expecting them to have the same zealous work ethic he had, and inevitably being disappointed. Walter and Sidney both acquired debts; two of his sons went to Australia to find new opportunities: Alfred in 1865 when he was twenty years old, and three years later Edward (or Plorn as he was known in the family), when he was only sixteen. Charley followed the family business, writing for Dickens's journals *Household Words* and *All the Year Round*, eventually editing the latter after his father's death. Dickens had a whole new generation of family to think about now, not to mention a brand new expenditure when he separated from his wife in 1858 and began a new relationship with his young mistress Ellen Ternan. Dickens's dependants continued to grow, and so too there was continued reason for him to pursue a profitable income. That hunger can be seen in his eventual decision to conduct a public reading tour across the UK and USA (with another leg planned in Australia which never came to pass). Forster raised his eyebrows at the idea of an author parading himself like this, but the financial benefits were simply too great to be ignored. As will be discussed in Chapter 12, it is highly likely that the stress and strain of the reading tours and their punishing schedule worsened Dickens's health dramatically and contributed to his death; it is not an exaggeration then to link Dickens's relentless pursuit of new projects, and the financial security they promised, with his demise: the man worked himself to death.

The story that emerges from this consideration of Dickens and money is one of restlessness. This restlessness materialises in several forms and moments through Dickens's life. There is the restlessness that shows in his pursuit of new activities: mesmerism, playwriting, amateur dramatics, editing, stage magic, foreign languages, charity, public readings – it's a wonder he ever found time to write the novels. In each pursuit Dickens was keen to show his skill and virtuosity; it was never purely a diversion, but an opportunity for him to prove his prowess and ability. His restlessness was born from the desire to prove himself as much as the desire to achieve financial security; many of the pursuits he took up were non-profitable after all, but each served either to demonstrate his skill or to further his wider reputation. His financial anxiety was linked to a social one; and his shame of the blacking factory incident was caused by the impact on his status as much as the monetary implications. His time working at Warren's was time not spent in education, and now that he was moving among literary gentleman he felt it keenly. When G. H. Lewes asked Dickens a question about the writing of *Oliver Twist* and its philosophical influences, Dickens's answer was evasive, having no particular theoretical framework behind his writing, but something more instinctive instead: 'It came like all my other ideas, such as they are, ready made to the point of the pen – and down it went. Draw your own conclusion and hug the theory closely.'[13] Likewise, his aggressive dismissal of art in *Pictures from Italy* is a proactive defence of a man who had not been educated in art as a gentleman should be. He prefers his own 'natural perception of what is natural and true' rather than blindly following critical opinions, regularly attacking famous works of art for not deserving their reputation, suggesting 'that the indiscriminate and determined raptures in which some critics indulge, is incompatible with the true appreciation of the really great and transcendent works.'[14] When he returned to Italy in 1853 with Wilkie Collins and Augustus Egg he wrote with growing annoyance about Collins's assumed knowledge on art:

> The Fine Arts afford a subject I never approach; always appearing to fall into a profound Reverie when it is discussed. Neither do I ever go into any Gallery with them. To hear Collins learnedly holding forth to Egg (who has as little of that gammon as an artist *can* have) about reds,

and greens, and things 'coming well' with other things, and lines being wrong, and lines being right, is far beyond the bounds of all caricature. I shall never forget it.[15]

Dickens's annoyance with Collins is provoked by the apparent pomposity of Collins's views and Dickens's own suspicions that he knows more than Collins. The gaps in his education and his subsequent success gave Dickens both an inferiority and superiority complex. He once wrote to his wife a surprisingly frank self-portrait:

> You know my life too, and my character, and what has had its part in making them successful; and the more you see of me, the better perhaps you may understand that the intense pursuit of any idea that takes complete possession of me, is one of the qualities that makes me different – sometimes for good; sometimes I dare say for evil – from other men.[16]

Restlessness is at its heart an inability to relax. Dickens spent his life in 'intense pursuit' of several ideas, each time insisting his own natural prowess and brilliance in that field, be it acting, stage-magic, mesmerism or, of course, writing. But with intense pursuit came also intense avoidance. The more successful he became, the more his past haunted him: Dickens's anxieties fuelled that fear of being found out. It would be curious to see whether Dickens would have identified with the term 'Imposter Syndrome' had it been coined in his time, but there are certainly enough indicators to suggest that he might. The depiction of Mr Merdle in *Little Dorrit*, and his constant fear of his own butler, 'the sight of which splendid retainer always finished him', is a telling portrait of a man who has an overbearing sense of his own inadequacy that is only exacerbated, rather than appeased, by his growing success.[17] Dickens enjoyed the experience of relative anonymity in Italy, and later his relationship with Ellen Ternan would require Dickens, by necessity, to spend time away from the public gaze. This suggests a man who was wearied by his reputation as much as buoyed by it. Success came at a cost for Dickens.

Case Study: Becoming a Gentleman in *Great Expectations*

Dickens used first-person narrative sparingly in his novels; after a brief attempt (quickly abandoned) in *The Old Curiosity Shop*, he then used it for the entirety of *David Copperfield*, alternately in *Bleak House*, and then once more in its entirety in *Great Expectations*. Pip, the hero of the latter book, shares some common traits with David Copperfield: both have humble beginnings but emerge into a greater and more secure future. In the case of David, this future is achieved through the support of his aunt when David is still relatively young, allowing him opportunity to receive an education, then become a clerk and so work his way up towards fortune. In Pip's case however, greatness is thrust upon him when the lawyer Mr Jaggers arrives one day on behalf of an anonymous benefactor, to announce Pip as the inheritor of a large sum of money and the insistence that he should give up his current life as a blacksmith's apprentice to become a gentleman in London at once:

> 'I am instructed to communicate to him,' said Mr. Jaggers, throwing his finger at me sideways, 'that he will come into a handsome property. Further, that it is the desire of the present possessor of that property, that he be immediately removed from his present sphere of life and from this place, and be brought up as a gentleman, – in a word, as a young fellow of great expectations.'[18]

The citing of the book's title in Jaggers's announcement is no accident, but a reinforcement of the book's purpose and the significance of this moment by Dickens. What does it mean to be 'a young fellow of great expectations'? Pip, unlike David, has no gradual introduction to his new life but is swiftly and jarringly moved from one sphere into another, with little to no sense of expected etiquette or education to support him in his new role. This is seen in the conversation he has with his new housemate, Herbert Pocket, who proves himself a kind friend with gentle hints of social practices:

> 'Let me introduce the topic, Handel, by mentioning that in London it is not the custom to put the knife in the mouth, – for fear of accidents, – and that while the fork is reserved for that use, it is not put further in than necessary. It is scarcely worth mentioning, only it's as well to do as other people do. Also, the spoon is not generally used over-hand, but under. This has two advantages. You get at your mouth better (which after all is the object), and you save a good deal of the attitude of opening oysters, on the part of the right elbow.'
>
> He offered these friendly suggestions in such a lively way, that we both laughed and I scarcely blushed.[19]

Just as Dickens exaggerated the difficulties of his own childhood in depicting the childhood of David Copperfield, so too Pip's sudden and immediate switch into polite society can be seen as a hyperbolic retelling of his own early experiences of becoming a London gentleman. Pip's awareness of his own shortcomings stands as a constant check against his enjoyment of his new life; his early experiences as a blacksmith's apprentice – which is by no means a shameful life – nonetheless becomes a shameful secret in Pip's eyes, who desperately tries to conceal it from those he meets. This manifests itself in Pip's painfully awkward interactions with Joe, the kind blacksmith who is married to Pip's sister, and has raised Pip up and cared for him. No sooner is Pip made a gentleman but he begins to worry about Joe mixing with his new society. He confides as much to Biddy (a girl Pip's age who acts as a maid in Joe's house after his wife becomes an invalid): 'if I were to remove Joe into a higher sphere, as I shall hope to remove him when I fully come into my property, they would hardly do him justice.'[20] Biddy notes that Joe knows this, and when she tries to curb Pip's growing pride and distance, Pip harshly retorts:

> 'Now, Biddy,' said I, 'I am very sorry to see this in you. I did not expect to see this in you. You are envious, Biddy, and grudging. You are dissatisfied on account of my rise in fortune, and you can't help showing it.'
>
> 'If you have the heart to think so,' returned Biddy, 'say so. Say so over and over again, if you have the heart to think so.'[21]

What is remarkable in *Great Expectations* is that if we are to consider Pip's character as drawing upon Dickens's experience, then it is not a particularly flattering self-portrait. Pip becomes proud, ungrateful, denying his past life and acting ashamed of it while simultaneously embracing a more wanton life of extravagance. It is immediately clear to a reader that Joe is truly a *gentle man*, while Pip's desperate attempts to become a gentleman expose his own hypocrisy and the moral emptiness at the heart of social climbing. The other great influence in Pip's life is Estella, a fine and beautiful young lady who treats him with disdain. Pip hopes his new fortunes will make him worthy of her at last, but he always retains the sense of his perceived 'failings' while pursuing her. It is after his first meeting with Estella as a boy that Pip first begins to loathe himself and the life he was previously happy in:

> I set off on the four-mile walk to our forge; pondering, as I went along, on all I had seen, and deeply revolving that I was a common labouring-boy; that my hands were coarse; that my boots were thick; that I had fallen into a despicable habit of calling knaves Jacks; that I was much more ignorant than I had considered myself last night, and generally that I was in a low-lived bad way.[22]

Pip is therefore a character who finds himself in a glittering and prosperous society while despising himself and his upbringing. He is a character defined by pride and shame. He embraces his new life as a means of bettering his position, but doing so only increases his own fears and insecurities. Jaggers invites Pip to dinner with Bentley Drummle, a rival for Estella who has the experience and position Pip lacks, and in this situation Pip resorts to showing off about his fortune:

> Dinner went off gayly, and although my guardian seemed to follow rather than originate subjects, I knew that he wrenched the weakest part of our dispositions out of us. For myself, I found that I was expressing my tendency to lavish expenditure, and to patronise Herbert, and to boast of my great prospects, before I quite knew that I had opened my lips.[23]

The emphasis is not simply on having money, but displaying it. Pip expresses 'his tendency to lavish expenditure' in a bid to impress, despite himself, and even while doing so there is a sense that this is actually rather a shameful and naïve thing to do. Is this so very different from Dickens's own lavish expenditures in his early days? The money Dickens invested in wine and entertainment of his new friends in London speaks of the same need to *demonstrate* fortune in order for that fortune to truly impress. To be rich without others knowing it is not enough; money is linked to status, and therefore to be truly rich one must show that to others in order to secure the status one would expect from such riches.

Countered against these moments of boastful extravagance is Pip's more private interactions with his new fortunes (and its limitations). Jaggers is appointed his guardian, and as such has control of Pip's fortunes, which Pip only has to apply for as and when he wants it. This subsequently leads to an awkwardness as Pip attempts to establish what is, or is not, an appropriate amount of money to ask for, not wishing to ask for too much nor too little:

> 'It is so difficult to fix a sum,' said I, hesitating.
> 'Come!' said Mr. Jaggers. 'Let's get at it. Twice five; will that do? Three times five; will that do? Four times five; will that do?'
> I said I thought that would do handsomely.
> 'Four times five will do handsomely, will it?' said Mr. Jaggers, knitting his
> brows. 'Now, what do you make of four times five?'
> 'What do I make of it?'

'Ah!' said Mr. Jaggers; 'how much?'

'I suppose you make it twenty pounds,' said I, smiling.

'Never mind what *I* make it, my friend,' observed Mr. Jaggers, with a knowing and contradictory toss of his head. 'I want to know what *you* make it.'

'Twenty pounds, of course.'[24]

Jaggers teases Pip rather maliciously about it, and the dynamic that is shown here is of a young man feeling his way into a new world of figures he could previously only dream of, attempting to negotiate with a seasoned professional. It is not inconceivable, if we are to link this with Dickens's own experiences, to see in it the young Dickens as he negotiates contracts with his publishers, trying to decide if he is asking for too much, or selling himself short. Pip's inexperience, and his careful testing of Jaggers to see what is or is not appropriate to ask for, speaks of that same uncertainty the young Dickens may well have faced when first encountering the profits available to him as an author.

Tellingly, Pip's fortunes are tempered with an awareness of the limitation of money. As much as we are told he has inherited a great fortune, more than enough for anyone to live on comfortably, we are shown that Pip frequently reaches the limits of that fortune for no reason other than his lavish expenditure:

> We spent as much money as we could, and got as little for it as people could make up their minds to give us. We were always more or less miserable, and most of our acquaintance were in the same condition. There was a gay fiction among us that we were constantly enjoying ourselves, and a skeleton truth that we never did. To the best of my belief, our case was in the last aspect a rather common one.[25]

Money is shown to be as much a cause for unhappiness as it is for happiness, if not more so, due to Pip's extravagant spending on temporary pleasures rather than prudent investment in longer-term security. Pip and Herbert's response to such moments is comical (and relatable), in so much as they make grand plans for how things will change, without actually acting upon them. A great ceremony is made of writing up their finances and accounts, with the sense that simply doing so is enough to solve the problem without actually following that plan through: 'I sometimes found it difficult to distinguish between this edifying business proceeding and actually paying the money' notes Pip, 'In point of meritorious character, the two things seemed about equal.'[26] Writing up their accounts proves to be a ceremony rather than a course of action; amounts are estimated, and the writing down of figures imitates a control over them.

> I established with myself, on these occasions, the reputation of a first-rate man of business, – prompt, decisive, energetic, clear, cool-headed. When I had got all my responsibilities down upon my list, I compared each with the bill, and ticked it off. My self-approval when I ticked an entry was quite a luxurious sensation. When I had no more ticks to make, I folded all my bills up uniformly, docketed each on the back, and tied the whole into a symmetrical bundle. Then I did the same for Herbert (who modestly said he had not my administrative genius), and felt that I had brought his affairs into a focus for him.[27]

The illusion of control is everything here. The reader almost screams at Pip with impatience; he has a steady income from Jaggers, an annual payment to enjoy and live upon quite happily if only he could control his spending, but he does not. Pip, and Herbert with him, is playing the part of gentleman, and a respectable man of finance. But it is a fallacy. Pip is but a young man playing with amounts of money he has no prior experience with, and falling into bad habits as a consequence. There is no self-control, no sense of limiting his expenses or recognising those costs which are unnecessary. And yet, the act of writing out his accounts in this manner provides a pleasing sense of ownership:

> But there was a calm, a rest, a virtuous hush, consequent on these examinations of our affairs that gave me, for the time, an admirable opinion of myself. Soothed by my exertions, my method, and Herbert's compliments, I would sit with his symmetrical bundle and my own on the table before me among the stationery, and feel like a Bank of some sort, rather than a private individual.[28]

To bring this back to Dickens, clearly Pip's case is more exaggerated than his. But the central truth of the experience is there. It is important to note therefore that *Great Expectations* is narrated by Pip at a much older age, looking back upon the actions of his younger self with an appropriate sense of wry amusement mixed with embarrassment. If the reader can see the young Pip's folly, that is because the older Pip can see it too. At the time of writing *Great Expectations* in 1859 and 1860, Dickens was in his late forties. He had purchased Gad's Hill, and was coming to the end of his tenancy of Tavistock House. The older Dickens may well have looked back upon the spending of his younger self with the same sense of weary reproach that the older Pip displays while writing of young Pip's adventures. But by having *Great Expectations* narrated by the older Pip, it allows that sense of self-knowledge to be evident even when young Pip seems most ignorant. We are assured as readers that a lesson will be learned, and maturity achieved. Pip discovers the truth behind his mysterious benefactor and reconciles himself with his past. Not dissimilar to Dickens's fictional reimagining of the conversation with his father outside Gad's Hill, in which his own adult self replaces his father to offer his younger self reassurance, so too in *Great Expectations* Pip reaches a position of closure, where rather than be haunted by his upbringing, and limited by his insecurities, he reaches acceptance and grows into his new role at last.

Notes

1 Charles Dickens, *David Copperfield*, ed. by Nina Burgis (Oxford: OUP, 1981), Chapter 12, p. 150.

2 For information on Dickens's finances I am indebted to Warren Weiss, who is currently transcribing the entirety of Dickens's personal accounts for a doctoral project. He discusses Dicken's wine expenditure in 'An Account of Charles Dickens's Personal Finances in the Early Years of his Career with Observations on his Aptitude for Managing Them', University of Buckingham MA Thesis (unpublished), 2019.

3 Robert Patten, *Charles Dickens and His Publishers* (Oxford: OUP, 1978), p. 10.

4 Dickens, Letter to Angela Burdett-Coutts, 2 June 1843, in Madeline House, Graham Storey and Kathleen Tillotson (eds.), *The Letters of Charles Dickens*, Volume Three 1842–1832 (Oxford: Clarendon Press, 1974), pp. 499–500 (p. 500).

5 Dickens, Letter to John Forster, 15 November 1838, in Madeline House and Graham Storey (eds.), *The Letters of Charles Dickens*, Volume One 1820–1839 (Oxford: Clarendon Press, 1974), p. 454 (p. 454).

6 Michael Slater, *Charles Dickens* (New Haven: Yale, 2011), p. 131.

7 Slater, p. 131.

8 Weiss, p. 116.

9 Dickens, Letter to Dudley Costello, 25 April 1849, in Graham Storey and K. J. Fielding (eds.), *The Letters of Charles Dickens*, Volume Five 1847–1849 (Oxford: Clarendon, 1981), p. 527 (p. 527).

10 The sign is now displayed at the Charles Dickens Museum, London.

11 Dickens, 'Travelling Abroad', *Household Words*, Volume II (7 April 1860), pp. 557–562 (p. 557).

12 Dickens's servants is a surprisingly under-researched area; in Joy Tetley *Other Voices: An Exploration of The Role of Servants in the Life of Charles Dickens,* University of Buckingham MA Thesis (Unpublished), 2021, Tetley discusses the photograph of the servants (p. 127); it is also discussed in Leon Litvack, 'Dickens in the Eye of the Beholder: The Photographs of Robery Hindry Mason', in *Dickens Studies Annual,* Volume 47, 2016, pp. 165–199 (pp. 174–175).

13 Dickens, Letter to G. H. Lewes, 9 June 1838, in *Letters,* Volume One, pp. 402–404 (p. 403).

14 Charles Dickens, *Pictures from Italy,* ed. by Pete Orford (Oxford: OUP, 2023), p. 133. For more on Dickens's reaction to art, see Leonee Ormond's essay 'Dickens and Italian Art' in Charles Dickens, *American Notes and Pictures from Italy,* ed. by F. S. Schwarzbach and Leonee Ormond (London: Everyman, 1997), pp. 499–503.

15 Charles Dickens, Letter to Catherine Dickens, 21 November 1853, in Graham Storey, Kathleen Tillotson and Angus Easson (eds.), *The Letters of Charles Dickens,* Volume Seven 1853–1855 (Oxford: Clarendon, 1993), pp. 203–206 (p. 204).

16 Charles Dickens to Catherine Dickens, 5 December 1853, in *Letters,* Vol. 7, pp. 223–225 (p. 224).

17 Charles Dickens, *Little Dorrit,* ed. by Harvey Peter Sucksmith (Oxford: OUP, 1979), Book 1, Ch. 33, p. 390.

18 Charles Dickens, *Great Expectations,* ed. by Margaret Cardwell (Oxford: OUP, 1993), Book 1, Ch. 18, p. 137.

19 *Great Expectations,* Book 2, Ch. 3, pp. 177–178.

20 *Great Expectations,* Book 1, Ch. 19, 147.

21 *Great Expectations,* Book 1, Ch. 19, p. 148.

22 *Great Expectations,* Book 1, Ch. 8, p. 66.

23 *Great Expectations,* Book 2, Ch. 7, p. 213.

24 *Great Expectations,* Book 2, Ch. 5, pp. 197–198.

25 *Great Expectations,* Book 2, Ch. 15, p. 273.

26 *Great Expectations,* Book 2, Ch. 15, p. 275.

27 *Great Expectations,* Book 2, Ch. 15, p. 275.

28 *Great Expectations,* Book 2, Ch. 15, p. 276.

9

Dickens's Literary Network

Focal Point: The 1850s

Case Study: The Haunted House

By definition, a biography will tell the story of a life; in so doing it will make that life the central character of the narrative, whereas in reality we all of us live our lives as one among many, all of whom are the central character of their stories in turn. It is important then that even while studying the life of Dickens, we consider that life in context, and acknowledge the influence and interaction of others around him. Throughout his life and career Dickens built up a network of writers, publishers, editors, actors and illustrators with whom he enjoyed varying degrees of mutual support. The young Dickens reached out to those who were more established for initial opportunities, as well as his peers for collaborative opportunities from which they could both benefit; as Dickens's fortunes rose so the balance shifted and frequently it was he who was the established partner offering opportunities to new starters. This chapter will consider the way in which Dickens worked with others.

It can be difficult to distinguish between friends and colleagues of Dickens; many professional colleagues turned out to be lifelong friends, and many friends were called upon by Dickens to collaborate with him in later life. In particular, I will be thinking about those who had a direct involvement in his writing, focusing on the team of writers Dickens assembled for his journals *Household Words* and *All the Year Round* for the last twenty years of his life. In these there is a definite and explicit relationship between Dickens and other writers in his role as editor, but obviously there are many more ways in which the people around an author will influence their work. Melisa Klimaszewski notes that '[i]n practice, collaboration includes all sorts of interactions that extend past two people sitting in a room together while one of them writes ideas down on a page.'[1] Biographical experiences frequently inform Dickens's writing, and friends and family often became unwitting inspirations for fictional characters. Then there is the invisible labour so hard to define but not to be ignored: I have already noted in Chapter 3 Catherine's involvement with assisting Dickens for *Barnaby Rudge*

The Life of the Author: Charles Dickens, First Edition. Pete Orford.
© 2023 John Wiley & Sons Ltd. Published 2023 by John Wiley & Sons Ltd.

and *Pictures from Italy*. In both instances she was writing down Dickens's words, something which has traditionally not been recognised as collaboration, but is increasingly being seen as the incremental influences of others (especially wives) that contribute to the completion of a text.

The implication of these brief insights, preserved through writing or anecdote, is the potential for many more, never recorded: the ephemeral passing comments and conversational feedback which might occur in the Dickens house. We do know that Dickens regularly discussed plot ideas with Forster, and that he would read chapters aloud to his friends to gauge their reactions. Most famously perhaps is the intervention of Edward Bulwer Lytton which resulted in Dickens changing the ending of *Great Expectations* to something more ambiguous and potentially more hopeful. 'You will be surprised to hear that I have changed the end of *Great Expectations*' he told Forster, but Bulwer-Lytton 'so strongly urged it ... and supported his views with such good reasons' that Dickens was convinced.[2] 'No man is an island', as John Donne proclaimed, and as much as Dickens pronounced himself as 'the Inimitable', he was always collaborating on some level.

Dickens's Early Network: The 1830s and 1840s

For obvious reasons our interest in Dickens's associates are primarily with those who were involved in his writing, but this can skew our understanding of him. It is worth noting in brief then, three lifelong friends, whose names appear frequently as correspondents in the letters of Dickens: Thomas Beard, Thomas Mitton and Henry Austin. All three were work colleagues of Dickens before he was famous, none were involved in writing fiction, and all were lifelong friends of Dickens. Mitton was a clerk with Dickens when he worked at Molloy's; their working relationship lasted just a year, from 1828 to 1829, but their friendship was for life. While Dickens left the law to write, Mitton stayed in the career and acted as Dickens's solicitor from 1838 through to 1858, overseeing the agreement of various publishing contracts. Beard was a journalist at the *Morning Chronicle*; once again, he and Dickens began as colleagues but became close friends; Beard was best man at Dickens's wedding. Also at the *Chronicle*, Dickens met Henry Austin, who would become another life-long friend and married Dickens's younger sister Letitia. These three men show the life Dickens had *outside* of writing. The enduring friendship of Mitton, Beard and Austin also stands as testament to the idea that Dickens could be and was making genuine friends through work. This is important to note as a number of the names coming in this chapter are all somehow linked to Dickens's profession and it would be easy to dismiss some of them as opportunistic, without Beard, Mitton and Austin to stand as counterpoint to that.

This is not to say that Dickens might not sometimes have chased names; for example, one of his earliest literary friends was W. H. Ainsworth, who was one of the most successful writers at the time. There are several letters from Dickens to Ainsworth in the 1830s, most of them regarding meeting up, and when Mary Hogarth died Dickens wrote to Ainsworth 'You cannot think how glad I should be to see you just now.'[3] Forster noted that Ainsworth was 'especially welcome' to himself and Dickens at the time, and 'shared with us incessantly for the three following years in the companionship which began at his house' in 1836.[4] However, as Ainsworth's fame faded, he and Dickens saw less and less of one another, the latter's star ascending over the former's. When Ainsworth bought *Bentley's Miscellany* in 1857, one might assume that the purchase of a journal Dickens had once edited, by a man he was formerly good friends with, would warrant some reaction, yet in a letter to Bentley Dickens confesses ignorance and indifference:

> I certainly had been aware that you had disposed of the Miscellany to Ainsworth, but I had as entirely forgotten it, until you reminded me of the fact, as if I had never heard of such a thing in my life.[5]

Unlike Dickens, Ainsworth's career did not live up to its initial promise. He wrote prolifically, but commanded smaller and smaller fees for them. His novel *Jack Sheppard* (1839–1840) told a tale of a young boy in a life of crime, not so different from the world of *Oliver Twist*, but the novel proved popular with the masses while being savaged by the critics for its inappropriateness, as they worried it might inspire the populace to crime: 'as the millions who see it [...] will not distinguish between now and a hundred years back, all the Chartists in the land are less dangerous than this nightmare of a book.'[6] As Ainsworth continued to be condemned as a writer of sensational and unsavoury tales, Dickens was being hailed for his domestic scenes and happy morals: their work and reputations diverged dramatically. Dickens himself bristled at the comparisons raised between Ainsworth's work and *Oliver*, complaining privately about the 'jolter-headed enemies' who 'most unjustly and untruly charged me with having written a book after Mr. Ainsworth's fashion'.[7] Despite his critical disdain, Dickens attended a housewarming party at Ainsworth's new home in 1842, but by 1853 as Ainsworth's fortunes dwindled, he moved to Brighton, and as his biographer Stephen Carver notes, 'with this move, the old circle of Forster, Dickens, Thackeray *et al* broke up, and although Ainsworth continued to privately entertain, the great literary gatherings were over'.[8] Dickens's apparent distancing from him does not come from any animosity; in a letter dated 9 June 1856 to Alfred Hachette, Dickens offered to write a letter of introduction to Ainsworth.[9] But neither did Dickens make any attempt to help his friend, nor invite him to write for either of his journals. There was no great conflict to cause the split, but rather a gradual growing apart. This contrast with Dickens's friendship with Edward Bulwer Lytton for example, another famous author of the time (and ultimately more successful than Ainsworth). He met Dickens in the 1830s, but it was not until the 1840s that they became friends, and in later years Bulwer Lytton would publish in Dickens's journals. Dickens took direct involvement in securing Bulwer Lytton for the journal, but couched it in the language of friendship:

> Not to overload the plainness of these statements with other matters interesting to us as private friends and not associated with a question of business, I break off here, and hope to hear from you soon.[10]

The lasting impact of Ainsworth on Dickens is that it was he who introduced Dickens to John Forster. After meeting initially at Ainsworth's house sometime in late 1836, Forster reviewed Dickens's play *The Village Coquettes* for the *Examiner* in December that same year, in which he stated 'a great respect and liking for Boz'.[11] By March 1837 the pair were in regular correspondence and a lifelong friendship had begun. As I have said, Forster looms large in Dickens's biography not least because he *wrote* the biography, which stood as lasting testament to the closeness of their friendship, but also to an extent advertised and confirmed the strength of their relationship to a wider audience. The proximity of Forster to Dickens offers advantages and disadvantages to modern scholars – most notably the biography makes no mention of Dickens's affair with Ellen Ternan– but if Forster falls short as a biographer it is because he steps forward as a friend, prioritising the story Dickens wanted to be told, and how Dickens wanted to be remembered, over the opportunity to tell the whole truth. In their first few months of meeting, Dickens was already writing to Forster to acknowledge the value of his insight:

> Believe me that it affords me great pleasure to hear that you continue to read my writings, and far greater gratification than I can well describe to *you* to hear from your own lips that poor Oliver "affects" you – which I take to be the highest of all praise.[12]

Forster would soon progress from reading the story after completion to acting as a sounding board for new, unwritten, plot ideas; he was regularly involved in conversations with Dickens at the planning stage, and was generally a trusted and dependable friend. When Dickens quit as editor of the *Daily News*, it was Forster who stepped in to pick up the reins, and when Dickens died, he not only entrusted his manuscripts and notes to Forster, but also made him joint guardian of his children alongside Georgina Hogarth. He received no commission, but nonetheless was often instrumental in supporting and promoting Dickens's work. He would also introduce Dickens to others, such as William Charles Macready, with whom he could collaborate and further his name. As it happened, Macready too would become a lifelong friend to Dickens, and the pair shared a mutual respect for one another and their professional skills. Nonetheless in facilitating their initial meeting, Forster operated in a capacity that nowadays would be recognised as a literary agent.

But Forster was not the only person whose feedback Dickens sought. A clear example of this is Dickens's bizarre and desperate insistence in travelling back from Italy in December 1844 just to read *The Chimes* out to his friends. Forster was amazed at Dickens's insistence, not being certain that such a trip was necessary, but Dickens did it anyway. He and his courier Roche travelled for several days either side just to be back in London for three days before Christmas. Daniel Maclise has created a wonderful sketch that captures the moment; in it can be seen Dickens in the centre like a parody of *The Last Supper*, surrounded by family, friends, and creatives, including Thomas Carlyle, Douglas Jerrold, William Blanchard, and Clarkson Stanfield [see Figure 9.1]. They were brought there to praise Dickens and confirm the quality of this, his latest work. It seems incredibly needy of Dickens to travel all this way just to get feedback in the flesh, and it shows two key aspects of Dickens's relation with others. First is the ego or insecurity of the man, that he should need to do this and get verbal confirmation that the book was okay, but second is that recognition and respect for the opinion of others and the value it adds to his writing process. Dickens was not a lone genius, but instead a writer who frequently checked with others, seeking both their feedback and the opportunity to present his work and gain approval.

The other close friends/colleagues of this early period are of course Dickens's illustrators, of whom the two main collaborators were George Cruikshank and Hablot Knight Browne, aka Phiz. Cruikshank was twenty years older than Dickens but the pair became good friends; Cruikshank provided the illustrations for *Sketches by Boz* and *Oliver Twist*, after which their professional relationship came to a close. Cruikshank joined the temperance movement, having previously been an alcoholic, and his strict adherence to the movement was at odds with Dickens's own belief in moderation. But a surviving letter during the writing of *Oliver Twist* offers a valuable insight into their partnership:

Figure 9.1   Daniel Maclise, Sketch of Dickens reading *The Chimes*, 1844.

My dear Cruikshank,

I have described a *small* kettle for one on the fire – a *small* black teapot on the table with a little tray & so forth – and a two ounce tin tea cannister. Also a shawl hanging up – and the cat & kittens before the fire.

Ever faithfully yours
Charles Dickens[13]

Dickens is giving precise details for the illustration 'Mr. Bumble and Mrs. Corney taking tea', and the brevity of the letter indicates it is one of a series: either Dickens has seen Cruikshank's initial sketches and is offering feedback, or else he is attempting to provide as much information as possible to ensure the illustration matches and complements the text as closely as possible. It is a very involved relationship between author and artist. But while Cruikshank's working relationship with Dickens would prove to be brief, Phiz proved to be a much longer and profitable collaboration.[14] After his initial involvement on *Pickwick*, he would then go on to do illustrations for a further nine novels by Dickens. Phiz's illustrations have become synonymous with Dickens's writings, and vice versa; the frantic energy of Phiz's drawings capture perfectly the vibrant buoyancy of Dickens's works. Their relationship seems to be predominantly professional; Phiz accompanied Dickens on trips, but always with a purpose for the new work. In contrast, Dickens's relationship with Maclise was predominantly personal with an occasional professional collaboration. Maclise provided pictures for some of Dickens's *Christmas Books*, as well as a couple for *The Old Curiosity Shop*. It seems strange that the two could have been such good friends and not collaborated more together; Maclise did several portraits of Dickens and his family, including the picture of the children which Dickens and Catherine took to America with them, and the portrait of Dickens which would be reproduced in copies of *Nicholas Nickleby* and so at last introduce the world to the man behind Boz. Another artist who would remain more a personal rather than professional acquaintance was Clarkson Stanfield. He produced some illustrations for the Christmas books, and Dickens had hoped Stanfield would illustrate *Pictures from Italy* in 1846, but the strong anti-Catholic tone of the work meant Stanfield simply could not be associated with it. The decision came at short notice, but Dickens accepted it with good grace:

> Of your decision (of course) I have not a word to say. You are the best judge whether your Creed recognises and includes, with men of sense, such things as I have shocked you by my mention of. I am sorry to learn that it does-and think far worse of it than I did.[15]

The pair remained good friends regardless – like Maclise, Stanfield was a friend first, artist second. When Dickens published the volume edition of *Little Dorrit* in 1857 he dedicated the work to Stanfield from 'his attached friend'. So in his early career we can see how Dickens, with the assistance of Forster, cultivated a society of creative talents, be they actors, artists, editors or writers. In the 1850s Dickens would now capitalise on that network as he embarked on a new collaborative project.

Dickens's Midlife Network: The 1850s

On 27 December 1849, Dickens launched his journal *Household Words*, the editing of which would prove significantly more successful and prolonged than his earlier attempts for *Bentley's Miscellany* and the *Daily News*. A key appointment was W. H. Wills, who had previously worked with Dickens as his secretary during his short stint on the *Daily News*. Now Wills was being appointed as sub-editor, and in the capacity became one of Dickens's most enduring professional colleagues, working together with him on both that and its successor *All the Year Round* for the rest of Dickens's life. Wills was the perfect balance to Dickens: he was dependable, reliable, and got the job done. At the beginning of the appointment, Dickens said rather dismissively of Wills that he did not have 'the ghost of an idea in the imaginative way', but instead had 'a union of qualities very necessary to the business-part of such a design'.[16] Ultimately though Wills's capacity for work and organisation was a necessary counterpoint to Dickens's more sporadic sense of genius and energy which would often see him employed on other projects and spreading himself thin - and Dickens knew it, eventually referring to Wills as 'my other self'.[17] Throughout Dickens's various reading tours, Wills kept a steady hand at the helm of the journal to keep it going.

Not every writer was queueing up to be in Dickens's circle. George Eliot, despite invitations, did not publish in Dickens's journals. Dickens was friends with her partner George Lewes, and expressed great admiration for Eliot's work, but to no avail. It is also worth noting that just as Dickens had friends in the literary world, so too he had rivals. George W. M. Reynolds was a constant sparring partner. Reynolds had written his own sequel to *The Pickwick Papers* entitled *Pickwick Abroad* which 'helped launch his writing career on the back of Dickens's success.'[18] It was a cause of irritation on several fronts; it shamelessly used Dickens characters and placed them in a new narrative, copyright laws allowing him to do so without paying a penny to Dickens, and worst of all, it was a great hit. Politically, the two were often opposed. They had similar aims but different ideas of how to achieve those aims, with Reynolds being the more radical of the pair. Another rival writer was William Thackeray, but this rivalry was not so pronounced: they could agree as often as they disagreed, and there was mutual respect between the pair. Thackeray's greatest novel, *Vanity Fair* was serialised at the same time when *Dombey and Son* was in circulation, and Thackeray famously went to his own publishers one day with a copy of *Dombey* and told them, in awe, 'There's no writing against such power as this – one has no chance!'[19]

With *Household Words* Dickens entered the arena of the nineteenth-century press, literally. The offices for the journal were located on Wellington Street in London, as were the offices for 'more than 20 newspapers or periodicals and 13 booksellers or publishers' during the period of 1843 through to 1853.[20] It was a literary hub, and from his office Dickens was but a stone's throw away from other literary figures such as his friend Henry Mayhew, and his frenemy Reynolds (although hopefully no actual stones were thrown in this case). It is in the journals where we see a significant increase in Dickens's collaborative work. The title page for both *Household Words* and *All the Year Round* announced that the journals were 'Conducted by Charles Dickens'. No-one is entirely clear what this means; it takes immediate inspiration from *Chamber's Magazine* which Dickens was using as a model template for his new journal, but that word 'conducted' has subsequent connotations which puts Dickens in the guise of an impresario, running a show rather than editing a paper. His was the only name to appear regularly in the journal; other names would occasionally pop up in a short advertisement at the end to announce the publication of one of the novels serialised in the journal, but for the most part articles were published anonymously. Despite the multitude of writers pouring their work into the journal, not to mention the work of Wills and others in the office, the one name presented to the readers week in week out was Dickens. As a result, there is a sense of house style; a whimsy which many articles allude to that mimics the style of Boz. The full impact of this was accidentally discovered by a computational mistake in 2012, when the editors of *Dickens Journals Online* conducted authorship analysis tests on some of the anonymous pieces, and one, 'Temperate Temperance', was identified as very likely to be by Dickens himself.[21] Subsequently, however, a complete set of *All the Year Round* was discovered by Jeremy Parrott which showed the author of the article to be Charles Collins (brother of Wilkie Collins, and husband to Dickens's daughter Katey).[22] The fact that the computer was fooled can indicate either the extent to which Dickens himself was editing and shaping the writing submitted by his authors, or how they in turn had learned to imitate the inimitable and present works in the Dickens house style. Parrott's discovery has allowed us at last to read *All the Year Round* with a confidence in who was writing what; for *Household Words*, we have Wills's account books which give a relatively complete set of information for writers – I say 'relatively', because the various voluntary correspondents who did not get paid thus do not appear in the account books, leaving some gaps for researchers to fill.[23] But both of these sources are after the event. For the original readers of these journals, with neither a marked-up copy nor computational analysis to aid them, they were presented with a weekly journal under the banner of Dickens, and his name was the one they had in mind while reading.

The journals combine serialised fiction with poetry and a range of stylised non-fiction that covers topics from overseas politics to the new arrival of a hippopotamus at London Zoo. As the conductor, Dickens had direct involvement in the work and writing of established writers and several emerging authors: Elizabeth Gaskell published in the journal, as did Bulwer Lytton and Wilkie Collins. He also received and encouraged new works: Amelia B. Edwards and Adelaide Ann Procter both made their first appearances in Dickens's journals. They remain relatively obscure today, but were regular contributors to the journal, as were Dickens's 'young men', as they came to be known, who were all keen writers working under the Inimitable's gaze, of which the most famous now are George Sala, Edmund Yates and Percy Fitzgerald.[24] Dickens's journals remain relatively understudied, but that is changing. An increasing amount of work is being done on them, and as we learn more about them and the people working for them, so we can begin to question the extent to which their time with Dickens helped or hindered them. There are instances where writers may have been pushed into a particular type of writing: in the case of Henry Morley, another regular contributor, he showed interest in writing fantasy and super-natural tales, but Dickens repeatedly commissioned him to write science arti-cles instead. Daragh Downes suggests the 'magnitude of the calamity of the *Household Words* years for Morley's own artistic development is ultimately incalculable.'[25] The resulting work that Morley produced is good, and it paid, so we can argue this is Dickens recognising Morley's true talent and guiding him towards it; or we can see it more dismally as Dickens suffocating Morley's imagination and stifling his creativity.

As written works, Dickens's journals constitute a definite and concrete example of Dickens's networking at this time. Writers would send things to him on speculation, but equally he would reach out to writers to commission them. Dickens had established himself at the centre of a literary circle, the god-father of writing. It's hard to see how this could have been anything other than immensely satisfying to his ego. Like his failed attempt to be a playwright, Dickens's circle of writers, and his joint role as novelist and editor, afforded him a sense of prestige as well as the opportunity to emulate his own literary heroes like Smollett, Fielding and Goldsmith. He had recreated his own ver-sion of the literary salon where the Augustan and Regency writers would gather and collaborate.

This recreation of his heroes' literary circles was further explored in the ama-teur dramatics he engaged in, allowing him to indulge on the stage as well as the page. Among his fellow actors were Mark Lemon and Augustus Leopold Egg. Lemon was editor for *Punch*, and wrote the original script for *Mr. Nightingale's Diary* which Dickens would then rework extensively. Egg was an artist who painted Dickens in his role as Sir Charles Coldstream in Bulwer Lytton's play *Used Up!* Neither were involved with Dickens professionally, but operated in parallel lines of work, just like Maclise and Macready. Lemon was a friend of the family; his children played with Dickens's children. Egg did not have a family; he did propose to Dickens's sister-in-law Georgina, but was refused. While Lemon was the family friend, Egg offered a bachelor perspec-tive, and along with Wilkie Collins joined Dickens on his return visit to Italy in 1853. This was a distinct change to the family tour he had done in 1844–1845; now the three men went on a lads' trip abroad. Those assuming that these three creative talents must have experienced a deep and spiritual awakening in their time together are due for a disappointment: Dickens's letter home involve a running commentary on the facial hair of the other two – 'Collins's mous-tache is gradually developing' – which seems to have formed the basis of a competition to see who could grow the biggest.[26] This is hardly high-intellec-tual discourse. What is noticeable is that Forster was not one of the party; the old reliable was still being called upon as a sounding board for work, and a dependable support, but increasingly Dickens was widening his horizons and social circles, and Forster had competition.

While enjoying and consolidating longstanding friendships, Dickens also continued to work with younger writers and artists. Sala, Yates and Fitzgerald – all regular contributors to Dickens's journals – were sixteen, nineteen and twenty-two years younger than Dickens respectively, and represented a new generation; in turn Dickens saw himself as the founder of the feast. As with Collins, there was some antagonism here; when Sala was due to give a speech to the Newspaper Press, Dickens commented that 'he is certain to be drunk' and wondered whether he should 'forewarn the innocent Committee'.[27] Sala for his part complained about 'the slavery of a visit to Gad's Hill' where 'Everybody must work at something from 10 to 2':

> Sala used to take down an old bundle of proofs and make believe correct them, while he amused himself like a school boy with a book on the sly. Poor Wilkie Collins who needed rest used to sneak off to the library and go to sleep with a cigar, Dickens found him out and said 'none of this – no smoking in the library in the day time – you must work at something'[.][28]

To the young men, Dickens was both a person of respect and a figure of fun; his exacting routines and expectations that all should work to his own punishing schedule was a source of disdain and ridicule, but it got results. As much as they complained, they were all loyal to Dickens. Edmund Yates defended him after the separation from his wife, with Dickens defending Yates in turn when Thackeray accused Yates of spying on him at the Garrick Club and reporting his private comments in the press. After Dickens's death, these young men would lionise and memorialise Dickens, writing books about the inimitable and his work. Sala, for all his mocking of Gads Hill, wrote that 'To me he was literally *everything*.'[29]

The dynamic between Dickens and Wilkie Collins is much debated; with the young author being framed at different times as Dickens's protégé or rival. In 1860, during the publication of *The Woman in White* (in Dickens's *All the Year Round*), Dickens told Collins 'You know what an interest I have felt in your powers from the beginning of our friendship, and how very high I rate them.'[30] A number of letters from Dickens offer constructive criticism of Collins's work – 'I should have given Mr. Pendril some touches of comicality' he wrote of *No Name*, while in *The Woman in White* Dickens told Collins that 'the great pains you take express themselves a trifle too much; and you know I always contest your disposition to give an audience credit for nothing'.[31] The pair met in 1851 via Augustus Egg, and when the three of them visited Italy together two years later, Dickens frequently expressed annoyance and exasperation with Collins, usually provoked by a sense that Collins always wants to be in the right:

> It is the drollest thing in the world to see Egg and Collins burst out into economy – always on some wretched little point, and always on a point they had previously settled the other way. For example. This morning at breakfast, they settled that there was no need for them to have the Servitore di Piazza today. I waited until the discussion was over, and then said 'But when we met at dinner yesterday, you told me you had engaged him.' – 'O yes, so we did – almost – but we don't want him, and it will be all the same.' It is then eleven o'Clock. Downstairs we all go. In the hall, is the Servitore. To whom Collins – in Italian, of which Georgy will give you an adequate idea – expounds that they don't want him. Thereupon he respectfully explains that he was told to come, has lost his day, and has been waiting an hour. Upon that, they are of course obliged to take him; and the only result of the great effort is (as always is) that it has been a profoundly mean, and utterly fruitless, attempt at evasion.[32]

Moreover, there is a particularly condescending letter to Collins when he was ill in which Dickens offers to write the next instalment of *No Name* for him:

> I am quite confident that, with your notes and a few words of explanation, I could take it up at any time and do it. Absolutely unnecessary to say that it would be but a make-shift! but I could do it, at a pinch, so like you as that no one should find out the difference.[33]

Dickens evidently saw himself as the superior writer, both in his criticism, helpful suggestions and the belief he could write so as to be indistinguishable from Collins if he so chose. In turn, years after Dickens's death, Collins savagely dismissed his final work, *The Mystery of Edwin Drood*, as 'the melancholy work of a worn-out brain'.[34] These moments of tension and conflict suggest a tempestuous relationship, but equally the younger Collins was a good match for Dickens in his later years. Collins was certainly in no position to judge Dickens over his affair with Ellen Ternan, given that he himself was in relationships with two women, neither of whom he was married to. So far as their professional relationship is concerned, the two were writing distinct types of novels and no real competition as such existed, nor is there any real sense of Collins maturing under Dickens's tutorage; that said Dickens did provide a publishing space for Collins's novels in his journals and the pair did work together on a number of collaborative projects, including projects written solely by the two of them such as *The Lazy Tour of Two Idle Apprentices* and *No Thoroughfare*.

Another writer who Dickens helped was his own son Charley. Charley Dickens was the one child to go into the family business, writing short articles for his father's journals. But Dickens also helped another Charley, another impressionable young mind, and one of the more prolific contributors to Dickens's journals: Charles Allston Collins, though his name is mostly unknown today. The younger brother of Wilkie, and first husband to Dickens's daughter Kate, poor Charley, as he was often referred to, was quite a sickly young writer. He was originally an artist but quit the profession after a moment of imposter syndrome had him worrying that he was not original enough. The tragedy is that he then started writing for Dickens who proved to be an even more dominant influence. Just as Dickens redirected the path of Morley's career, so too he moulded Charley Collins into a mini-Dickens, a dependable and malleable writer who could produce several pieces in the Dickens whimsical style.[35]

There are happier instances of Dickens's influence on young minds. When his friend and neighbour Frank Stone died in 1859, Dickens took Stone's sons Arthur and Marcus under his wing. He personally tutored Arthur in the same fiendish method of shorthand he had learned in his youth, and commissioned Marcus to provide the illustrations for his penultimate novel, *Our Mutual Friend*. Dickens had moved on from the playful caricatures of Phiz; despite their long collaboration, Phiz did not illustrate the final three Dickens novels: – *Great Expectations, Our Mutual Friend* and *The Mystery of Edwin Drood*. Dickens drew instead on Stone and Luke Fildes to provide the illustrations. The pictures for the last three novels are very different in tone from Phiz's: more static, but also more detailed and realistic, they mark a change in public taste, which had moved away from caricature towards realistic illustration by 1860. It is worth considering how different the reception of the last three books might have been had they been furnished with the familiar Phiz illustrations, whether his work would have brought out the comic side of the works just as the actual illustrations exacerbate the gloomier tone of the novels. Did Dickens change his style, or did the difference in illustrations lead readers to emphasise and prioritise different aspects of the novel? The decision was hard upon Phiz, who by this point was struggling financially. One might have hoped Dickens would show some loyalty to his long-standing illustrator, but he was trying to adapt and evolve to a new style, not simply recreate the works of the past. Dickens had begun writing in the 1830s, but as he moved through the 1860s he found himself surrounded by a new generation of writers, and a new emerging form of literature that would eventually result in modernism. Dickens did not want to be a relic in his own lifetime and so adapted and changed as required.

After his death, Dickens's legacy was secured by his network: his son Charley took over editorship of the journal, according to his 'father's wish, expressed in writing only a week before his death'.[36] Sala wrote a piece in the *Daily Telegraph* which he subsequently expanded and published as *Charles Dickens* that same year. And of course Forster produced his three-volume biography. It was Dickens's wish that he did so, but nonetheless the result is that Forster established himself in the public eye as Dickens's true friend and confidante, revealing unknown wonders to the reader such as the blacking factory years. But Forster did not live many years after Dickens, so that as time wore on it was the young men, people like Sala, Yates and Fitzgerald, who carried the name of Dickens forward. As societies and fellowships formed, these were the people speaking out, sharing their memories of Dickens and encouraging further discussion of his work. The network Dickens created carried his name on, to some extent traded upon it too, but this meant that Dickens was remembered as a mentor as well as a writer.

Case Study: Dickens Writing with Others in *The Haunted House*

After the initial success of *A Christmas Carol* in 1843, Dickens repeated the experiment with four further Christmas books, before adopting a new strategy for his Christmas publications: the establishment of *Household Words* provided opportunity for a Christmas special. At first this was simply one of the December issues, but in subsequent years it became its own distinct publication released alongside the regular issues of the journal. In these Christmas numbers, Dickens invited a group of writers to contribute short stories which he would then connect together with a framing narrative. Initially that framing narrative was relatively straightforward: *A Round of Stories by the Christmas Fire* (1852) and its imaginatively titled sequel *Another Round of Stories by the Christmas Fire* (1853) both supposed a group of friends and family sharing stories, so that the frame narrative offered little interest beyond its purpose of connecting the disparate stories together. As the Christmas numbers continued, Dickens began to construct more elaborate framing narratives: *The Wreck of the Golden Mary* imagines survivors of a shipwreck telling tales in the lifeboats to maintain their spirits; *Somebody's Luggage* (1862) looks upon the belongings of an unknown person and imagines tales suggested by each item – 'His Boots', 'His Umbrella' etc. The 1859 number *The Haunted House* supposed the narrator to take possession of an isolated house believed by locals to be haunted; annoyed by the superstitious fears of his servants, he dismisses all but one of them, and along with his sister invites various friends to join them and stay in the house for a given time, at the end of which each one shares their story of the haunting they have received. Like all the Christmas numbers, the stories were published anonymously, so that Dickens's initial readers would have read one unified work under the Dickens banner; but subsequent scholarship allows us to now appreciate and recognise all the authors involved:

'The Mortals in the House' by Charles Dickens
'The Ghost in the Clock Room' by Hesba Stratton
'The Ghost in the Double Room' by George Augustus Sala
'The Ghost in the Picture Room' by Adelaide Anne Procter
'The Ghost in the Cupboard Room' by Wilkie Collins
'The Ghost in Master B's Room' by Charles Dickens
'The Ghost in the Garden Room' by Elizabeth Gaskell
'The Ghost in the Corner Room' by Charles Dickens

In some instances, identifying the work is no real challenge: Elizabeth Gaskell published her story under her own name in a subsequent collection of her works, which was quite common.

In one sense *The Haunted House* represents a coherent and unified work, with Dickens's framing narrative fulfilling its purpose of connecting the separate stories together. Reading them with an awareness of the different authors challenges this cohesion, but equally it is fair to say that the collection offers a varied range of style and content which trades upon and celebrates the strengths of its different authors. Adelaide Anne Procter's is the most distinct, being a poem. Proctor was a poet, not a novelist, after all; her 1858 collection *Legends and Lyrics* proved popular, and she contributed a number of poems to *Household Words*. Bringing her in to write a poetic narrative acts like a musical interlude in a variety show: the change in form acts both as a palate cleanser and respite between the various narratives, as well as sharpening our focus upon the piece and its writer specifically because of its distinction from the others. Elizabeth Gaskell's story is typical of her style; it tells the sad tale of a Yorkshire couple, with appropriate dialect, who work hard on the farm while their son attends school and grows increasingly haughty and ungrateful, ultimately leading to his attempted robbery of the family home to get the money he feels entitled to. It is the longest story in the collection, which speaks also of Dickens's respect for Gaskell. She was an established author, and his correspondence with her is mindful of that, showing far more tact and understanding than some of the more direct criticism he offered to new and younger writers. Wilkie Collins was about to go stellar; the first instalment of *The Woman in White* had been published in *All the Year Round* on 26 November

1859, just three weeks before the publication of *The Haunted House*; his contribution is a sensational suspense tale of a sailor transporting gunpowder to South America during a conflict, only to be captured and left to die in the ship's hold, tied up and watching with horror a candle burning lower and lower next to an ominous trail of powder designed to explode the many kegs surrounding him. George Sala's tale is more satirical, telling of a young man with 'the ague', which is clearly a pseudonym for being drunk, while Hesba Stratton's story adopts a more moral tone of a coquettish young girl finding true love and devotion in the arms of a serious but faithful scholarly man.

Reading the work as one volume is rather a disorientating experience then, as we move from writer to writer; with each shift we find ourselves in a different genre, tone and style of writing. The framing narrative was designed to both excuse and celebrate this diversity, giving the illusion of cohesion while ultimately allowing free rein to each writer to do what they do best. To consider the stories as one single work, we must look to Dickens's efforts in the framing narrative and interlinking paragraphs which introduce each new tale. While the other writers were working independently, Dickens sat at the centre of the hub, offering feedback, directing and organising the individual stories and reacting to them in his overarching narrative. Just as the other contributions betray familiar aspects of their authors, so too Dickens's segments can be analysed for distinctively Dickensian traits. The narrator, like Dickens, has a dog named Turk, which seems a rather curious Easter Egg to include. It is unlikely that readers would recognise the reference, so this may have been a hidden joke for Dickens's friends, or an indication that Dickens is drawing on his own experience while writing the section. The Christmas Numbers often had to compete for Dickens's attention with his novels – he had finished *A Tale of Two Cities* just a few weeks earlier – so the use of his own dog's name is an easy shortcut to make for a man writing in a hurry. Equally, the narrator speaks of how in 'an old Italian palace, which bore the reputation of being very badly haunted indeed, and which had recently been twice abandoned on that account, I lived eight months, most tranquilly and pleasantly', a seeming nod to his own stay for eight months in the Villa delle Peschiere.[37] Moreover, the narrator also alludes to his dead father (Dickens's own father had died in 1851):

> I once saw the apparition of my father, at this hour. He was alive and well, and nothing ever came of it if, but I saw him in the daylight, sitting with his back towards me, on a seat that stood beside my bed.[38]

The opening narrative expresses strong scepticism of ghosts, very similar to Dickens's own views of the supernatural. The narrator finds himself on a train with a man who 'might be what is popularly called a Rapper', which is to say a spiritualist, 'one of a sect for (some of) whom I have the highest respect, but whom I don't believe in.'[39] The gentleman's subsequent reference to his discussions with Socrates, Pythagoras, Galileo, Milton, Prince Arthur and others is a scathing swipe at his egotistical delusions. The narrator arrives at his destination in the morning 'in a heathen state of mind' and in this state of scepticism tells us why morning, rather than night-time, is truly a spiritual time:

> No period within the four-and-twenty hours of day and night, is so solemn to me, as the early morning. In the summer time, I often rise very early, and repair to my room to do a day's work before breakfast, and I am always on those occasions deeply impressed by the stillness and solitude around me. Besides that there is something awful in the being surrounded by familiar faces asleep – in the knowledge that those who are dearest to us and to whom we are dearest, are profoundly unconscious of us, in an impassive state anticipative of that mysterious condition to which we are all tending – the stopped life, the broken threads of yesterday, the deserted seat, the closed book, the unfinished but abandoned occupation, all are images of Death. The tranquillity of the hour is the tranquillity of Death.[40]

In his mocking of the spiritualist, and his reappraisal of morning as a time of death, Dickens turns conventional ideas about ghosts upon their head before the other writers have opportunity to share their stories. He is controlling the overall narrative of the work, and even in a work that is purportedly about hauntings he is framing these stories within his own sceptical views of the reality of such ideas. Upon arriving at the house the narrator is told by the locals how haunted it is, and sure enough finds there are several strange noises to disturb him, at which the narrator takes action which proves both subtle and very, very direct while inviting the local, Ikey, to inspect his gun:

> "Ikey," said I, "don't mention it; I have seen something in this house."
> "No sir?" he whispered, greedily opening his eyes. "Ooded lady, sir?"
> "Don't be frightened," said I. "It was a figure rather like you."
> "Lord, sir?"
> "Ikey!" said I, shaking hands with him warmly: I may say affectionately; "if there is any truth in these ghost-stories, the greatest service I can do you, is, to fire at that figure. And I promise you, by Heaven and earth, I will do it with this gun if I see it again!"
> The young man thanked me, and took his leave with some little precipitation, after declining a glass of liquor. I imparted my secret to him, because I had never quite forgotten his throwing his cap at the bell;

because I had, on another occasion, noticed something very like a fur cap, lying not far from the bell, one night when it had burst out ringing; and because I had remarked that we were at our ghostliest whenever he came up in the evening to comfort the servants.[41]

Like Scrooge, Dickens cries humbug at the idea of ghosts, inviting us to share his scepticism and find rational explanations for apparently supernatural events. It predisposes us against the stories which follow. Curiously, the stories themselves bear little connection to the supernatural; instead each ghost has told their story to the room's occupant, and it is that, rather than the haunting, which is then told to the group. A lot of the 'ghosts' turn out to be something else: Stratton's tale, supposedly told by the narrator's cousin John Herschel, is revealed in Dickens's closing narrative not to have been relayed by a ghost, but a subterfuge to reveal the true story of Herschel's wife. Dickens's narrator tells of his haunting by a young child, only to reveal in the close of the story that this is not a ghost but rather the narrator's own childhood self, coming back to him through memories: 'No other ghost has haunted the boy's room, my friends, since I have occupied it, then the ghost of my own childhood, the ghost of my own innocence, the ghost of my own airy belief.'[42] The closing narrative, written by Dickens again, is the story of Joe's friend Jack Governor, who while listening to the others stories has been sitting closely to Joe's sister:

> 'All night long, I have been haunted by one figure. All day, the same figure has so bewildered me in the kitchen, that I wonder I haven't poisoned the whole ship's company. Now, there's no fancy here. Would you like to see the figure?'
>
> 'I should like to see it very much.'
>
> 'Then here it is!' said Jack. Thereupon, he presented my sister, who had stolen out quietly, after us.
>
> 'Oh, indeed?' said I. 'Then, I suppose, Patty, my dear, I have no occasion to ask whether *you* have been haunted?'
>
> 'Constantly, Joe,' she replied.[43]

Dickens's sections may show a consistency among themselves, but offer a contrast to the other contributors: the cheerfulness of Jack Governor's short narrative above comes rather abruptly after the dismal and depressing ending of Gaskell's story. The contrast between Dickens's framing narrative and the stories is highlighted in the formatting of the issue; each individual story is presented in two columns, with the interspersed narrative in one column across the page. Reading *The Haunted House* is therefore an odd but interesting experience. Klimaszewski notes the 'paradoxical combination of continuity and differentiation' in the work and argues that 'variation in writing style helps the number avoid monotony and demonstrates that multiple voices enhance overall quality'.[44] But equally, as diverse a work as it may be, we can also see first-hand Dickens interacting with other writers, responding to their ideas, commenting on them and enveloping them into his own narrative. The final page offers summarising comments on the various sub-narrators:

> It occurs to me to mention that I observed Belinda [Procter's narrator] and Alfred Starling [Sala's narrator] to be rather sentimental and low, on the occasion, and that they are since engaged to be married in the same church. I regard it as an excellent thing for both, and a kind of union very wholesome for the times in which we live. He wants a little poetry, and she wants a little prose, and the marriage of the two things is the happiest marriage I know for all mankind.[45]

As the writer of the framing narrative, Dickens gets the final word and is in a position to provide additional conclusions to the individual works of his contributors, and their characters. There is also an implied commentary on the authors too, if one wants a little poetry and the other a little prose, in which Dickens is marking the strengths and failings of both and recommending a compromise. Dickens's attempt to do a one-man journal in *Master Humphrey's Clock* proved to be too exhausting; supporting and utilising the work of others in *Household Words* and *All the Year Round* proved a far more sustainable approach, but Dickens nonetheless managed to stamp his authority upon the piece. The anonymity and uncertainty of provenance that the collaborative Christmas numbers afforded also allowed 'the protection in risk-taking', where authors could experiment with their usual style and touch upon more controversial elements if they so chose.[46] Yet among all this diversity of style and content, the work of several people was ultimately 'conducted by Charles Dickens'. His name loomed large over the project even while he benefitted from (and encouraged) each individual's work. If he learned from them, he also maintained his own brand and sense of self over and above them.

Notes

1 Melisa Klimaszewski, *Collaborative Dickens: Authorship and Victorian Christmas Periodicals* (Athens: Ohio University Press, 2019), p. 13.

2 Dickens, Letter to John Forster, 1 July 1861, in Graham Storey (ed.), *The Letters of Charles Dickens*, Volume Nine 1859–1861 (Oxford: Clarendon Press, 1997), pp. 432–434 (pp. 432–433).

3 Dickens, Letter to W. H. Ainsworth, 17 May 1837, in Madeline House and Graham Storey (eds.), *The Letters of Charles Dickens*, Volume One 1820–1839 (Oxford: Clarendon Press, 1965), p. 260 (p. 260).

4 Forster, *The Life of Charles Dickens*, Volume One (London: Chapman and Hall, 1870), p. 158.

5 Dickens, Letter to Richard Bentley, 28 July 1857, in Graham Storey and Kathleen Tillotson (eds.), *The Letters of Charles Dickens*, Volume Eight 1856–1858 (Oxford: Clarendon Press, 1995), pp. 390–391 (p. 390).

6 Mary Russel Mitford, cited in Stephen Carver, *The Man Who Outsold Dickens: The Life and Work of W. H. Ainsworth* (Barnsley: Pen & Sword, 2020), p. 101.

7 Dickens, Letter to R H Horne, February 1840, in *Letters*, Vol. Two, pp. 20–21 (p.20).

8 Carver, p. 176. For details of the 1842 party, see Carver, pp. 155–156.

9 Dickens, Letter to Alfred Hachette, 9 June 1856, in *Letters*, Vol. 8, p. 133 (p. 133).

10 Dickens, Letter to Edward Bulwer Lytton, in *Letters*, Vol. 9, pp. 345–346 (p.345).

11 John Forster, 'Review of *The Village Coquettes*', *The Examiner*, 11 December 1836, p. 792.

12 Dickens, Letter to John Forster, 26 May 1837, in *Letters*, Vol. 1, p. 262 (p. 262).

13 Dickens, Letter to George Cruickshank, January 1838, *Letters*, Vol. 1, p. 353 (p. 353).

14 For more about Hablot K Browne, see Valerie Browne Lester, *Phiz: The Man who Drew Dickens* (London: Pimlico, 2006).

15 Dickens, Letter to Clarkson Stanfield, 12 March 1846, in Kathleen Tillotson (ed.), *The Letters of Charles Dickens*, Volume Four 1844–1846 (Oxford: Clarendon Press, 1977), p. 517 (p. 517).

16 Dickens, Letter to Henry Austin, 21 March 1850, in Graham Storey, Kathleen Tillotson and Nina Burgis (eds.), *The Letters of Charles Dickens*, Volume Six 1850–1852 (Oxford: Clarendon Press, 1988), pp. 69–70 (p. 69).

17 Dickens, Letter to Robert Lytton, 26 August 1855, in Graham Storey, Kathleen Tillotson and Nina Burgis (eds.), *The Letters of Charles Dickens*, Volume Seven 1853–185 (Oxford: Clarendon Press, 1993), pp. 694–695 (p. 694).

18 Shannon, p. 42.

19 Thackeray cited in George Hodder, *Memories of my time* (London: Tinsley, 1870), p. 277.

20 Mary Shannon, *Dickens, Reynolds, and Mayhew on Wellington Street: The Print Culture of a Victorian Street* (London: Routledge, 2019), p. 3.

21 John Drew and Hugh Craig, 'Did Dickens write "Temperate Temperance"?: (An Attempt to Identify Authorship of an Anonymous Article in *All the Year*

Round)', in *Victorian Periodicals Review*, Volume 44, Number 3, Fall 2011, pp. 267–290.

22 Jeremy Parrott, 'The Skeleton out of the Closet: Authorship Identification in Dickens's *All the Year Round*', *Victorian Periodical Review*, Vol. 48, No. 4 (Winter 2015), pp. 557–568.

23 For a comprehensive list of the contributors to *Household Words*, see Anne Lohrli, *Household Words: A Weekly Journal 1850–1859, Conducted by Charles Dickens. Table of Contents, List of Contributors and their Contributions* (Toronto: University of Toronto Press, 1973).

24 For more on this see P. D. Edwards, *Dickens's 'Young Men'* (London: Routledge, 1997).

25 Daragh Downes, 'Morley was alive: to begin with. The Curious Case of Dickens and his Principle Household Wordsmith', in Hazel Mackenzie and Ben Winyard (eds.), *Charles Dickens and the Mid-Victorian Press, 1850–1870* (Buckingham: University of Buckingham Press, 2013), pp. 185–200 (p. 199).

26 Charles Dickens, Letter to Catherine Dickens, 27 November 1853, in *Letters*, Vol. 7, pp. 203–206 (p. 204).

27 Dickens, Letter to Georgina Hogarth, in Graham Storey (ed.), *The Letters of Charles Dickens*, Volume Twelve 1868–1870 (Oxford: Clarendon Press, 2002), pp. 323–326 (p. 325).

28 Samuel Ward cited in *Letters*, Vol. 12, p. 325n.

29 George Augustus Sala, 27 June 70, cited in *Letters*, Vol. 12, p. 325n.

30 Dickens, Letter to Wilkie Collins, 7 January 1860, in *Letters*, Vol. 9, pp. 194–195 (p. 195).

31 Dickens, Letter to Wilkie Collins, 24 January 1862, in Graham Storey, *The Letters of Charles Dickens*, Volume Ten 1862–1864 (Oxford: Clarendon Press, 1998), pp. 20–21 (p. 20); Dickens, Letter to Wilkie Collins, 7 January 1860, in *Letters*, Vol. 9, pp. 194–195 (p. 194).

32 Charles Dickens, Letter to Catherine Dickens, 27 November 1853, in *Letters*, Vol. 7, pp. 215–217 (p. 216).

33 Dickens, Letter to Wilkie Collins, 14 October 1862, in *Letters*, Vol. 10, pp. 142–143 (p. 142).

34 Wilkie Collins, 'Wilkie Collins about Charles Dickens', *Pall Mall Gazette*, 20 January 1890, repr. Philip Collins (ed)., *Charles Dickens: The Critical Heritage* (London: Routledge, 1971), pp. 587–588 (p. 588).

35 The career of Charley Collins is another under-researched area, but was the recent focus of Saad Al-Maliky, *Charles Alston Collins (1828–1873): A Literary and Artistic Life*, Unpublished PhD Thesis, University of Buckingham, 2018.

36 Charles Dickens Jnr, 'Personal', *All The Year Round*, 25 June 1870, Vol. 4, p. 73.

37 Charles Dickens et al, *The Haunted House*, The Extra Christmas Number of *All the Year Round*, 13 December 1859, p. 571.

38 *The Haunted House*, p. 570.

39 *Haunted House*, p. 569.

40 *The Haunted House*, p. 570.

41 *The Haunted House*, p. 574.

42 *The Haunted House*, p. 598.

43 *The Haunted House*, p. 616.

44 Klimaszewski, p. 118.

45 *The Haunted House*, p. 616.

46 Seth Whidden, cited in Klimaszewski, p. 94.

10

Dickens and Separation

Focal Point: 1855–1859

Case Study: Our Mutual Friend

Dickens's separation from his wife Catherine in 1858 was announced to the world in two very different public letters. The first one appeared in the *Times* on 7 June 1858 and speaks of the matter in a very distant, clinical manner:

> Some domestic trouble of mine, of long-standing, on which I will make no further remark than that it claims to be respected, as being of a sacredly private nature, has lately been brought to an arrangement, which involves no anger or ill-will of any kind, and the whole origin, progress, and surrounding circumstances of which have been, throughout, within the knowledge of my children.[1]

With that letter, a marriage of twenty-two years was brought publicly to an end, described as 'domestic trouble', brought to 'an arrangement'. This is a stark contrast to the outpourings of emotion in the letters which began the relationship. Then, a couple of months later, on 30 August 1858, another letter appeared in the press, which has since come to be known as 'The Violated Letter' given Dickens's insistence that he never intended it to be printed. While it may have been published later, the writing of this letter actually predates the formal declaration in *The Times*, and was sent to Dickens's tour manager Arthur Smith in May 1858 with a note giving 'full permission to show this [...] to any one who wishes to do [Dickens] right, or to any one who may have been misled into doing [Dickens] wrong.' The Violated Letter, under the cover of being a more private correspondence, does not hold back in the way *The Times* letter would, and states in the opening sentence that 'Mrs. Dickens and I have lived unhappily together for many years.'[2]

Dickens was caught in the eye of a hurricane, as we will see, of rumour, speculation and public relations, so he decided to write his way out. In the two letters and their contrasting message we see an attempt to present a calm and mutual decision on the one hand, and to put the blame upon Mrs Dickens on

The Life of the Author: Charles Dickens, First Edition. Pete Orford.
© 2023 John Wiley & Sons Ltd. Published 2023 by John Wiley & Sons Ltd.

the other. That claim that they 'lived unhappily together for many years' is loaded, and has prompted Dickensians to look back upon their marriage as doomed almost from the beginning. This can and should be challenged as there is no evidence to suggest the early years of their marriage were unhappy; but nor should we subscribe to the other extreme that everything was perfect until Ternan arrived. Instead between these two absolute lies various potential times where we can suggest the troubles began: yes, there is his first meeting with Ellen Ternan in 1857 that some might consider the catalyst; but we can also go further back to disagreements and disappointments in Dickens's life which may have been dismissed as minor issues at the time, or be the seeds from which the later forest of discontent would grow. Therefore, before we analyse the events of 1857 and 1858, I will take a brief moment into what may – or may not – be the beginning of the end.

Rivals, Reunions and Realisations: Mme de la Rue and Maria Beadnell

Some have suggested that troubles may have begun in the Dickens marriage as early as 1844–1845 during their stay in Genoa. It was here that Dickens met Augusta de la Rue, wife to the banker Emile de La Rue. Mme de La Rue was experiencing some form of mental distress, so with her husband's blessing, Dickens embarked on an intense series of sessions in which he would practice his mesmerism skills to bring Mme de la Rue into a trance-like state and so attempt to root out the source of her disquiet. It sounds fantastical, and the sort of narrative which might well appear in Dickens's fiction; in fact, it did, in his 1852 short story *To Be Read at Dusk* and, arguably, in his last novel *The Mystery of Edwin Drood* and the possessive, dominating presence of John Jasper over the heroine Rosa Bud. In this latter instance there is an overt sexual tension behind Jasper's power over Rosa, so it is not unreasonable that others might perceive a similar tension in Dickens's mesmerism of Mme de la Rue. Dickens's letters do not suggest this, however. We should of course bear in mind that many of these letters were being written to Monsieur de la Rue, so any such discussion is unlikely to be in print, but even so the letters which Dickens writes are passionate about the symptoms, not the patient:

> The impression made on the disorder, generally, is beyond all question very great. But the extent to which her thoughts are directed to, and clustered round, that bad phantom – and the manner in which she watches the effect upon it, and trusts to my influence over it, and refers all her suffering to it – is most remarkable.[3]

Dickens's obsession with Mme de la Rue seems to be primarily borne by his appreciation of his own brilliance rather than hers. In one letter he marvels how while practising his skills he accidentally mesmerises Catherine, who happens to be sat next to him, and this in turn fascinates Dickens immensely as an indication of his power: 'It was really quite a fearful thing, and the strongest instance of the strange mysteries that are hidden within this power, that I have ever seen or heard of'.[4] There is no indication that Dickens ever took advantage of this power over Mme de la Rue, but there is certainly a sense that he is intoxicated by the position he finds himself in. As he travelled around the rest of Italy he wrote back to the de la Rues asking for frequent updates and offering to cut short his travels to come straight back. There is an urgency in his writing which speaks as much of his own desire to be back in that position of power as it does of a genuine desire to help Mme de La Rue. If there was an attraction in this relationship, it was that potency of his role as mentor, healer and guru which fascinated Dickens so immensely.

However, Catherine was not impressed. Initially, she was kept in the dark about it, with Dickens assuring Emile de La Rue that 'No word had ever passed my lips in reference to my compact with Madame de La Rue' and that Catherine 'was as utterly ignorant of it, as she is of any business-secret in your banking house'.[5] But clearly she was not happy about Dickens spending so much time in the company of another man's wife. After their return to England, Dickens was eager to go abroad again, and wanted to return to Genoa, but declined this in a letter to Mme de la Rue on the grounds that 'Mrs. Dickens, who was never very well there, cannot be got to contemplate the Peschiere – though I have beset her in all kinds of ways'.[6] A later letter to Catherine implies this was a white lie, and that the real reason was her jealousy of Mme de La Rue:

> Nine years have gone away since we were in Genoa. Whatever looked large in that little place may be supposed in such a time to have shrunk to its reasonable and natural proportions [...] Whatever made you unhappy in the Genoa time had no other root, beginning, middle, or end, than whatever has made you proud and honoured in your married life, and given you station better than rank, and surrounded you with many enviable things. This is the plain truth, and here I leave it.[7]

Again, we are left with only Dickens's say on the matter, and no sense of how accurate this reflection is. Dickens may well be rewriting his own history: after the separation Catherine's jealousy is cited as further evidence of their longstanding discord; but back in 1846 Dickens acquiesced to his wife's wishes: they did not go to Genoa, but Switzerland instead. If Catherine was jealous, Dickens was aware enough to heed the warning; either to concede she had a point, or to realise that a harmonious marriage relied upon listening to the needs of his wife as well as his own desires. The ambiguity of the de La Rue relationship is thus twofold: first there is the question of whether there was any genuine attraction between Dickens and Mme de La Rue; then there is the question of how Dickens responded to his wife's concerns at the time, as opposed to retrospectively after their separation. What can be confidently inferred from the situation is that notion of power. Dickens felt a power over Mme de la Rue and was enthralled by it; he also recognised the power of his wife and bowed down to that, later to resent it.

Away from the battle of wills and domination, there is another root of disquiet to be considered, and that is what we would nowadays term as a midlife crisis. Dickens was getting older; the reworking of his childhood biography into *David Copperfield* allowed him opportunity to confront (and capitalise on) his insecurities and inner demons, but it also prompted a nostalgia for the past. The character of Dora, David's first wife, bore similarities to Dickens's first love Maria Beadnell. In a subsequent letter he wrote of David and Dora's romance that:

> People used to say to me how pretty all that was, and how fanciful it was, and how elevated it was above the little loves of very young men and women. But they little thought what reason I had to know it was true and nothing more nor less.[8]

Anyone who has read *David Copperfield* might be surprised to see this relationship talked about so fancifully; after all, David's first marriage ends tragically, and even before that it is shown frequently to be an ill-fated match, with David's second wife being a much better choice and a true marriage of equals. *Copperfield* could, and perhaps should, then be seen as a recognition of Catherine's superiority over Maria Beadnell, and Dickens's recognition that he chose his wife well despite his initial infatuation. But the letter above does not take that stance, instead thinking back wistfully and nostalgically on the prettiness of that earlier romance. The context for the letter makes it clear as to why this should be: Dickens was writing to Maria Beadnell herself. The object of the young Dickens's attraction, who was once out of his reach, was now approaching him, as a famous author and toast of the town, to re-establish contact – and Dickens was thrilled.

When Maria, now Mrs de Winter, wrote to Dickens in February of 1855 he responded initially in a tone that harkens straight back to twenty years earlier:

> As I was reading by my fire last night, a handful of notes was laid down on my table. I looked them over, and, recognizing the writing of

no private friend, let them lie there, and went back to my book. But I found my mind curiously disturbed, and wandering away through so many years to such early times of my life, that I was quite perplexed to account for it. There was nothing in what I had been reading or imme-diately thinking about, to awaken such a train of thought, and at last it came into my head that it must have been suggested by something in the look of one of those letters. So I turned them over again, – and sud-denly the remembrance of your hand, came upon me with an influence that I cannot express to you. Three or four and twenty years vanished like a dream, and I opened it with the touch of my young friend David Copperfield when he was in love.[9]

The balance of power had shifted; last time they met he was but the lowly reporter and she the gentlemen's daughter, now he was the one with the greater reputation, and she the one flattered by the connection. As with Mme de la Rue, Dickens's thrill at this reconnection is explained as much by his own vanity as by any lingering attraction to Beadnell. She, like Dickens, was now married, so Maria de Winter was never a serious threat to the Dickens's marriage. But what she offered was a fantasy, a wistful consideration of what might have been, with the lingering question of whether that other life might have been happier. This is the classic midlife crisis, one that even Dickens, for all his success, was still vulnerable to. As it transpired, his romantic fantasis-ing would have an abrupt end. Dickens's memories of Maria were vacuum-packed, preserving her forever as the young girl he had wooed. Obviously, this was nonsense: the real Maria had grown older, and Dickens was horrified. She had also grown fatter, which was a further blow to Dickens's fragile perception of her perfect past self. The final blow was that she continued to behave in the same coquettish manner she had when they were younger, and what had seemed charming and arousing now seemed gro-tesque and deluded. Dickens famously, and mercilessly, used the experience a few years later to create the character of Flora Finching in *Little Dorrit*. Just like Dickens, the book's male protagonist Arthur Clennam is excited to see the girl he had unsuccessfully tried to woo in his youth, and is disappointed by the meeting with her older self:

> Flora, always tall, had grown to be very broad too, and short of breath; but that was not much. Flora, whom he had left a lily, had become a peony; but that was not much. Flora, who had seemed enchanting in all she said and thought, was diffuse and silly. That was much. Flora, who had been spoiled and artless long ago, was determined to be spoiled and artless now. That was a fatal blow.[10]

Dickens's depiction of Flora seems brutal, and there's certainly a thoughtlessness here in so blatantly using his own personal experience in creating this character – there is no doubt that Maria must have recognised Flora to be a portrait of herself. But if Dickens is attacking Maria here, he is also attacking himself. He, like Flora, was wrapped up in the fantasy of the past, and if she is ridiculous for doing so then he is no less so. In particular, Flora's manner of speaking directly imitates the letters Dickens himself had written at the time, full of long sentences in dire need of punctuation, such as this one:

> Our meetings of late have been little more than so many displays of heartless indifference on the one hand while on the other they have never failed to provide a fertile source of wretchedness and misery and seeing as I cannot fail to do that I have engaged in a pursuit which has long since been worse than hopeless and a further perseverance in which can only expose me to deserved ridicule I have made up my mind to return the little present I received from you sometime since (which I always prized as I still do far beyond anything I ever possessed) and the other enclosed mementos of our past correspondence which I am sure it must be gratifying to you to receive as after our recent relative situations they are certainly better adapted for your custody than mine.[11]

That entire paragraph is just ONE SENTENCE. Dickens had written to Beadnell after the end of the courtship to request the return of all his letters to her, so although this letter was written twenty years prior to *Little Dorrit*, it would have been available to him, and likely to have been retrieved and read by him during his initial nostalgic fantasising prompted by Beadnell reinitiating contact. This is evident when we see Flora's method of speech:

> You mustn't think of going yet [...] you could never be so unkind as to think of going, Arthur–I mean Mr Arthur–or I suppose Mr Clennam would be far more proper–but I am sure I don't know what I am saying–without a word about the dear old days gone for ever, when I come to think of it I dare say it would be much better not to speak of them and it's highly probable that you have some much more agreeable engagement and pray let Me be the last person in the world to interfere with it though there was a time, but I am running into nonsense again.[12]

The style of writing is exactly the same as the letter by the young Dickens: he is satirising himself. Even Flora's recurring slip of referring to Clennam by his first name is a reflection on what Dickens himself had done after Beadnell had written to him in 1855, opening one of his replies with: 'My dear Mrs. Winter

(I had half a mind when I dipped my pen in the ink, to address you by your old natural Christian name.)'[13] Thus when Dickens fictionalises this in *Little Dorrit*, he is not only mocking the style and tone of his younger self, but also laughing at his more recent folly too. Flora may well be based physically on Maria Beadnell, but her character is all Dickens.

Clearly then the reunion provided Dickens with cause for reflection. He had immediately reverted to his younger self, and quickly seen the foolishness of that behaviour in order to then mock in his writing. He may have been able to laugh at himself in exposing Flora's foolishness, but that laughter covers a nervousness. For the short interim between receiving Beadnell's letter and meeting her, Dickens had been entirely transported. It may have ended in disappointment, but clearly Dickens was susceptible to temptation and ready to consider other paths. What was now evident was that he could not go back, only forward, and if he was unhappy then he would not find his solution in the past, but the future.

The Beadnell infatuation teaches us two things about Dickens's state of mind at the time. First, his fascination with meeting his former sweetheart certainly speaks of a playful flirtation with what might have been. The eagerness with which he responds and the fondness with which he looks back upon that time are not positive signs for marital satisfaction. Secondly, his disappointment that the young girl has become a woman, and 'grown to be very broad', is horrifically sexist, but also a potential indication of his dissatisfaction with his wife as much as with Maria. By 1855, Catherine Dickens had now had ten children; unsurprisingly that had taken its toll on her physical appearance. The postpartum disorder she had experienced with her first child turned into a recurring event. From Dickens's perspective this could be – and was – interpreted as further failings on her part as a mother, that another woman was required to give their child milk. In 1857 Dickens wrote to Forster that 'Poor Catherine and I are not made for each other' and suggests 'What is now befalling me I have seen steadily coming on, ever since the days you remember when Mary was born'.[14] Thus Dickens retrospectively pinpointed the beginning of the end as far back as 1838 and the birth of their second child. The reference to 'Poor Catherine' somewhat patronisingly positions Dickens as the kind but regretful benefactor who looks upon his wife with pity rather than disdain, while the connection to the birth of their daughter reinforces the inference that the problems are connected to Catherine's role as a mother and her perceived failure in that role. He told Angela Burdett Coutts that Catherine 'does not – and she never did – care for the children; and the children do not – and they never did – care for her.'[15] In the violated letter he says with an assumption of magnanimity that is frankly audacious, 'In the manly consideration towards Mrs.

Dickens which I owe to my wife, I will merely remark of her that the peculiarity of her character has thrown all the children on someone else.'[16] Such is the way Dickens would come to write of it, with postnatal depression reduced to a 'peculiarity of her character'; but far more important than that is a consideration of Catherine's perspective, and the trauma of experiencing childbirth ten times and the subsequent stigma of not being a 'proper' mother, whatever that might be. If Catherine was proving to be a disappointment to Dickens, that speaks more of his own unrealistic expectations of what the perfect partner should be, and the inability to see his wife for who she was, rather than who he wanted her to be.

Ellen Ternan

In January 1857 Dickens, along with friends and family, was acting in an amateur performance of Wilkie Collins's play *The Frozen Deep* (heavily amended by Dickens) and Edward Bulwer Lytton's comedy *Uncle John*. The performances were a great success and so plans were made to present them to a wider audience. As much as Dickens relished being in theatre himself, he was uncomfortable with the women of his family going on the public stage. Roles first played by his sister-in-law Georgina and his daughters Katey and Mamie were now to be played by professional actors: enter Ellen 'Nelly' Ternan. She was just eighteen years old at the time, while Dickens was forty-five. She joined his acting company along with her older sister Fanny (who would go on to marry Dickens's friend Thomas Trollope) and their mother, Frances. We can only speculate as to when precisely the attraction began, and how it was instigated: some defenders of Dickens prefer to cast Ternan as the scheming opportunist, but the predominant view is that Dickens, as the more powerful of the two, is likely to have been the primary mover. *The Frozen Deep* has subsequently been interpreted and reinterpreted as the fatal backdrop for this emotional and tempestuous affair, but really this is rather ridiculous. Dickens and Ternan spent little time on stage together in the drama; she did not play the romantic lead but rather the sister of the romantic lead. The play itself offered little opportunity for Dickens and Ternan to interact; she was not playing his romantic interest, but the sister of his romantic interest with whom he shared little interaction, and so attempts to unpick the drama for subliminal messages are therefore rather futile. The accompanying play *Uncle John* is far more interesting in this respect as Dickens played the older Uncle John while Ternan plays the 'dear little girl, just nineteen' who he intends to marry.[17] The playing of those roles therefore provides far more scope for tension and interpretation given the dynamic of the two actors off-stage. Even though the resulting play is a comedy, it nonetheless offers a much more uncomfortable instance of life imitating art.

The Manchester performances went ahead in August 1857. In September that year, Dickens and Collins went on a trip to the North of England which they would then write up as *The Lazy Tour of Two Idle Apprentices*. The trip was borne out of restlessness, but it was also an opportunity to meet up with Ternan who was acting in Doncaster at the time. In *The Lazy Tour*, Dickens and Collins describe their trip to Doncaster races where Dickens's fictional alter-ego falls 'into a dreadful state concerning a pair of little lilac gloves and a little bonnet that he saw there'; a likely reference to Ternan.[18] We can confidently trace the beginnings of the affair here, whether physical or purely flirtatious. Dickens writes in infuriatingly arch innuendo to Wills, who was back in London running the journal (as usual):

> I wish I was as good a boy in all things as I hope I have been, and mean to be in this.

> But Lord bless you, the strongest parts of your present correspondent's heart are made up of weaknesses. And he just come to be here at all (if you knew it) along of his Richard Wardour! Guess *that* riddle, Mr Wills![19]

Wardour was the character Dickens played in *The Frozen Deep*, so the riddle seems to be linked to the idea of Dickens being among his cast again (specifically, the actresses). It is the worst kind of joke: funny to the speaker, meaningless to the audience. For all his apparent self-awareness in Flora in *Little Dorrit*, Dickens was acting like a love-sick puppy again. As Dickens became more infatuated with Ternan, so too the letters depicting his long-standing dissatisfaction with his wife began to appear, which is why the question arises as to how accurate those letters might be. Just as Dickens rewrote his childhood in *David Copperfield* to render his youth even more tragic and pitiful than it actually was, so it is likely that his regretful musings over his marriage are not entirely true. Minor points of disagreement that may have been cheerfully passed over at the time become reimagined as the certain signs of a doomed marriage long in the making. Dickens is allowing the end to change the narrative of the relationship. But when we look back at the letters he sent both to and about Catherine through their marriage, there is no indication of discontent, instead he writes to her as his darling and dearest. It suited the older Dickens to imagine the marriage was doomed from the start, as a means to ease his own guilt and share the blame for the separation, but in reality there were many happy moments shared between the pair, and however sour things might have gone, that initial happiness should never be dismissed.

As the partner who was having an affair, it would be Dickens who would be recognised as the guilty party in a divorce court. Dickens's attitude towards the separation accordingly takes on a defensive stance, and readily adopts the mantra of the best defence being a good offence. In the violated letter he cites Anne Brown, Catherine's loyal servant who had since married and left their service, as a witness to their long-standing unhappiness:

> An attached woman servant (more friend to both of us than a servant), who lived with us sixteen years, and is now married, and who was, and still is in Mrs Dickens's confidence and mine, who had the closest familiar experience of this unhappiness in London, in the country, in France, in Italy, wherever we have been, year after year, month after month, week after week, day after day, will bear testimony to this.[20]

Here we see Dickens reaching back, suggesting flaws in the marriage as early as 1844 and the trip to Italy. Brown had also accompanied them to America in 1842, but this is not mentioned, thus suggesting the troubles started later; his statement to Forster contradicts this with the earlier start of 1838. The contradiction in the narrative betrays its flimsiness; Dickens is reaching for a point, to share the blame for his misdemeanour. In fact, if anything, he is almost attempting to shift the blame entirely onto Catherine. In the violated letter he continues:

> For some years past Mrs Dickens has been in the habit of representing to me that it would be better for her to go away and live apart; that her always increasing estrangement made a mental disorder under which she sometimes labours – more, that she felt herself unfit for the life she had to lead as my wife, and that she would be better far away. I have uniformly replied that we must bear our misfortune, and fight the fight out to the end; that the children were the first consideration, and that I feared they must bind us together 'in appearance'.[21]

This is extraordinary. Dickens's narrative of events would have us think that he was the one trying to keep them together while Catherine wanted to leave. The facts simply do not support this. Dickens built a barrier between him and Catherine – *literally*. He wrote to his wife's maid Brown (now married and going by the name Anne Cornelius) that he wanted 'the recess of the doorway between the Dressing-Room and Mrs. Dickens's room, fitted with plain white deal shelves, and closed in with a plain light deal door, painted white'. Though he writes about it in purely practical terms, he also insists 'The sooner it is done, the better' and opens by explaining that he prefers Cornelius to oversee matters as he 'would rather not have [the arrangements] talked about by comparative strangers'.[22] The devastating symbolism of Dickens blocking off the passageway between his wife's bedroom and his own has understandably caught the attention of subsequent biographers.[23] This is not the action of a man who wants to 'fight the fight out to the end'. The referencing of her 'mental disorder' is another attempt to undermine her credibility and capability; putting blame upon her failures while also planting seeds of doubt in any contradictory statements she might release in the future. Likewise, the idea that 'she felt herself unfit for the life she had to lead as my wife' is horribly self-ignorant on Dickens's part. Any such expectations on that life would have come from him; the implicit sense of honour in being his wife which Dickens felt in turn implies the crushing disappointment that Catherine should fail to fulfil the role of Mrs Dickens. Lilian Nayder rightly notes the unavoidable disparity caused by Dickens's fame, meaning Catherine Hogarth will forever be known and considered primarily as the wife of Dickens rather than as her own woman.[24] But the truly shocking and awful thing about the violated letter is not the things Dickens wrote, but that he made Catherine's mother and sister co-sign it.

Throughout the separation Dickens continued to place the blame anywhere but on his own shoulders. It is clear he was both angry and embarrassed by the situation, and that anger was unfairly poured upon others. When early rumours circulated that Georgina was the other woman, Dickens blamed this on 'Mrs. Dickens's weakness, and her mother's and her youngest sister's wickedness' even though Dickens had apparently 'warned them in the strongest manner.'[25] It is likely this warning was more threat than genuine selfless concern. Moreover, when the first letter was published he wrote to Catherine to blame her for the necessity of its appearance:

> I will not write a word as to any *causes* that have made it necessary for me to publish the enclosed in *Household Words*. Whoever there may be among the living, whom I will never forgive alive or dead, I earnestly hope that all unkindness is over between you and me.[26]

Even as an enthusiastic fan of Dickens's work, I readily concede that his treatment of his wife and the handling of their separation was despicable. Horrifically misguided, Dickens handled the situation very badly indeed. He goes too far – far too far. The cause of this can be identified partly in his fixation with reputation. He was Charles Dickens™ – the man of the people, the 'Household Word' who came into people's houses through his writings of domestic scenes. His career rested upon this perception of him as the champion of the home, and now he had broken his own home. He was on the defensive, and he lashed out as a consequence. Had he been alive today, where the stigma of divorce and separation is significantly less than in the nineteenth century, then he might have been thought of more kindly for meeting someone else, and there would have been no need for his extreme reaction. The tragic irony is that today it is that reaction we judge him for rather than the separation itself. It is a horrific treatment of his wife in the process, not to mention an aggressive rewriting of the narrative that descends into gaslighting. One particularly malicious example is the anecdote of a bracelet, from Dickens and intended for Ellen, being mis-delivered to Catherine, the jeweller assuming, not unreasonably, that Dickens would be requesting such a present for his wife.[27] Catherine was of course perturbed by this, in response to which Dickens affected strong offence, insisting that Catherine should go to Ternan's house herself to deliver the present and thus show that nothing untoward was happening between Dickens and Ternan. He put his wife through unnecessary emotional turmoil to pervade the myth of his innocence and respectability.

In 2020 John Bowen suggested that Dickens might have even considered committing Catherine to an asylum. This sort of strategy was not unheard of; Dickens's friend Bulwer Lytton had done exactly this with his own wife in June 1858. The references to Catherine's 'mental disorder' in the violated letter accordingly takes on a much more sinister meaning in this context. Placing Catherine in an asylum might remove the problem; more importantly it would place blame upon her and position Dickens as the unfortunate but well-meaning husband. Though Bowen makes a compelling case, it is not conclusive; the accusations are second-hand, appearing 'in a letter from Edward Dutton Cook, Catherine's next-door neighbour in Camden'.[28] We cannot say that this was definitely Dickens's plan then, and should be wary of doing so, there's also a sense that it might be more trouble than help. Bulwer Lytton's committal of his wife had provoked outcry, resulting in her release; and had Catherine been committed this would still not provide grounds for divorce. It is not unreasonable to think Dickens may well have *considered* the move, but ultimately it went no further, and for good reason.

For all of his insecurity, the truth is Dickens had the advantage from the start. He was a man in a patriarchal society; moreover, he was a successful novelist with the money and resources to tell his story. Catherine had no such means to tell her story, and ultimately had to concede to Dickens's will. Dickens could not divorce her; to do so would have meant taking the case to court and outlining the reasons for separation, and ultimately it was Dickens who was having the affair. He had no justifiable reason to divorce his wife in the eyes of the law; Catherine *did* have justifiable reason to divorce him, but doing so would mean Dickens's secret becoming public.[29] So instead the couple separated, with Dickens providing financial support for Catherine in return for his affair with Ellen remaining a private matter.

Rumours did spread however, and the press speculated on the possible causes for this shocking separation.[30] Many people assumed Georgina was the other woman, something which Dickens addressed in the public letters. Thackeray wrote to his mother to refute the rumour, saying instead (accurately as it turns out) 'No says I no such thing – it is with an actress'.[31] Georgina for her part chose to stay with Dickens. This certainly raises questions (and eyebrows); it feels like a betrayal of her sister, but we could be generous and see it as devotion to the children. By staying with Dickens she stayed with the family, and the children she had helped to raise. It's also true to say she chose security in staying with Dickens over her sister; she also remained loyal to him long after his death. In contrast, Mark Lemon fell out with Dickens over the affair for his sympathy to Catherine, as well as the decision of Lemon as editor of *Punch* to not publish Dickens's statement defending his role in the separation. As Slater notes, this is unfair and irrational of Dickens that he 'should have wished, or should have thought it appropriate, for such an item to appear in the pages of a comic miscellany'.[32] Dickens and Lemon would not speak for several years, Dickens instructing Catherine that 'I positively forbid the children ever to see or to speak to him', until the two men finally reconciled their differences after meeting at a funeral in 1864.[33] As for Ternan, she and Dickens would continue their relationship until his death, in the shadows by necessity. Dickens secured accommodation for them in hidden locations, in France and in England. She is rarely mentioned in his letters, nor in Forster's biography. She is named in Dickens's will, and rumours emerged after Dickens death, escalated by Gladys Storey's account of what Dickens's daughter Katey had told her.[34] By the mid-twentieth-century, Dickens and Ternan was an open secret among Dickensians, barely known to the wider world despite publications and discussion, until Claire Tomalin's biography popularised the tale of Ternan and made her name prominent at last.

Case Study: Commentaries on Marriage and Love in *Our Mutual Friend*

In his penultimate novel *Our Mutual Friend* Dickens explores a varied range of relationships, from the idyllic to the diabolic. Within this diverse display we can infer several personal commentaries and ruminations on Dickens's own experience of marriage, domestic life and sexual urges. The dynamic between the heroine Bella Wilfer and her father is a telling indication of how Dickens might prefer himself to be seen. Mr Wilfer is a 'clerk in the drug-house of Chicksey, Veneering, and Stobbles' and described as rather shy, unassuming and markedly childlike: 'If the conventional Cherub could ever grow up and be clothed, he might be photographed as a portrait of Wilfer.'[35] Mrs Wilfer, on the other hand, presents a very different figure:

> Mrs Wilfer was, of course, a tall woman and an angular. Her lord being cherubic, she was necessarily majestic, according to the principle which matrimonially unites contrasts.[36]

There is a role-reversal in the relationship of the Wilfers compared to that of Dickens and his wife. Though Dickens certainly maintained a childlike view in many respects, it is clear that he was the one in control of the household. But the portrayal of Wilfer and his wife captures the image that Dickens would have wished to present to the public at the time of the violated letter. It shows a marriage that has fallen apart due to the wife's tyranny, but continues because of the husband's complicity. He is a victim in his own marriage, a nice man who would have been much happier if only he had married another woman, not so cold and tyrannous. Of course, the tall, angular Mrs Wilfer has nothing in common with Mrs Dickens, but those who had not met her, and only read the violated letter, might be forgiven for assuming she did. What is most telling in the portrayal of the Wilfers is the way in which Mr Wilfer is shown to have a genuine and loving bond with his children where Mrs Wilfer does not. After Bella Wilfer is taken into the home of the Boffins, and provided with an allowance, she returns home to visit her family. Her meeting with her mother and siblings is cold and awkward, but afterwards she goes to meet her father alone after work, and treats him to a new suit and day out:

> 'Don't you wish, my dear,' said R. W., timidly, 'that your mother was here?'
> 'No, I don't, Pa, for I like to have you all to myself to-day. I was always your little favourite at home, and you were always mine. We have run away together often, before now; haven't we, Pa?'
> 'Ah, to be sure we have! Many a Sunday when your mother was – was a little liable to it,' repeating his former delicate expression after pausing to cough.[37]

One of the key elements of Dickens's narrative during the separation was that Catherine was a bad mother, and that he, by inference, was a good father. Photos taken at Gad's Hill show him sat in the garden with his daughters Katey and Mamie, a charming scene of father and children [see Figure 10.1]. It is possible for this to be both true and fantastical; Dickens certainly had a good relationship with his children, but that relationship suffered during his

Figure 10.1   Robert Hindry Mason, Photograph of Dickens and his daughters Katie and Mamie at Gad's Hill, c. 1866.

separation from their mother. Charley chose to live with Catherine rather than Dickens; Katey married Charles Allston Collins and it is widely suspected this was motivated primarily by a desire to escape her father's household. Bella Wilfer's desire to have her father all to herself is ultimately a father's fantasy, an implicit praise of the man's qualities as a father that have been unrecognised by his harsh and selfish wife. Dickens makes the point emphatically by comparing this stolen day between Wilfer and Bella with Wilfer's wedding day:

> A happy and a chatty man was Pa in his new clothes that day. Take it for all in all, it was perhaps the happiest day he had ever known in his life; not even excepting that on which his heroic partner had approached the nuptial altar to the tune of the Dead March in Saul.[38]

The narrative betrays him. Dickens could not leave his wife for a mistress and be the hero; but a man could express dissatisfaction with his wife and show love for his children and thus redeem himself. This is the narrative of Mr Wilfer, and the narrative that Dickens tried to portray at the time of his separation.

If Dickens is fantasising here in *Our Mutual Friend*, elsewhere in the novel he gives vent to his bitterness on matrimony. Mr and Mrs Lammle are married in the tenth chapter of the book; in the very same chapter that recalls their happy union, Dickens then cuts to two weeks later where they discover that both are poor, and both were lying about their own prospects in order to ensnare a wealthy partner, much to one other's bitter disappointment.

> 'Do you pretend to believe,' Mrs Lammle resumes, sternly, 'when you talk of my marrying you for worldly advantages, that it was within the bounds of reasonable probability that I would have married you for yourself?'
>
> 'Again there are two sides to the question, Mrs Lammle. What do you pretend to believe?'
>
> 'So you first deceive me and then insult me!' cries the lady, with a heaving bosom.
>
> 'Not at all. I have originated nothing. The double-edged question was yours.'[39]

This is a scathing attack on the falsity of marriage. Each has been attracted by the other's perceived position over and above any genuine affection for them as a person. Is it possible Dickens felt similar dissatisfaction at the end of his marriage with the daughter of George Hogarth? Would he have married Catherine for her own merits, or was he attracted to her position and family when making his choice of bride? The bitterness of the Lammles continues beyond their initial disappointment to the claustrophobic realisation of their now being stuck with one another, and the shame of public scrutiny which would attend any sense of their unhappiness:

> But the folly is committed on both sides. I cannot get rid of you; you cannot get rid of me. What follows?'
>
> 'Shame and misery,' the bride bitterly replies.
>
> [...] 'it's enough to have been done, without the mortification of being known to have been done. So we agree to keep the fact to ourselves. You agree?'
>
> 'If it is possible, I do.'
>
> 'Possible! We have pretended well enough to one another. Can't we, united, pretend to the world? Agreed.'[40]

The Lammles' attempts to swindle each other are sensational enough to be dismissed as fiction, but this commitment to hiding their subsequent disappointment and pretending to be a happy couple is more universal: their regret at their choice of partner is compounded by the recognition that they cannot part, and their inner misery is tempered by a desire never to let the wider world know they are unhappy. The divorce act of 1857 meant that unhappy marriages were a topical subject, but for all the fears of widespread divorce the reality for most couples was that the situation remained unchanged: marriage was for life. Thus comes the great British tradition of keeping up appearances – to let others know that your marriage was unhappy was to pour additional shame upon yourself. The Wilfer and Lammle marriages both propose the same commentary, that most married couples are unhappier than they let on to the wider word. This is rather a gloomy outlook, but coming from Dickens's experience it makes more sense. The author is writing about what he knows, and his experience of marriage is decidedly this sort of arrangement. His brief flirtation with Maria Beadnell shows that the separation was not due specifically to Ellen Ternan, but rather that he was already dissatisfied at that point and looking wistfully at other opportunities both past and present. The more he presented the façade of being the perfect family man, in a happy marriage, the more his resentment is likely to have grown.

In contrast to this sensation of entrapment in a loveless marriage, Dickens also explores the idea of repressed love and uncontrollable urges in *Our Mutual Friend*. Eugene Wrayburn, a listless gentleman with financial security but no real ambition, becomes enamoured with Lizzie Hexam, a poor but earnest girl who works on the river. They are an incompatible match in the eyes of society, and Eugene knows it. The assumption of all is that he must have untoward designs to the young girl, similar to that of the many rakes in literature who seduce then abandon poor unsuspecting victims. Eugene's friend Mortimer challenges him on this point:

> 'Are you in communication with this girl, Eugene, and is what these people say true?'
> 'I concede both admissions to my honourable and learned friend.'
> 'Then what is to come of it? What are you doing? Where are you going?'[41]

Eugene is stuck between his desires and the limitations of social expectations. Mortimer's questioning reveals the underlying gossip and scandal surrounding the relationship, whatever it may be. It could very well be the same questions addressed to the author about Ellen Ternan. The specificity of Mortimer's questions identifies the different options available to Eugene alongside the unsuitability of them all:

'Eugene, do you design to capture and desert this girl?'

'My dear fellow, no.'

'Do you design to marry her?'

'My dear fellow, no.'

'Do you design to pursue her?'

'My dear fellow, I don't design anything. I have no design whatever. I am incapable of designs. If I conceived a design, I should speedily abandon it, exhausted by the operation.'[42]

Eugene does not know what to do. He does not choose to abandon Lizzie, nor to use for her a brief affair and then move on. He cannot marry her – the social uproar is too much for him to consider. But yet he still sees her, spends time with her, knowing the rumours that will circulate, but still needing to see her regardless. It is difficult *not* to see Dickens's own predicament in this. What were his intentions towards Ternan, and how did these come into conflict with what the society of the time would not allow? If Eugene is without a design, then so too was Dickens in 1858. Ternan offered him what he wanted, but not what he was allowed. To be with her he had to part from his wife, but a divorce was out of the question. Separating from his wife to be with another woman was equally incompatible with his position and public relations. And yet he chose to be with her. The way in which he writes about it in Eugene and Lizzie's relationship both puts Lizzie on a pedestal, as a diamond in the rough, while also implicitly holding her responsible for Eugene's actions. As much as she can be seen as a positive influence on him, she is an influence nonetheless, prompting him to take action that causes consternation in his peers. If Dickens is using his fiction to fantasise about tyrannical wives and hapless husbands, so too he is exploring the idea of young innocent sirens leading otherwise rational men astray. This is brought to a height in the character of Bradley Headstone, who is also infatuated with Lizzie. But if Eugene's feelings for Lizzie are ultimately positive and benevolent, Headstone is decidedly destructive and malevolent. His ravings give full rein to the darkest side of Dickens's imagination:

Yes! you are the ruin – the ruin – the ruin – of me. I have no resources in myself, I have no confidence in myself, I have no government of myself when you are near me or in my thoughts. And you are always in my thoughts now. I have never been quit of you since I first saw you. Oh, that was a wretched day for me! That was a wretched, miserable day![43]

This is hardly romantic. Headstone's reaction to meeting this beautiful woman is entirely negative, full of self-pity and self-loathing. How much simpler his life would have been, he assumes, had he never met Lizzie. Did Dickens ever wonder this himself about Ternan? If he did, it is as deluded a thought as Headstone's. If Dickens had not met Ternan, there is a strong chance he would have met someone else instead; however genuine their relationship may have been, it is difficult to avoid the sense that its origin stemmed equally from a dissatisfaction with Catherine, and his own midlife crisis of finding himself to be in a mundane marriage rather than the high romance of his fantasies. Dickens would return again to the psyche of Headstone in the character of John Jasper in his final book *The Mystery of Edwin Drood*: he too has uncontrollable, but inappropriate, urges for a young woman leading to self-loathing and destruction. Before we completely abandon all hope in Dickens, it is worth remembering just how much he exaggerated his childhood sufferings in *David Copperfield*, and to state, for any who have forgotten it, that Dickens was a writer of fiction. His writings do not immediately translate to strict autobiography, and whenever he does use his own experiences he will frequently adapt, change, edit and heighten that experience to create a suitable dramatic result. In Headstone and Jasper, Dickens is indulging the darker side of his personality; it does not mean that these thoughts held any real sway in his own life, but it does show the potential within him which he unleashed for this fiction. For a man who so carefully maintained the public perception of himself as 'Mr. Popular Sentiment', giving rein to his darkest urges in his fiction must have been a therapeutic release.[44]

Notes

1 Dickens, 'Personal Statement'. The statement first appeared in *The Times* on 7 June 1858 and was published in *Household Words*, 12 June 1858, p. 601.

2 Dickens, The Violated Letter, in Graham Storey and Kathleen Tillotson (ed.), *The Letters of Charles Dickens*, Volume Eight 1856–1858 (Oxford: Clarendon Press, 1995), pp. 740–741 (p. 740).

3 Dickens, Letter to Emile de la Rue, 25 January 1845, in Kathleen Tillotson (ed.), *The Letters of Charles Dickens*, Volume Four (Oxford: Clarendon Press, 1977), pp. 249–250 (p. 249).

4 Dickens, Letter to Emile de la Rue, 27 January 1845, in *Letters*, Vol. 4, pp. 252–255 (p. 254).

5 Dickens, Letter to Emile de La Rue, 27 January 1845, in *Letters*, Vol. 4, pp. 252–255 (pp. 253–254).

6 Dickens, Letter to Augusta de La Rue, 17 April 1846, in *Letters*, Vol. 4, pp. 533–535 (p. 534).

7 Charles Dickens to Catherine Dickens, 5 December 1853, in Graham Storey, Kathleen Tillotson and Angus Easson (ed.), *The Letters of Charles Dickens*, Volume Seven 1853–1855 (Oxford: Clarendon Press, 1993), pp. 223–225 (p. 224).

8 Dickens, Letter to Maria Beadnell, 5 February 1855, in *Letters*, Vol. 7, pp. 538–539 (p. 539).

9 Charles Dickens to Maria Winter (nee Beadnell), 10 February 1855 in *Letters*, Vol.7, pp. 532–534 (pp. 532–533).

10 Charles Dickens, *Little Dorrit*, ed. by Harvey Peter Sucksmith (Oxford: OUP, 1979), Book 1, Chapter 13, p. 143.

11 Dickens, Letter to Maria Beadnell, in Madeline House and Graham Storey (ed.), *The Letters of Charles Dickens*, Volume One 1820–1839 (Oxford: Clarendon Press, 1965), pp. 16–17 (pp. 16–17).

12 *Little Dorrit*, Book 1, Chapter 13, p. 144.

13 Dickens, Letter to Maria Winter(nee Beadnell), 15 February 1855, in *Letters*, Vol. 7, pp. 538–539 (p. 538).

14 Letter to Forster, 1857 (cited in Michael Slater, *The Great Charles Dickens Scandal* (New Haven: Yale University Press, 2012), p. 10).

15 Dickens, Letter to Angela Burdett Coutts, 23 August 1858, in *Letters*, Vol. 8, pp. 632–634 (p. 632).

16 Dickens, The violated Letter, in *Letters*, Vol. 8, pp. 740–741 (p. 740).

17 John Baldwin Buckstone, *Uncle John: a petite comedy in two acts* (London: John Miller, 1833), p. 12.

18 Charles Dickens and WIlkie Collins, *The Lazy Tour of the Two Idle Apprentices*, Chapter the Fifth, *Household Words*, 31 October 1857, pp. 409–416 (p. 411).

19 Dickens, Letter to W. H. Wills, 17 September 1857, in *Letters*, Vol. 8, pp. 448–449 (p. 449).

20 Dickens, The violated Letter, in *Letters*, Vol. 8, pp. 740–741 (p. 740).

21 Dickens, The violated Letter, in *Letters*, Vol. 8, pp. 740–741 (p. 740).

22 Dickens, Letter to Anne Cornelius, 11 October 1857, in *Letters*, Vol. 8, p. 465 (p. 465).

23 Claire Tomalin, *The Invisible Woman* (London: Penguin, 1991), p. 108.

24 Nayder, p. 1.

25 Dickens, Letter to William Macready, 7 June 1858, in *Letters*, Vol. 8, pp. 579–580 (p. 579).

26 Dickens, Letter to Catherine Dickens, 4 June 1858, in *Letters*, Vol. 8, pp. 578–579 (578).

27 Tomalin, p. 111.

28 John Bowen, 'Unmutual friend: How Dickens tried to place his wife in an asylum', *Times Literary Supplement*, 22 February 2019, https://www.the-tls.co.uk/articles/how-dickens-tried-to-place-wife-in-asylum-essay-john-bowen.

29 I am grateful to Deborah Siddoway, who generously shared her professional expertise of the law in many enjoyable conversations about Dickens and the Divorce act.

30 For a full account of the press reaction to Dickens's separation, see Patrick Leary, 'How the Dickens Scandal Went Viral', in Hazel Mackenzie and Ben Winyard (ed.), *Charles Dickens and the Mid-Victorian Press, 1850–1870* (Buckingham: University of Buckingham Press, 2013), pp. 305–325.

31 William Thackeray, Letter to his mother, May 1858, cited in Michael Slater, *Charles Dickens* (New Haven: Yale, 2011), p. 453.

32 Slater, p. 455.

33 Dickens, Letter to Charles Dickens Jnr, 10–12 July 1858, in *Letters*, Vol. 8, pp. 602–603 (p. 603).

34 Gladys Storey, *Dickens and Daughter* (London: Frederick Muller, 1939). For a full account of how awareness of Dickens and Ternan's relationship grew, see Slater, *The Great Charles Dickens Scandal*.

35 Charles Dickens, *Our Mutual Friend*, ed. by Michael Cotsell (Oxford, OUP, 2008), Book 1, Ch. 4, p. 32.

36 *Our Mutual Friend*, Book 1, Ch. 4, pp. 33–34.

37 *Our Mutual Friend*, Book 2 Ch 8, pp. 316–317.

38 *Our Mutual Friend*, Book 2, Ch. 8, p. 318.

39 *Our Mutual Friend*, Book 1, Ch. 10, p. 124.

40 *Our Mutual Friend*, Book 1, Ch. 10, p. 126.

41 *Our Mutual Friend*, Book 2, Ch. 6, p. 295.

42 *Our Mutual Friend*, Book 2, Ch. 6, p. 294.

43 *Our Mutual Friend*, Book 2, Ch. 15, p. 395.

44 Anthony Trollope, *The Warden*, ed. by Robin Gilmour (London: Penguin, 1984), Ch. 15, p. 131.

11

Dickens on Tour

Focal Point: 1858–1870

Case Study: Sikes and Nancy

Imagine the opportunity to hear Dickens himself reading his own works aloud – it is a tantalising prospect and one that understandably proved popular with his contemporaries. Dickens's public reading tours took him across the UK and USA, closing the gap between reader and writer, allowing them to experience the story together at point of transmission. Dickens's experience of reading to an audience started much earlier, and on a non-professional basis, to small groups of friends and family, before extending to charity performances in public. However, the success of these and the lucrative potential they offered tempted Dickens into launching his professional readings. If they proved financially beneficial, they also satisfied another need in Dickens, to see the reactions of his readers, and witness first-hand the power he held over them as they grew transfixed by his stories; it also allowed him to further indulge his long-held dreams of acting. Today, the readings are a difficult animal to study: Dickens was performing while recording technology was in its very early stages, so no audio of any performance exists. Instead, we have the edited texts he used, with annotations and notes, and the first-hand accounts of various audience members from which we can piece together what it would have been like to be in the room as Dickens read, but this still accounts to a historical re-enactment of the experience.

The remaining question is how we qualify the readings in relation to Dickens's writings: are they an act of creation in themselves or merely reprisals of previous works of creation? When Dickens read from his works, was he creating or recreating art? Do the resulting works, and any edits involved, carry less or more authority than the earlier forms of the texts? These are some of the questions I'll be considering in this chapter, but for Dickens and his contemporaries both the appeal and concern were more straightforward: fans were excited to hear the author read his works (and sometimes disappointed if certain elements did not meet their expectations), while detractors felt it was unbecoming of an author to parade himself upon the stage. Whether

The Life of the Author: Charles Dickens, First Edition. Pete Orford.
© 2023 John Wiley & Sons Ltd. Published 2023 by John Wiley & Sons Ltd.

supporting or criticising the tour, one thing was clear: Dickens taking to the road promoted himself specifically, turning him into a nineteenth-century celebrity as recognised and popular as his works.

The Early Readings

How do we define when Dickens's readings began? The extreme would be to point back to those early performances with his father in the local pub performing comic monologues from Charles Matthews's repertoire, or the stories Dickens told to his family and school friends while a child. In *David Copperfield* he imagines David telling stories at school to Steerforth, an arrangement which David recalls 'inspired me with great pride and satisfaction'.[1]

> What ravages I committed on my favourite authors in the course of my interpretation of them, I am not in a condition to say, and should be very unwilling to know; but I had a profound faith in them, and I had, to the best of my belief, a simple, earnest manner of narrating what I did narrate; and these qualities went a long way.[2]

It is not unreasonable to imagine the young Dickens engaged in a similar pursuit in his schooldays. Similarly, another fictional retelling of Dickens's past recalls ghost stories 'by my nurse before I was six years old'; and this nurse has traditionally been interpreted as Mary Weller who worked for the Dickens family in Chatham.[3] None of these recollections are conclusive, and the fictional texts in particular need to be treated carefully, but together they create a reasonably accurate impression of the young Dickens as audience and speaker. As a member of an audience Dickens could witness the power of storytelling; as a speaker he could experience that power first-hand. Dickens continued exploring this power as he matured, performing sections of his work to friends and family. What did Dickens hope to gain from this – and for that matter, what was in it for his audience? For Dickens, it was an opportunity to test out his writing and get immediate feedback before publication; it was also opportunity for praise and recognition. For his audience, there was a privilege in being first to hear the latest instalment and to be part of that select circle. There is also an indication that Dickens was a very effective reader of his own works – and he knew it. When he gave the private reading of *The Chimes* to Macready on 1 December 1844, Dickens reports Macready 'undisguisedly sobbing, and crying on the sofa, as I read', and when he performed it again the following night for a larger circle of friends, Daniel Maclise said 'there was not a dry eye in the house' and, significantly, then contextualised the private reading in a theatrical framework: [4]

> We should borrow the high language of the minor theatre and even then not do the effect justice – shrieks of laughter – there were indeed – and floods of tears as a relief to the – I do not think that there was ever such a triumphant hour for Charles[.][5]

Often the responses to Dickens's early readings were in praise of his performance as much as the content. When he had trialled his play *The Lamplighter* to Macready, the actor may have dismissed 'the meagreness of the plot' but he nonetheless marvelled at the execution of Dickens's reading: 'He reads as well as an experienced actor would – he is a surprising man.'[6] But in many senses the performance and content were linked, as can be witnessed in Dickens's writing practice. His daughter Mamie recalls seeing her father writing one day in Tavistock House when she was ill and allowed to join him in the study while she rested:

> I was lying on the sofa endeavouring to keep perfectly quiet, while my father wrote busily and rapidly at his desk, when he suddenly jumped from his chair and rushed to a mirror which hung near, and in which I could see the reflection of some extraordinary facial contortions which he was making. He returned rapidly to his desk, wrote furiously for a few moments, and then went again to the mirror. The facial pantomime was resumed, and then turning toward, but evidently not seeing, me, he began talking rapidly in a low voice. Ceasing this soon, however, he returned once more to his desk, where he remained silently writing until luncheon time.[7]

For Dickens, writing was a performance, in which he would embody each character, and then report that performance as seen either in the mirror or his mind. The implication then is that Dickens had a specific reading of his works in mind, a particular way to intone and emphasise particular words and beats. But once the words were written down, it was then up to the reader how to interpret them. Punctuation can do so much, but ultimately Dickens was relinquishing control to each reader to adapt his words to their own reading style. There are contemporary accounts of household readings, where the father would read the latest instalment first, then read it again to the family. Dickens and the reader became collaborators in the performed version that the rest of the family would experience. By being the reader himself, Dickens assumed complete control of the performance. The reading of *The Chimes* was a welcome treat for Dickens as much as, if not more than, his select audience – so much so that he travelled several miles on a return trip from Italy specifically to do these readings. But he was still only reaching a small amount of people compared to the multitudes who were reading his works. Unsurprisingly, Dickens began to do larger readings.

Once again, that stigma over professional performances played a part. Dickens was able to enjoy a gentleman's status while acting through the loophole of 'amateur' performances; the same logic meant that doing readings for money rather than charity raised concerns about commercialism and vulgarity. Being an author was a literary pursuit, but to go on stage and perform his works crossed the line into acting, and suggested too much familiarity with the audience. Charity performances allowed Dickens to indulge his fantasy without compromising his reputation. The first public readings, for charity, were on 27, 29 and 30 of December 1853 at Birmingham Town Hall, where Dickens read *A Christmas Carol* on two nights and *The Cricket on the Hearth* on the middle night. The following December he performed the *Carol* three times in different locations, followed by sporadic readings in March, October and December of 1855, and June, July and December of 1857, all of the *Carol*. There is no overarching schedule dictating these performances; they appear to be mostly responsive rather than heavily planned, with Dickens agreeing to help out various institutions by offering his time. The performances were predominately in London and Kent, with some readings further afield in Reading, Bradford, Peterborough, Sheffield, Manchester and Coventry. For the most part these were individual events rather than a planned tour, centred around helping local institutions and charities. The choice of the *Carol* for each of these readings further emphasised their charitable nature in the story's implicit call to do more for the people around us. Nonetheless, however much these events were billed as charitable, they proved popular, and it must have been clear to Dickens that the potential lay there for a more organised and prolonged series of readings. Dickens's charitable performances would continue through to 1866, but from 1858 onwards they would not be his sole public readings, but rather would be interspersed between the professional reading tour he now commenced on.

The First UK Tour

The decision to go professional was made against the advice of Forster. Dickens had first aired the idea as early as 1846, highly conscious himself that '[i]t would be an *odd* thing' but convinced that 'it would take immensely.'[8] Forster advised against it, later calling it 'a substitution of lower for higher aims, a change to commonplace from more elevated pursuits', and Dickens initially conceded.[9] It is noticeable that Dickens's early suggestion comes only eight years after Forster himself had been encouraging Dickens into writing for the stage; clearly a distinction was felt between writing and performing. Forster worried that to actually go on stage would have 'so much of the character of a public exhibition for money as to raise, in the question of respect for his calling as a writer, a question also of respect for himself as a gentleman.'[10] However, Dickens had proved there was a public appetite for the readings through the subsequent charity performances, which encouraged him to once again consider 'reviving that old idea of some Readings from my books'.[11] What had changed since 1846? Well, two things: first, the status of the actor was improving. Russell Jackson notes that 'by the end of the century, the profession had found a new kind of recognition'; he cites Henry James who in 1879 noted that in addition to actors joining society, so too 'the people of society appear on the stage ... as if the great gate which formerly divided the theatre from the world had been lifted off its hinges.'[12] This was a gradual movement that had been taking place incrementally throughout Dickens's life; Malcolm Andrews notes that the 1861 census was the first to recognise actor as a professional status.[13] The second evolution to pave the way for Dickens's readings was that other public readings had become increasingly popular in the 1850s, though it was still rare for the authors themselves to read their own works.

Nonetheless, steps were taken to avoid the readings being too much like a theatrical performance. Dickens put great care and attention into the details of his staging, which would be decidedly simple and low-key [see Figure 11.1]. A plain backdrop would be suspended behind, and a reading desk was built, to Dickens's own designs, which he would stand behind or next to. The desk was tall, with a raised platform for the book to rest on, and a glass of water. Lighting was low and homely, illuminating Dickens's face and figure. This all had two effects: the first was to create the illusion of a cosy home atmosphere; despite the packed theatre, the intended experience was a recreation of all those private readings Dickens had done before, so that audiences were not see-ing a dramatic performance but rather a gentleman reading in his study. The staging stressed the unsensational aspect of the readings to create the illusion of appropriate decorum. Conversely, the second effect was that there were no distractions on stage to divert the audience's eye away from Dickens, who thus enjoyed their full attention. This was a star performance, with Dickens him-self as the main draw for those queuing up to buy tickets. The presence of a book proved to be as much of a prop as a required tool; Andrews notes that 'by the time Dickens turned professional, he was already partly independent of the script, so the book in his hand could be lowered away from time to time, and even rested down on the prop.'[14] The readings, for all their homely

Figure 11.1   C. A. Barnes, 'Charles Dickens as he appears when reading', 1867.

presentations and insistence upon their non-theatricality, increasingly evolved into dramatic performances rather than mere recitals.

Dickens's first professional reading was *The Cricket on the Hearth* on 29 April 1858. He had performed this just once before, among the many readings of the *Carol*, and the fact that he did not start his professional readings with the more tried and tested work shows an eagerness on his part to experiment and vary the performances, much like a band on tour eager to do more than just 'play that one song' that everyone knows. Slater notes how '[t]he Christmas books were an obvious quarry for Dickens's readings repertoire' due to 'their novella-type length' allowing an almost complete reading in under two hours, something that would simply not be possible with the novels.[15] When we look at the texts performed by Dickens, we can see performances of *The Chimes* also included; Dickens also prepared a version of *The Haunted Man* though this never got performed. The *Carol* still loomed large as the most often performed text, but he also began to balance the clear popularity and desire for this text with intermissions of different works, creating new readings based on extracts and subplots of his larger novels so he could, in his own words, take 'a swim in the broader waters of one of my long books.'[16] From *Dombey and Son* he took the narrative of Paul Dombey and performed 'The Story of Little Dombey',

Martin Chuzzlewit was diluted to produce the reading 'Mrs. Gamp'; *Pickwick* edited to present just 'Bardell and Pickwick'; 'David Copperfield' did not attempt the entirety of the novel but rather focused on the characters of Ham and Little Em'ly; *Nicholas Nickleby* produced 'Nicholas Nickleby at the Yorkshire School'; and *Pickwick* was drawn upon a second time for 'Mr. Bob Sawyer's Party'. In creating these readings, Dickens was identifying either those episodes within the novels which could operate as standalone narratives, or instead selecting a particular character and focusing purely on their story. Theoretically this would allow a newcomer to follow the episode more easily, but in practice the majority of the audience would most likely be familiar with the parent text already, so that the reading did not operate as an introduction to the text so much as a revisiting of it. These episodic readings were joined by others based on the Christmas Numbers Dickens had been writing along with others for his journals: 'The Poor Traveller', 'Boots at the Holly-Tree Inn', 'Doctor Marigold', and 'Barbox Brothers' and 'The Boy at Mugby'. A letter in January 1866 is particularly insightful in relation to Dickens's requirements for a reading text, and the way in which the perception of the readings was changing. He discusses the possibility of adapting *Mrs. Lirriper* and *Doctor Marigold* (of which only the latter was performed):

> Mrs Lirriper has also occurred to *me*. The difficulty is (the old lady herself being the narrator) that it must be done with little change of voice; and I am afraid I have accustomed the audience to expect variety in that wise. If I do Doctor Marigold – objection would be strengthened by his being in much the same plight. It would be a small objection in a small place but expands in proportion to the size of the Hall. The greater the room and the larger the audience, the more imperative the necessity for something dramatic. Remember the little unchanging figure, seen from afar off, and the very little action that can be got from a bird's-eye view of that table.[17]

After the initially cautious approach of ensuring the readings were definitely not theatrical, Dickens was now talking of them in precisely that way, focusing on the need for action to please great rooms and large audiences. A simple reading was no longer enough, nor what the audience wanted: a more dramatic performance was called for instead. This was not only the audience's desire; the preference for readings with multiple voices also betrays Dickens's own preference. Inspired by his childhood hero Charles Matthews and his monopolylogues, such readings allowed Dickens the opportunity to show off his virtuosity – an opportunity he had previously indulged in with the 1851 farce *Mr. Nightingale's Diary*, in which his character Mr Gabblewig has to adopt a number of different personas.

It is particularly interesting that a number of the readings were based on recent works, some of which were written after Dickens had begun his reading tour: *Doctor Marigold's Prescriptions* and *Mugby Junction* were written in 1865 and 1866 respectively. Given that other Christmas numbers had already proved their potential for readings, how much was Dickens thinking about the possibility of future readings while writing these stories for print? *Doctor Marigold* in particular has a much more coherent structure and concept than some of the earlier Christmas numbers. Dickens was writing it in November 1865, and performing it as a reading in April 1866; as the letter above shows, he was discussing adapting it as early as January 1866, with reservations. Even in March those reservations persisted; he told Forster 'I have gotten him [*Doctor Marigold*] up with immense pains', betraying the work involved, yet he also admitted 'I rely for mere curiosity' for sales.[18] At barely four months it was a new and untested work next to the likes of the *Carol*. His fears were unfounded and he ended up performing *Doctor Marigold* seventy-six times. Perhaps because of this, he shows far more confidence later that year; in December (by which point he had performed *Doctor Marigold* sixteen times already) he was already planning to adapt that year's Christmas number, *Mugby Junction*:

> Now, as I propose to read the Boy, when we want anything new – and Barbox also – and as so many thousands of people have this fresh interest in my books, I am very strong for beginning as soon after, Xmas as possible.[19]

Dickens's confidence was well-founded; the day after he wrote to his sister Letitia saying that *Mugby Junction* was already an 'astonishing number of *40,000* ahead of even Doctor Marigold at the same time'.[20] Given the success of he had experienced adapting the last year's number into a reading, this new number, with its higher sales, must surely be a hit. He prepared three pieces: 'Barbox Brothers', 'The Boy at Mugby' and 'The Signalman', though the last one was never performed (which is somewhat ironic as today it is the most celebrated story in the collection). But lightning did not strike twice, and the readings based on *Mugby Junction* did not prove as successful as 'Doctor Marigold'; Dickens's tour manager George Dolby records the new reading 'was received cordially by the audience, but it was apparent that it would never take rank with the other works of its kind' and were it not 'for the fact that the Reading was already announced for some of the towns in the early part of the tour, it is probable that "Barbox" and "The Boy" would have been shelved, then and there.'[21] Given that Dickens had been thinking about the number as a reading so early, it is not unreasonable to consider that the public readings might have reversed the level of influence, so that rather than being adaptations of the published works, they began to directly inform the composition of new works: in other words, Dickens may well have been writing the prose with a mind to performing it dramatically. While 'Barbox' and 'The Boy' both have first person narrators, they also offer multiple voices within that narration to offer Dickens precisely the type of performance he favoured. This is especially evident in the opening of 'Barbox'; not just it's reading version, but the original story that appeared in print first:

> 'Guard! What place is this?'
> 'Mugby Junction, sir.'
> 'A windy place!'
> 'Yes, it mostly is, sir.'
> 'And looks comfortless indeed!'
> 'Yes, it generally does, sir.'
> 'Is it a rainy night still?'
> 'Pours, sir.'
> 'Open the door. I'll get out.'[22]

Dickens wrote the opening as pure dialogue; it may as well be the script for the reading (which replicates this opening exactly). Likewise, the unperformed script for 'The Signalman' is barely edited from the print copy. Just as Dickens's experience as a shorthand writer had rewired the way he saw words, his prolonged time doing the readings was impacting on how he conceived and wrote the Christmas numbers, anticipating their potential performance.

The UK tour was a great success, with positive reviews confirming the sagacity of Dickens's decision despite Forster's misgivings. However much the readings might compromise his position as a gentleman, the sheer financial success of them put any such doubts to rest. Moreover, Dickens's reputation was not diminished by the experiment, but enhanced. Mr Household Words was now forging a more direct link with his audience. The timing of the professional readings with the very public separation between Dickens and his wife is unlikely to be purely coincidental. Both can be said to be prompted by the same symptoms of restlessness. It is unlikely that the tours were intended as crisis management, but nonetheless Dickens going on the road to meet his readers proved an effective way to protect his brand and establish himself as the people's writer regardless. The most likely reason for Dickens's continued involvement with the tours – beyond the financial benefits, of course – is the potential for a more personal need for the reassurance these readings offered. Stand-up comedians regularly note the satisfaction and confirmation that comes from performing in front of an audience who have all come to hear and enjoy their words; at a time when his personal life was in crisis, going on the road to meet rooms of adoring fans must have been a welcome and alluring respite. Buoyed by both the financial success and adulation, Dickens planned to take the tour overseas, returning to America.

Throughout his reading tours, Dickens was accompanied by a tour manager: first Arthur Smith, then Thomas Headland, then George Dolby. Slater notes that Dickens had 'considerable fondness' for Smith, who proved a loyal companion during Dickens's public separation from his wife; it was to Smith that Dickens wrote the violated letter, which Smith showed liberally as per Dickens's request to ensure his side of the story was publicised and ticket sales unaffected.[23] Sadly, Smith died in 1861. Dolby had been suggested to Dickens three years earlier, by Dolby's sister Charlotte, a singer for whom her brother had already acted as a tour manager. At the time Dickens politely declined, as he had not 'the remotest idea of severing [him]self from Arthur Smith', claiming 'I have every conceivable reason to regard him as one of my most trusty friends, nor can I easily imagine myself treading the same road again without him.'[24] But now, in 1861, Dickens had no choice but to imagine that situation.

> Poor Mr Arthur Smith is dead; and as I knew very little of the Reading arrangements he had made for me, I have been greatly at a loss – only knowing generally that I was bound to read fifty times, and but dimly knowing where or when.[25]

What is remarkable in this is the reliance Dickens shows upon Smith (and furthermore his admittance of that reliance). In many aspects of his life Dickens frequently exerted his authority and control, whether that be in his amateur dramatics, the writing of his works or his marriage. Now he was beginning to recognise the benefits of delegation, whether that be to his tour manager, or trusty Wills back in the office. With Smith gone, his assistant Headland was temporarily appointed, but it was Dolby who would ultimately take on the role, proving to be an equal match for the Inimitable. Not dissimilar to the Brave Courier Louis Roche, the relationship which sparked between them was a fine balance between master, servant and friends. Dolby helped organise Dickens on the road while Wills was back in London organising the journals. His memoirs of their time together have emphasised their relationship in a similar manner to how Forster's biography has forever established him as one of Dickens's closest confidantes in the public imagination.

The USA Tour

The last time Dickens had been in America, he had travelled with his wife and been alternately bemused and exasperated by the constant intrusions into their privacy by eager Americans wanting to come in and meet him. Now he was visiting America again in a much stricter professional capacity, capitalising on that eagerness of his American audience and deliberately putting himself out to market. This came at a cost: Ternan did not accompany him. Given that he would be in America for five months, this was an unwelcome separation (although it should be recalled that he experienced a longer separation from his children during his first American tour). As noted in Chapter 10, Dickens agreed to send Ternan a coded message once in America: telegraphing 'all well means *You come*' whereas telegraphing 'Safe and well means *You don't come*'; Dickens was keen for Ternan to join him but had to survey the lay of the land first, which proved too public and the second message was sent on 22 November 1867.[26] Nonetheless, the elaborate planning of this coded message evidence the desire on Dickens's part that she could join him.

The American tour proved to be a punishing schedule, both in the physical amount of travelling required and the amount of time, effort and energy expended both in the readings themselves and the significant number of public dinners and events which Dickens was subsequently invited to. This was not a relaxing break away but a professional tour. Dickens was now in his mid-50s, and the boundless energy that had propelled him through life was beginning to wear thin. But the audience enthusiasm was insatiable. The second USA tour allowed opportunity for Dickens to repair his reputation after the controversies of his first visit and his subsequent comments in *American Notes*. While copyright laws had not changed, Dickens had become more proactive in working with American publishers to ensure he enjoyed some profit from transatlantic sales. He had been sending advance copies of manuscripts to select publishers to allow them to publish ahead of their competitors. Now that he was touring the states, he worked with his friend James Fields to ensure a ready supply of merchandise. Ticknor and Fields produced the Diamond Edition of Dickens's works, and special reading copies were also produced so that audiences could, in theory, read along (or attempt to recreate a reading after the event). One of the regular visitors to Dickens's performances in America was Kate Field, who would later go on tour herself performing 'An Evening with Charles Dickens' where she passed on what she had learned to others.[27] In this way, the experience of seeing Dickens extended from a first-hand one to a second-hand one, with audiences remaining keen for that glimpse of proximity to the author.

Of course, the weight of expectation could prove too much in some cases. Mark Twain expressed disappointment with Dickens's voice, which was not as warm and welcoming as he had imagined:

> Mr Dickens' reading is rather monotonous, as a general thing; his voice is husky; his pathos is only the beautiful pathos of his language – there is no heart, no feeling in it – it is glittering frostwork.[28]

The disappointment is informed as much by Twain's expectations of what Dickens would (or should) sound like as much as an objective review of the performance before him, with Dickens's pronunciation of Steerforth as 'St'yawfuth' prompting Twain's bizarre (and one might think, obvious) criticism that Dickens was 'a little Englishy in his speech'.[29] Yes, the reading tours allowed Dickens to stamp his own reading of the texts upon the public ear, but for many years his readers had been hearing these characters and plots in their own voice. To what extent could Dickens now claim authority over his own works when they had existed in the public imagination for so long? Dickens himself seemed to recognised the multiplicity of readings even while conducting his own; in 1866 he wrote to the Rev Henry Blink who planned to perform *A Christmas Carol* for his local Penny Reading Society:

> I beg to assure you that you have my full permission to carry out your purpose of reading my Christmas Carol in public. But my correspondents are far too numerous, to leave me leisure for explaining how I am accustomed to condense it when I read it myself.[30]

Dickens is happy for there to be other people reading his works; but the brevity of the reply, and Dickens's reluctance to share details on his own reading (which Blink had already attended as an audience member), shows the limitations of Dickens's goodwill. It was advantageous for there to be multiple readings of Dickens's works, but even better to secure a sense of uniqueness to Dickens's own readings. No other reader could ever claim the same authority that Dickens himself could. Unsurprisingly then, despite the misgivings indicated by Twain, the overwhelming response to the reading tour was positive. In turn, Dickens's enthusiasm for America proved mutual; it was this return visit to the country which prompted his public apology for his earlier comments (discussed in Chapter 5), along with a commitment that this apology would be published in every subsequent edition of *Martin Chuzzlewit* and *American Notes*.

The Final UK Tour

After his return to the UK, Dickens added two new works to his repertoire: 'Mr. Chops, the Dwarf' from *A House to Let* and 'Sikes and Nancy' from *Oliver Twist*. The latter was a stark departure from Dickens's previous reading material. Other readings tended to be comic (e.g. 'Mrs. Gamp'), or sentimental, be that either cheering and heart-warming (e.g the *Carol*), or pathetically tragic (e.g. 'The Story of Little Dombey'). 'Sikes and Nancy' was quite different; a violent, sensational piece detailing the brutal murder of Nancy at Sikes's hands. This departed radically from the cosy, gentleman's salon atmosphere of the other readings and plunged headfirst into the more dramatic, theatrical element of the readings. It comes from a point of confidence in Dickens's reputation that he could take this risk now. He could not have opened his professional readings with such a performance, but having worked hard to establish the normality and appropriateness of an author performing public readings, he could now experiment further with those readings. Whether he was doing this to challenge his readers or himself is not clear; I suspect the latter was a more pressing concern, as the continued popularity of the *Carol* suggests Dickens could easily have continued to just perform that one reading on endless repeat and still draw in a crowd. But instead he sought to demonstrate his full dramatic range, to terrify the audiences who had come to enjoy a pleasant evening. Just like his earlier experiences of mesmerising Mme de la Rue, the real draw here was power: the power to command his audience's full attention, to elevate their heart rates and create sensational effects upon them. It coincides with the rise of the sensation novel that had been proving so popular for authors like Mary Elizabeth Braddon and Dickens's close friend Wilkie Collins, but it also speaks to Dickens's own dramatic dreams. After Dickens's reading of *Sikes and Nancy* he proudly told Georgina 'Macready is of the opinion that the Murder is "Two Macbeths".'[31] Part of this likely harkens back to Dickens's own whimsical fantasies of being an actor, that meant he was especially keen to hear feedback related to the performance of the reading as much as the content. This was no longer a reading but a fully dramatic performance.

If it elevated his audience's heart-rate, it had an even more dramatic effect on Dickens himself. The exhaustion of the tour was now exacerbated by the physical and psychological strain of performing this brutal and exerting scene on a regular basis. Dickens was killing himself for his craft. If he could, he would have carried on for much longer; he considered plans to take the tour to Australia and a brand new audience, but it simply was not possible. Now approaching his late fifties, Dickens was wearing himself out. Dolby speaks of the recurring health issues which plagued Dickens during this time, 'the return of the sleepless nights, with the additional trouble of pain in the swollen foot, which rendered walking an impossibility.'[32] Reluctantly, Dickens performed the last leg of his tour, a farewell series, and stepped back from the readings, his final performance being given on 15 March 1870, just a few months before he died. During this time his written output had taken a backseat. At the beginning of his career he was producing new works at a terrific rate, with the early parts of *Oliver* and *Nickleby* both coming out simultaneously with the later parts of *Pickwick* and *Oliver* respectively. In stark contrast, he did not write a novel in 1866, 1867, 1868 or 1869. There was a five-year gap between *Our Mutual Friend* and *The Mystery of Edwin Drood*, the longest pause between novels in his career. He had written shorter pieces in this interim, including his contributions to the annual Christmas number, but it is clear to see that the reading tour had come at the expense of his writing. Dickens was so busy reading to his public that he was no longer producing novels for them. The immediate allure of performing on the stage, financial as well as personal, was too attractive, and diverted his attention away from the career that had made his name.

There is speculation that had Dickens not done the reading tours, he might likely have lived for longer, and so in turn we might now have more of his novels to enjoy. This is likely to be true, but it is also important to note what would be lost. The reading tours may have prevented the writing of new works, but they cemented the reputation of Dickens and his existing works. Going on tour confirmed him as a celebrity: the familiar image of him with beard and moustache became fixed in the public imagination. Even now when we think of Dickens, for most people it is the older Dickens we see in our head; not the young clean-shaven man who produced *Pickwick* and *Oliver* to such great applause, but the bearded man as seen on his tours. The simple reason for this is the sheer amount of images produced of the older Dickens to accompany his tours. Postcards were sold in all the towns and cities he visited as merchandise and memorabilia. If Dickens was not producing new works, he was instead promoting himself, and very profitably too. The tour may have shortened his life, but they dramatically extended his reputation.

Case Study: 'Sikes and Nancy'

The material for 'Sikes and Nancy' is drawn from chapters 45, 46, 47, 48 and 50 of *Oliver Twist*. It is therefore quite late in the narrative, and shows Dickens's reliance on his audience already being familiar with the story. Some of the edits serve the purpose of introducing the reading as a standalone episode. Chapter 45 of *Oliver* begins:

> The old man was up, betimes, next morning, and waited impatiently for the appearance of his new associate, who after a delay that seemed interminable, at length presented himself, and commenced a voracious assault on the breakfast.[33]

Whereas 'Sikes and Nancy' begins:

> Fagin the receiver of stolen goods was up, betimes, next morning, and waited impatiently for the appearance of his new associate, Noah Claypole, otherwise Morris Bolter, who at length presented himself, and cutting a monstrous slice of bread, commenced a voracious assault on the breakfast.[34]

The changes offer the briefest amount of exposition necessary. The two characters of the dialogue are identified, but not really introduced. The audience is not told why Noah Claypole is using the name Morris Bolter – to find out they would need to read the book, but for the present circumstances they have the information they need for the episode at hand. Dickens's alterations serve more as a reminder than explanation. Note also how cuts have been made in some of the descriptions. For the most part Dickens was thinking about how to convey his words clearly and effectively to the audience. Longer bits of description could be removed if necessary to focus on the immediacy of the moment. In particular, Dickens removes text pertaining to 'he said' to transform the dialogue into something more approximating a play script. Again, compare *Oliver* and 'Sikes' below:

> 'Bolter,' said the Jew, drawing up a chair and seating himself opposite Morris Bolter.
> 'Well, here I am,' returned Noah. 'What's the matter? Don't yer ask me to do anything till I have done eating. That's a great fault in this place. Yer never get time enough over yer meals.'
> 'You can talk as you eat, can't you?' said Fagin, cursing his dear young friend's greediness from the very bottom of his heart.
> 'Oh yes, I can talk. I get on better when I talk,' said Noah, cutting a monstrous slice of bread. 'Where's Charlotte?'
> 'Out,' said Fagin. 'I sent her out this morning with the other young woman, because I wanted us to be alone.'
> 'Oh!' said Noah. 'I wish yer'd ordered her to make some buttered toast first. Well. Talk away. Yer won't interrupt me.'[35]

> _____

> 'Bolter, <u>Bolter</u>.'
> 'Well, here I am. What's the matter? Don't yer ask me to do anything till I have done eating. That's a great fault in this place. Yer never get time enough over yer meals.'
> 'You can talk as you eat, can't you?'
> 'Oh yes, I can talk. I get on better when I talk. <u>Talk away.</u> Yer won't interrupt me.'[36]

The reading is more in the moment. The interjections of Dickens's narrative voice are removed or relocated, in the case of the monstrous slice of bread which is mentioned instead in the opening paragraph of the reading. This allows for dialogue to pass uninterrupted; the past tense of Dickens's narrator is gone, leaving only the present tense of the dialogue: we are in the moment.

He does not need to include phrases like 'said Fagin' because his reading made it clear who was speaking; Fagin's annoyed tone, which is implied by his inward cursing of Claypole, can also be inferred more efficiently through Dickens's own tone of voice. In effect, the readings remove the need for Dickens to spell it out; he does not need to leave exact instructions of how each person is talking or feeling, as the reader himself he can project that through his performance. Note also the underlined words for emphasis. These are not underlined in print, but in Dickens's pen on his own prompt copy – it is not for the benefit of the reader but for Dickens's own purpose to remind him where to place emphasis. It reminds us therefore how the loss of Dickens's narrative voice on paper is effectively replaced by Dickens's actual voice on stage. The significance of this is seen later when Nancy is talking to Mr Brownlow, and Dickens introduces foreshadowing by emphasising keywords in her discussion:

> 'I told you before, that I was afraid to speak to you there. I don't know why it is,' <u>said the girl shuddering,</u> 'but I have such a fear and dread upon me to-night that I can hardly stand.'
> 'A fear of what?'
> 'I scarcely know of what,' replied the girl. 'I wish I did. Horrible thoughts of <u>death</u>, and <u>shrouds</u> with <u>blood</u> upon them, and a fear that has made me burn as if I was on fire, have been upon me all day. I was reading a book to-night, to wile the time away, and the same things came into the print.'[37]

Dickens is leaving his audience in no doubt as to what is about to occur. Again, the fact that he should choose an episode so late in the story of *Oliver* suggests an assumption that his audience has read the book; in which case the audience will also know that Nancy's murder is imminent. There is no mystery in the emphasis on 'death' and 'blood' therefore, no intrigue or speculation to be made, but rather absolute certainty that death is coming. In addition to underlining 'said the girl shuddering', a further note in the margin says 'shudder', presumably as a prompt to Dickens to do so. He is not simply reading out the lines of his characters, he is embodying them. Elsewhere the deletion of narrative voice telling us who is speaking implies Dickens is putting on voices; the marginal notes here tell us he is posturing as well. This is not a static armchair reading but a dynamic performance; this is not Dickens reading the words of Nancy in his own voice, but Dickens being Nancy in that moment. I specifically choose to emphasise this idea of being 'in the moment' because the immediacy of the performance is key to its effectiveness. Whether the brutal reading of 'Sikes and Nancy' or any of the more cheerful readings, part of the potency of Dickens performing his works was the allure of being with Dickens in that specific moment of time – everything is about the present. The audience will have read his works in the past, and can do so again in the future whenever they wish: what made them willing to pay the admission price was to be there at the specific time and place with the author, to experience being with Dickens as the story was unfolding. There is a tension between the foreknowledge of what will happen and the illusion of the present tense suggesting that anything could still happen. It allows the audience to be fully engaged in a story that was already familiar to them. Though the story continues to the death of Sikes, the climax in reality was the murder of Nancy.

> The housebreaker freed one arm, and grasped his pistol. The certainty of immediate detection if he fired, flashed across his mind; and he beat it <u>twice</u> with upon the upturned face that almost touched his own.
>
> She staggered and fell, but raising herself on her knees, she drew from her bosom a white handkerchief – Rose Maylie's – and holding it up towards Heaven, breathed one prayer for mercy to her Maker.
>
> It was a ghastly figure to look upon. The murderer staggering backward to the wall, and shutting out the sight with his hand, seized a heavy club and <u>struck her</u> down!![38]

The sheer amount of underlining in this section is almost comical; when everything is emphasised, what is there left to place emphasis on? But ultimately this is the moment of absolute heightened emotion. Contrast again with the original story and it becomes clear what we are not seeing:

> The housebreaker freed one arm, and grasped his pistol. The certainty of immediate detection if he fired, flashed across his mind even in the midst of his fury; and he beat it twice with all the force he could summon, upon the upturned face that almost touched his own.
>
> She staggered and fell: nearly blinded with the blood that rained down from a deep gash in her forehead; but raising herself, with difficulty, on her knees, drew from her bosom a white handkerchief – Rose Maylie's own – and holding it up, in her folded hands, as high towards Heaven as her feeble strength would allow, breathed one prayer for mercy to her Maker.
>
> It was a ghastly figure to look upon. The murderer staggering backward to the wall, and shutting out the sight with his hand, seized a heavy club and struck her down.[39]

In writing, Dickens has provided all manner of description of the actions his characters are making and the emotions they are feeling. A number of these passages are left out of the reading. We are not told that Sikes is 'in the midst of

his fury'; nor that Nancy raises herself 'with difficulty' or holds the handker-
chief up 'in her folded hands' as high 'as her feeble strength would allow'.
Instead these are left to be implied by Dickens's performance. He does not need
to say it out loud – he can show it. Dickens wrote of one performance of the
murder scene in April 1869 that

> I don't think a hand moved while I was doing it last night, or an eye
> looked away. And there was a fixed expression of horror of me, all over
> the theatre, which could not have been surpassed if I had been going to
> be hanged to that red velvet table. It is quite a new sensation to be exe-
> crated with that unanimity- and I hope it will remain so![40]

Dickens had initially been reluctant to perform the murder. He invited a small
circle of friends to a private reading on 14 November 1868 at St James's Hall in
London, as he could 'not decide whether the Art of the thing should exalt the
horror, or deepen it.'[41] When Wills and his wife were unable to attend, Dickens
told Mrs Wills that they would 'escape a rather horrible business!'[42] It seems
Forster remained unconvinced after the reading, but for all of Dickens's own
initial misgivings, the practice run had now convinced him of the reading's
potency:

> We might have agreed to differ about it very well, because we only wanted
> to find out the truth if we could, and because it was quite understood that
> I wanted to leave behind me the recollection of something very passionate
> and dramatic, done with simple means, if the art would justify the theme.[43]

Dickens echoes his earlier comment about the art justifying the theme; clearly
the content was horrific, but in that Dickens was finding something quite profound and truly terrific. If anything, Dickens would prove to be the most
enthusiastic audience member of all. Up till now his readings had been comic
or pathetic in tone; this was something new, and the power he held in that
moment was addictive. He was no longer dealing with an audience who
wanted to listen, but rather an audience who wanted *not* to hear any more but
could not stop. This was real power at last, to hold their attention and keep
them transfixed even while re-enacting a horrific crime. Dickens is not
ashamed of the 'fixed expression of horror of me' which he sees in the theatre
– he is proud of it. This was a new Dickens, a dark Dickens. A Dickens who
had confronted the cosy public perception of himself in the separation from
his wife, and was now finding himself in new territory. *Pickwick* was far
behind him; this author was ready for something much darker. The next book
he would write after performing 'Sikes and Nancy' would also be his last, but

The Mystery of Edwin Drood hints at something new. The tale of murder and obsession may likely have been informed by, if not borne from, Dickens's first-hand experience of re-enacting Nancy's murder and the compelling spell it cast upon those before him.

Notes

1 Charles Dickens, *David Copperfield*, ed. by Nina Burgis (Oxford: OUP, 1981), Ch. 7, p. 79.

2 *Copperfield*, Ch. 7, pp. 79–80.

3 Dickens, 'Nurse's Stories', *All the Year Round*, Vol. 3 (8 September 1860), pp. 517–521 (p. 518).

4 Dickens, Letter to Catherine Dickens, 2 December 1844, in Kathleen Tillotson, *The Letters of Charles Dickens*, Volume Four 1844–1846 (Oxford: Clarendon Press, 1977), pp. 234–235 (p. 235); Daniel Maclise, Letter to Catherine Dickens, 8 December 1844, in *Letters*, Vol. 4, p. 235n (p. 235n).

5 Daniel Maclise, Letter to Catherine Dickens, 8 December 1844, in *Letters*, Vol. 4, p. 235n (p. 235n).

6 William Macready, Entry for 5 December 1838 in *Diaries of William Charles Macready*, ed. by William Toynbee, Vol. 1 (London: Chapman and Hall, 1912), p. 480.

7 Mamie Dickens, *My Father as I Recall Him* (London: Roxsburgh Press, 1896), p. 48.

8 Dickens, Letter to Forster, 11 October 1846, in *Letters*, Vol. 4, pp. 631–635 (p. 631).

9 Forster, *The Life of Charles Dickens*, Volume Three (London: Chapman and Hall, 1874), p. 165.

10 Forster, Vol. 3, p. 165.

11 Dickens, Letter to Forster, 5 September 1857, in Graham Storey and Kathleen Tillotson (ed.), *The Letters of Charles Dickens*, Volume Eight (Oxford: Clarendon Press, 1995), pp.434–435 (p. 435).

12 Russell Jackson, *Victorian Theatre* (New York: New Amsterdam, 1989), p. 80; Henry James, *The Nation*, 1879, cited in Jackson, p. 80.

13 Malcolm Andrews, *Charles Dickens and His Performing Selves* (Oxford: OUP, 2006), p. 33.

14 Andrews, p. 136.

15 Michael Slater, *Charles Dickens* (New Haven: Yale, 2011), p. 462.

16 Letter to Arthur Ryland, 1855, cited in Slater p. 462.

17 Dickens, Letter to Henry Chorley, 12 January 1866, in Graham Storey (ed.), *The Letters of Charles Dickens* Volume Eleven, 1865–1867 (Oxford: Clarendon Press, 1999), pp. 136–137 (p. 137).

18 Dickens, Letter to John Forster, 11 March 1866, in *Letters*, Vol. 11, pp. 170–171 (p. 171).

19 Dickens, Letter to George Dolby, 12 December 1866, in *Letters*, Vol.11, p. 281 (p. 281).

20 Dickens, Letter to Letitia Austin, 13 December 1866, in *Letters*, Vol. 11, pp. 281–282 (p. 282).

21 George Dolby, *Dickens as I knew Him* (London: Everett & Co, 1885), p. 63.

22 Charles Dickens, 'Barbox Brothers', in *All the Year Round*, Volume Seven (25 December 1866), pp.573–582 (p. 573).

23 Slater, p. 451.

24 Dickens, Letter to Charlotte Dolby, 16 November 1858, in *Letters*, Vol. 8, p. 705 (p. 705).

25 Dickens, Letter to Mrs Richard Watson, 4 October 1861, in Graham Storey, *The Letters of Charles Dickens*, Volume Nine 1859–1861 (Oxford: Clarendon Press, 1997), p. 469 (p. 469).

26 See Claire Tomalin, *The Invisible Woman* (London: Penguin, 1990), pp. 179–181.

27 See Gary Scharnhorst, 'Kate Field's "An Evening with Charles Dickens": A Reconstructed Lecture', *Dickens Quarterly*, Vol. 21, No. 2 (June 2004), pp. 71–89.

28 Mark Twain, Review, *Alta California*, 5 February 1868.

29 Mark Twain, Review, *Alta California*, 5 February 1868.

30 Dickens, Letter to Henry Blink, 7 December 1866, in *Letters*, Vol. 11, p. 279 (p. 279).

31 Dickens, Letter to Georgina Hogarth, 24 January 1869, in Graham Storey (ed.), *The Letters of Charles Dickens*, Volume Twelve 1868–1870 (Oxford: Clarendon Press, 2002), pp. 282–283 (p. 282).

32 Dolby, pp. 293–294.

33 Charles Dickens, *Oliver Twist*, ed. by Kathleen Tillotson (Oxford: OUP, 1966), Ch. 45, p. 306.

34 Sikes, in Charles Dickens, *Sikes and Nancy and other public readings,* ed. by Philip Collins, (Oxford: OUP, 1983), p. 232.

35 *Oliver Twist*, Ch. 45, p. 307.

36 *Sikes and Nancy*, p. 232.

37 *Sikes and Nancy*, p. 235.

38 *Sikes and Nancy*, p. 243.

39 *Oliver Twist*, Ch.47, pp. 322–323.

40 Dickens, Letter to Mr and Mrs Fields, 9 April 1869, in *Letters*, Vol. 12, pp. 328–329 (p. 329).

41 Dickens, Letter to William Harness, 10 November 1868, in *Letters*, Vol. 12, p. 218 (p. 218).

42 Dickens, Letter to Mrs Wills, 14 November 1868, in *Letters*, Vol. 12, p. 219 (p. 219).

43 Dickens, Letter to John Forster, 15 November 1868, in *Letters*, Vol. 12, p. 220 (p. 220).

12

The End of Dickens

Focal Point: 1865–1870

Case Study: The Mystery of Edwin Drood

Dickens died on 9 June 1870. This is a fact; it is also a spoiler. Any attempt to consider and appraise the life of Dickens will always have a subconscious awareness of how the story ends, but this skews the way we explore Dickens's actions in his final years. *We* know Dickens will die on that date, *he* did not. When we look at posthumous discussions of Dickens's activities in the late 1860s there is a focus on his weariness, both physical and spiritual. There are elements of truth in this but we must also keep in mind our own bias, and how our certain knowledge of his approaching demise can encourage and exaggerate explorations of Dickens winding down in his later years. In this chapter I will look at the after-effects of the Staplehurst crash of 1865, and the last two years of Dickens's life, covering the final leg of his reading tour and his return to novel-writing. I will also explore the immediate reactions to his death in the public press and popular imagination, the outpouring of grief and the controversial decision to ignore Dickens's own wishes to be buried in Rochester in favour of a grand funeral and burial in Westminster Abbey. Finally, I will consider the contemporary responses to his final novel, *The Mystery of Edwin Drood*, both before and after his death, to see how perception of the work shifted as Dickens moved from a living to posthumous author.

The Beginning of the End: Finishing the Reading Tours, Starting *Drood*

As discussed in Chapter 11, the reading tours proved to be a physical strain upon Dickens's health, which was accelerated by the inclusion of 'Sikes and Nancy' in the repertoire. The regular re-enactment of Nancy's violent and brutal murder regularly got Dickens's heart racing and put him under enormous strain. But beyond the dramatic extremity of this one particular reading,

The Life of the Author: Charles Dickens, First Edition. Pete Orford.
© 2023 John Wiley & Sons Ltd. Published 2023 by John Wiley & Sons Ltd.

there was also the constant strain of regular travel across the UK and USA. This carried a psychological cost for Dickens in the aftermath of the Staplehurst Crash in 1865. On 9 June of that year, Dickens was travelling through Kent by railway with Ternan and her mother when the train derailed. It was a terrifying moment: Dickens's carriage was overturned but neither he nor his companions were hurt; others were not so lucky. Dickens is reported to have been an active helper at the scene, checking on others, providing support and distributing alcohol. The incident was reported in the news, and the next day Dickens wrote several letters reassuring his friends while also describing the incident.

> I was in the terrible accident yesterday, and worked some hours among the dying and dead.

> I was in the carriage that did not go down, but hung in the air over the side of the broken bridge. I was not touched – scarcely shaken, But the terrific nature of the scene makes me think that I should be the better for a gentle composing draught or two.[1]

The flurry of letters to his correspondents is reminiscent of the burst of messages he released after Mary Hogarth's death, but their similarity ends there. While the young Dickens spoke of Mary's death emotively and hyperbolically, the older Dickens speaks of Staplehurst with brevity and understatement. It is in the details that we can see how the latter incident had an equally strong impact upon him. His letter to his doctor has an attempt at his usual elaborate signature, but it is shaky, with a note from Dickens admitting 'I can't sign my flourish today'.[2] In a surprisingly brief letter to Forster he closes by saying simply 'No words can describe the scene'; a few days later he told Thomas Headland that he was still shaken, 'not by the dragging of the carriage itself, but by the work afterwards in getting out the dying and the dead, which was horrible.'[3] This was not the quiet, poetic passing of Mary in his arms, but the violent, brutal deaths and suffering of many people. It was a forcible reminder of the speed at which the trains were travelling and the dangers involved; for Dickens to continue with the reading tours meant continuing with this method of transport despite the experience of this incident, and Dolby notes a general anxiety which arises from this point forward:

> He never, he explained, had travelled since that memorable day (the 9th of June) without experiencing a nervous dread, to counteract which in some degree he carried in his travelling bag a brandy flask, from which it was his invariable habit, one hour after leaving his starting-point, when travelling by express train, to take a draught to nerve himself against any ordeal he might have to go through during the rest of the journey.[4]

For Dickens, every stop on the tour involved another train journey, another confrontation of past trauma. Like any major incident, it made Dickens aware of his own mortality. His publishing contracts for both *Our Mutual Friend* and *Edwin Drood* include details of what should happen in the event of his death, namely where the remaining payments should go to, and how much might need to be returned to the publisher in the instance of non-completion, which was a consideration he had never included in previous contracts. At the time of the Staplehurst crash Dickens was 53, not an especially old age by modern standards, but for Dickens it was clearly a point – emphasised further by the crash itself – at which death was no longer a distant event but something of ever-increasing proximity. This is not, as many Drood sleuths would like to think, a sense that Dickens knew he was going to die *soon*, but rather the broader awareness that he was going to die some day, as we all are. His parents were both deceased, and his children were now growing up, getting jobs and getting married, so Dickens was moving up to the next generation, no longer a young man but stepping ever closer to the status of the Aged P. More concerningly, death stalked his own generation: when Augustus Egg had died in 1863, Dickens had stoically told Wilkie Collins 'We must close up the ranks and march on', but in January 1870 Dickens noted how Macready had grown 'most distressingly infirm and unintelligible', and then in April that same year Dickens had 'the shock of first reading at a railway station of the death of our old dear friend and companion' Daniel Maclise.[5] Furthermore, all but one of Dickens's seven siblings died before him, despite him being the second-eldest of the family.

For Dickens to be increasingly aware of his own mortality at this time is therefore understandable. He had suffered from ill health for some time. Despite his love of walking, or because of it, he suffered with severe foot pains; in 1867 he told Forster 'I am laid up with another attack in my foot', and that word 'another' betrays the recurrence of this.[6] Shortly after, a report in the *Times* suggested Dickens was 'much out of health', which he vehemently denied.[7] As 'the innocent victim of a periodical paragraph-disease' Dickens wrote a series of increasingly exasperated letters to his friends to reassure them 'I never was better in my life'.[8] Dickens's insistence upon his health may have had an element of self-denial to them. Medical doctor Nick Cambridge has examined Dickens letters to diagnose the likely ailments which Dickens suffered from through his life, including gout, renal colic, haemorrhoids, and strokes.[9] In April 1869, Dickens wrote to Georgina complaining of a recent ailment and noting, four days later, that his 'weakness and deadness are all on the left side, and if I don't look at anything I try to touch with my left hand, I don't know where it is.'[10] Cambridge's diagnosis is that this was likely to be a stroke, and however much Dickens tried to underplay it, his doctor Frank Beard was 'evidently aware of the dangers involved' and 'immediately travelled up to Blackpool to meet Dickens and brought him to London to see Sir Thomas Watson, Physician Extraordinary to the Queen, who advised him to reduce his workload.'[11] Dickens's health was becoming a greater concern, and an impediment to his work.

Unfortunately, Dickens was not the sort of man who wanted to go slower. His separation from his wife, and relationship with Ternan, speaks partly of a midlife crisis as much as a disconnect between Dickens and Catherine, but it also speaks of his own need for an energetic partner, and that comes at a cost. Being with a woman several years younger might have reinvigorated Dickens but must also have reinforced his sense of his own age, and the growing number of ailments afflicting him. Dolby recalls that 'Had Mr. Dickens's health not given way, it was his earnest desire to make a voyage to Australia'; Dickens's dreams and ambitions were being explicitly stopped by his health.[12] The restless spirit of the man longed to travel and work, but the body was now dictating how much of that was actually possible. Thus the reading tours do take on a sense of urgency as well as defiance, with Dickens doing all that he can while he still can. In March 1870 Dickens gave his final public reading, and at the end of which he announced his return to novel-writing as a counterbalance to his departure from the readings:

> I have thought it well in the full flood tide of your favour to retire upon those older associations between us which date much farther back than these, and thenceforth to devote myself exclusively to the art that first brought us together.
>
> Ladies and Gentlemen, – in two short weeks from this time I hope that you may enter in your own homes on a new series of readings at which my assistance will be indispensable; but from these garish lights I vanish now for evermore, with a heartfelt, grateful, respectful, and affectionate farewell.[13]

The announcement is an equal mix of regret and optimism: regret of no longer being able to perform these readings and see his audience directly, but optimism at once again entering their homes in the familiar form. The announcement tells us a lot about how Dickens saw and valued his works. As a writer he became part of the household, a familiar friend with a presence in every home, even by proxy. It's significant to note that the disappointment of ending the reading tour is countered and compensated by the new work, both for Dickens and his audience. While our knowledge of his death just three months later can encourage that morbid sense of impending doom, Dickens is mostly hopeful about the future project. The planned work would be a monthly serial once again, but in only twelve parts rather than the usual twenty. It is not clear why

Dickens decided to do this; and again the pessimistic reading would be that he did not anticipate making it to the end of a twenty-month work. This could be true, or the alternative could be that Dickens was adjusting the format not out of fear of incompletion, but rather as the beginning of a new style of writing. Of his preceding three novels, two – *A Tale of Two Cities* and *Great Expectations* – had been shorter, weekly serialisations, while the other – *Our Mutual Friend* – was the familiar doorstopper. But the first two proved more popular; Dickens disliked the pressure of weekly writing, so producing a monthly novel allowed him the writing pace he preferred, while limiting it to twelve instalments was perhaps a recognition that slightly shorter works could reach a wider audience. The first instalment was published in April 1870; at the time of Dickens's death three numbers had been published and a further three were written out in manuscript. These final three were published posthumously according to the planned schedule of once a month, so that *Edwin Drood* ended not with Dickens death, but in September of that year. We thus have two moments for contemporary readers to consider as an ending to the novel: the last number published while Dickens was alive, and the last number written while he was alive. To this can be added the third, most tantalising ending which has intrigued us ever since: that which he would have written had he lived through to the completion of the novel.

It is important to note that the readers of the first instalment were categorically not reading Dickens's *last* novel, but rather his *latest* novel. Early reviews of *Edwin Drood* are mostly of an excited and congratulatory manner. The *Athenaeum* thrilled 'to see once more the green cover in which the world first beheld Mr. Pickwick' while the *Times* concurred that Dickens's 'latest effort promises to be received with interest and pleasure as widespread as those which greet those glorious Papers which built at once the whole edifice of his fame'.[14] If the reading tours had confirmed Dickens as a celebrity, and a cultural phenomenon as much as an author, then his return to writing was not a retreat but an expansion of the phenomenon: a brand new Dickens work. Like ABBA releasing a new album in 2021, this heralded both a wave of nostalgia in original fans as well as an opportunity for new fans to experience the sensation of reading a Dickens hitherto unread by anyone else. The *Athenaeum* notes the passage of time, and how readers of *Drood* would have grandparents who had read *Pickwick* at their age. Dickens had been around in the public consciousness for a long time and was almost an institution. It is unsurprising then that reviews of the new book would be seeking to celebrate the glory days and a sense of revival. Accordingly the *Athenaeum* praises the first number for its comic episodes and 'old Boz humour' – not something which most reviewers usually do today, but further evidence of that distinction between 'last' and 'latest' and the way in which it affect the way we read a book.[15]

Not every reviewer was thrilled to see yet another Dickens book appear on the shelves; some reviews attacked it specifically because it was so like every other book he'd ever written, rehashing the same character types, the same humorous mannerisms and speech patterns, the same bizarre names. An article in *Judy* spoofed the opening number, in which the proud and pompous Sapsea (now styled as 'Papsy') confirms boldly that his name 'is not Pecksniff', the proud and pompous villain of *Martin Chuzzlewit*.[16] Longevity is a double-edged sword: for fans it can be considered confirmation in itself of an author's greatness that their works continue to thrive and exists; but for detractors their enduring presence offers even more reason to grow weary of their work. Both positive and negative reviews centred on the same idea – it was *another* Dickens, with the promise (or threat) of more to come.

Dickens's Death

On 8 June 1870 Dickens wrote his last words of fiction. Later that day he had a stroke, dying the next day. These final words were written not in his study at Gad's Hill, but in a chalet just outside. The chalet had been a gift from the actor Charles Fechter for Christmas in 1864, and together he and Dickens had built it across the road from Gad's Hill, after which Dickens then had a tunnel dug to go under the road to allow Dickens to pass back and forth to it without having to encounter any members of the public who were travelling on the road (a further testament to Dickens's complicated relationship with celebrity, and his own desire for solitude when he wished it). Forster writes that at the time of the stroke on the evening of 8 July, he was alone with his sister-in-law Georgina, whose 'help alone prevented him from falling where he stood'.[17] Ternan's biographer Claire Tomalin offers a more exciting narrative, based on a rumour originating from the Rev. J Chetwode Postans, that 'Dickens did not die at Gad's Hill, as generally supposed, but at another house "in compromising circumstances".'[18] This then would imply Dickens had a stroke in Ternan's company, followed by a frantic rush to move him back to the family home where he could be treated without raising a scandal. This is a sensational idea, and at time of writing is still largely inconclusive, with Tomalin admitting 'there are undoubtedly a lot of awkwardness and rough edges to this version, enough to make it seem indeed much too good to be true.'[19] We cannot categorically say it did not happen this way, but the story as told by Forster is still taken to be the most likely event. What does ring true about Postans's version is the emphasis that Dickens and his close ones placed upon his reputation over his health.

Nonetheless, it is uncontentious to note that wherever the stroke occurred, Dickens died at Gad's Hill on 9 June, the anniversary of Staplehurst (which has

inevitably led to fantastical speculation about the haunting nature of that earlier incident on Dickens's psyche but it is, ultimately, just a coincidence). The
life of the author had come to a close, but not his story. So what happened
next? Dickens's daughters Katey and Mamey arrived the night before, while
Charley came in the morning. Leon Litvack has pieced together various sources
to reconstruct the immediate aftermath of Dickens's death:

> Katey hurried to London to tell her mother [...] while Henry Dickens
> (who had been at Cambridge) arrived two hours too late, having been
> told the news as Higham railway station [.] Letitia Austin (Dickens's
> surviving sister) also came. Thus by eight o'clock on the evening of 9
> June word had begun to spread.[20]

In terms of how to memorialise the man, this is where we see the strain between the private person and the public persona. Dickens had requested that
he be buried at Rochester Cathedral, close to his home in Gad's Hill. This did
not happen. Litvack's research has shown that the Dean of Westminster,
Arthur Stanley, was a key mover in 'overseeing the final journey of Dickens's
remains'.[21] It is astounding that the last wishes of a person should be disre-
garded in this way, but the argument was that the country's needs were
greater. Dickens was a great author, the pride of the nation, and as such he
deserved – no, needed – to be buried in the nation's capital. His body was
consequently removed from Rochester and taken to Westminster. Here it
was placed on public display where the people could come and bid farewell.
This was a combination of pomp and genuine sincerity. Dickens was the
man of the people, and in his death his body was delivered up to the people.
It is said that the authority to move his body from Rochester came from
Queen Victoria herself, thus his impact can be seen to stretch from the poor-
est household to the Empress who commanded half the world. Any criticism
of Dickens was temporarily muted in favour of universal outpourings of
admiration and loss.

There is a great irony in this. Dickens himself had roundly mocked the extravagant funeral arrangements of the Duke of Wellington in his provocatively titled
essay 'Trading in Death' which had reached an equal pitch of public grief:

> A system of barbarous show and expense was found to have gradu-
> ally erected itself above the grave, which, while it could possibly do no
> honour to the memory of the dead, did great dishonour to the living,
> as inducing them to associate the most solemn of human occasions
> with unmeaning mummeries, dishonest debt, profuse waste, and bad
> example in an utter oblivion of responsibility.[22]

Dickens's savage judgement condemned that sense of public display as distasteful, encouraging exaggerated responses rather than sincere condolences. Now his own death had sparked a public mourning on a par with Wellington's. Though Dickens's funeral itself remained private (partly so that Ternan could attend), the relocation to Westminster Abbey allowed for a much wider and more public mourning to occur; his own desires for a local burial were ignored, and all the press were united in singing his praises and outdoing each other in the extent of their grief.

Remembering Dickens

A flurry of illustrations emerged in the wake of Dickens's death depicting the man and his creations. Fildes's 'The Empty Chair' depicted Dickens's study in Gad's Hill without anyone in the picture, encapsulating that sense of absence; this in turn was copied and emulated in the national press, and eventually inspired pictures in which not only Dickens was present, but also his many fictional creations, the most famous being R. W. Buss's painting 'Dickens Dream' [see Figure 12.1]. In it we see Dickens in his chair, surrounded by his characters as spirit visions. It is as though the death of Dickens allowed the physical constraints of the man to be broken and permit the full fantastic spirit of his works to explode. With the death of Dickens his characters took on new life, new form. Dickens was still alive, not as the man, but as the author, as the

Figure 12.1   R. W. Buss, 'Dickens's Dream', 1875.

works themselves. We now refer to reading Dickens, in the present tense, with his name synonymous with anyone of the works he created: they have become Dickens, and Dickens has become them. Such is the process which all authors and their works will go through upon their death.

The obituary notices and subsequent opinion pieces are extraordinary in their hyperbole. 'One whom young and old, wherever the English language is spoken, have been accustomed to regard as a personal friend is suddenly taken away' wailed the *Times*.[23] 'The nation will learn with profound sorrow the loss it has sustained in the death of its "favourite novelist"' mourned the *Daily Telegraph*, 'if this, indeed, be a phrase which adequately describes a man of such rare genius that, in the creation of fictitious character and the evolution of fictitious narrative, he made his way straight to the hearts of all his millions of readers.'[24] Words could not do him enough justice: 'The shock of this event is too recent and too keenly felt to permit of any adequate attempt to estimate either the personal character or literary position of the great novelist whom we all mourn' mused the *Pall Mall Gazette*.[25] Many poems were written, all of them quite, quite terrible, such as:

> Charles Dickens dead! It is as if a light
> In every English home were quenched today;
> As if a face all know had passed from sight,
> A hand all loved to press were turned to clay.[26]

Or:

> And that sad circle stretching, still unbroken,
> Around the world to utmost regions sped,
> And tears were shed, where'er our tongue is spoken,
> To know CHARLES DICKENS – dead![27]

Or even:

> He's dead! Yet though he's passed away
> His peer although ' twere hard to find,
> He still will live in every heart,
> In every English home enshrined.[28]

Not only did people write these, but others saw fit to publish them. In hindsight, it is fair to say the press may have got a bit carried away, but equally it could be argued that their response, mawkish and exaggerated as it appears now a century and a half later, was in fact a fair and reasonable reflection of the public mood amid an extraordinary moment of national grief. In more recent times the death of Queen Elizabeth II heralded a similar outpouring of sorrow, prompting in turn either a sense of guilt that you might not be feeling sorry enough, or a sense of resentment that you were expected to feel sorry in the first place. News of her death dominated the cultural scene for several weeks; numerous celebrities stepped forward to offer their own personal anecdotes, while crowds of people journeyed to visit the coffin and say their farewell to a figure they had always known but never met. The same phenomenon can be seen to occur after Dickens's death. The sheer fame of the man meant that his death had a tremendous impact on the public psyche.

Dickens after Dickens

Dickens may have been dead, but *Drood* did not stop. There were still three numbers written out in manuscript, so Chapman and Hall continued publishing. It was now down to Forster to edit them ready for publication, and a lot of these edits involved undoing any deletions Dickens had made. Dickens's words were now finite, and every last one was precious. The last number was actually a chapter short, so Forster had to re-insert the deleted passages to bulk up the material, and move things around to evenly fill out the remaining three numbers. Numbers 4–6 of *Drood* are not solely by Dickens then, but rather a collaboration between Dickens and Forster. While the first three numbers had been met with excitement, these next three were reviewed with sorrow and solemnity. One reviewer declined from saying too much as it would not be appropriate so soon after Dickens's death: 'The recent calamity sustained alike by letters and society must be felt to exempt this latest production of Mr. Dickens from minute criticism.'[29] Others were quick to highlight the gloomier aspects of the story. Those comic episodes which had amused the reviewers of the first number were no longer on the radar, instead the book was already being rewritten as Dickens's last work, with every page a foreboding indication of the author's demise. One reviewer had already done this with the third number, pointing out that one scene in a graveyard 'has acquired a painful significance' and that Dickens's 'lamented departure points the moral with more than ordinary force' (although of course Dickens had frequently set scenes in a graveyard, such as the first chapter of *Great Expectations*, or Scrooge's gloomy vision of his Christmas yet to come, or Lady Dedlock's night-time visit to a cemetery in *Bleak House*).[30] It is curious to think what the experience must have been like for Dickens's readers outside of London: there, removed from the immediacy of the funeral and the corporeal proof of Dickens's death, it might have seemed like nothing much had changed, as the book carried on regardless, and each reader's relationship with the author continued uninterrupted. Dickens was, in a sense, still alive up until September 1870, when the last surviving manuscript was published, and the story stopped.

Except, it did not stop. Chapman and Hall may have issued a note in the sixth number saying that by not continuing the story they were doing what they believed 'what the author himself would have most desired', but it was not what the readers desired.[31] They wanted to know what happened next, and without Dickens to provide the answer, they started to create their own answers. The phenomenon of Droodism is one that has thrived since Dickens's death up to the present day, with its heyday in the early twentieth century. It is one I have already written about extensively, and is a tale that tells of the changing public perception of Dickens and the kind of writer he was.[32] The early responses reacted in much the same way as the many pirated and appropriated versions of his other works had – taking opportunity of a ready market eager for more stories about their favourite Dickensian characters, the completions which were written by other authors in the 1870s and 1880s were not concerned with uncovering what Dickens intended so much as using his first half as a springboard from which to launch their own story. This then gave way to a group that saw themselves as more serious (but who were in many ways no less ridiculous), who eagerly poured over the text to determine not just any possible ending, but rather the one, only, true ending as planned by Dickens himself. To do this often involved rejecting the testimonies of Dickens's friends and family. Forster, Charley Collins, Charley Dickens, Kate Dickens and Luke Fildes all stepped forward at different points to state, clearly, that yes, Edwin was dead and yes, Jasper was the murderer. Forster's summary was the most explicit:

> The story, I learnt immediately afterward, was to be that of the murder of a nephew by the uncle; the originality of which was to consist in the review of the murderer's career by himself at the close, when its temptations were to be dwelt upon as if, not the culprit, but some other man, were the tempted.[33]

The problem was Forster's statement did not appear in print until 1874, by which point readers had had plenty of time to ferment their own spectacular theories, next to which this was an anticlimax. The many subsequent amateur detectives taking up this case saw it as their mission to uncover the truth, and by so doing demonstrate that it was they, and they alone, who best knew and understood Dickens. With the man now dead, authority came not from those who knew *him*, but those who knew his works. Subsequent solutions have attempted to support Forster and reimagine the book not as a mystery at all, but a great psychological work that anticipates *Jekyll and Hyde* and Dostoevsky. Today, we continue to explore all manner of different possibilities for the story, not only in plot but in medium too: there have been stories, articles, monographs, plays, films and musicals attempting to complete Dickens's novel. We simply cannot leave it alone.

But there is something really rather cheering in this. Imagine, for a moment, that Dickens had completed *Edwin Drood*. Would that really be more satisfying? The incomplete nature of *Drood* has unwittingly preserved that experience, shared by all of Dickens's contemporary readers, of not knowing where the story is going to go. It is the essence of serialisation, that Victorians might discuss and ponder the fate of Oliver Twist and speculate about their own theories before Dickens closed the conversation with the final number. Each time Dickens ended a book, he ended the speculation. With *Drood*, that speculation remains; the conversation is still open. Instead of a full stop, he leaves us with an ellipsis. Any one of us can have our own idea about what might happen next, and ultimately, any one of us could be right. Dickens did not plan to leave *Drood* unfinished, but as it turns out he could not have planned it any better. Today, every reader of *Drood* becomes Dickens's collaborator, imagining the continuing adventures of the characters and picking up the pen that Dickens has dropped.

Case Study: Self-reflection and Anti-nostalgia in *The Mystery of Edwin Drood*

Dickens's final story tells of the disappearance, possibly murder, of the eponymous character Edwin Drood. It is a brooding, gothic, sensation story that plays with the ideas of dark personas laying hidden under bright and unassuming exteriors. Of all the places to set this tale, he sets it in 'an old Cathedral town' to which 'a fictitious name' must be given: 'Let it stand in these pages as Cloisterham.'[34] It is universally recognised that the inspiration for Cloisterham is Rochester. Visitors to the city today can see the gatehouse where John Jasper lived, or Eastgate House, the real-life equivalent of Miss Twinkleton's School for Ladies; and, of course, they can see the cathedral. Why, of all places, would Dickens set his tale here?

Partly there is that sense of writing what you know about. Dickens's home at Gad's Hill is on the outskirts of Rochester; for a man who had been forced to give up his travels due to ill health, it makes sense to focus his fictional imagination upon a landscape readily at hand. Nor was this the first time Dickens had used Rochester as a setting for his fiction. In his very first novel, *The Pickwick Papers*, it was the first destination which Pickwick and his companions travelled to. There, Dickens's description of the town veils criticism within mock cheerfulness, as Pickwick gladly writes of the 'wonders' of the town. Talking of the excessive 'consumption of tobacco' in the town Pickwick proclaims 'the smell which pervades the streets must be exceedingly delicious to those who are extremely fond of smoking', and while a 'superficial traveller might object to the dirt' which is said to be the 'leading characteristic' of Rochester and its surrounding towns, Pickwick decrees that 'to those who view it as an indication of traffic and commercial prosperity, it is truly grati-fying.'[35] In a more extended discussion, Pickwick also tells of the thuggish behaviour of various military personnel in the town in an equally cheery tone that shows Dickens's keen sense of parody.

> The streets present a lively and animated appearance, occasioned chiefly by the conviviality of the military. It is truly delightful to a philanthropic mind to see these gallant men staggering along under the influence of an overflow both of animal and ardent spirits; more especially when we remember that the following them about, and jesting with them, affords a cheap and innocent amusement for the boy population. Nothing [...] can exceed their good-humour. It was but the day before my arrival that one of them had been most grossly insulted in the house of a publican. The barmaid had positively refused to draw him any more liquor; in return for which he had (merely in playfulness) drawn his bayonet, and wounded the girl in the shoulder. And yet this fine fellow was the very first to go down to the house next morning and express his readiness to overlook the matter, and forget what had occurred![36]

There is a pleasant symmetry in Dickens visiting Rochester in his first and last novels. As much as *Pickwick* mocks Rochester through the unwitting irony of Mr Pickwick's commentary, the comedy of the episodes set there nonetheless leaves the impression of Rochester as jolly and energetic. Not so for the return visit in *Edwin Drood*. Here the town becomes simultaneously a sleepy, quiet town, while also being a place that harbours danger. Ironically, the book's char-acters frequently find safety and solace by travelling to London: Neville Landless finds a cold reception in Cloisterham and seeks sanctuary at Mr Grewgious's house in Staples Inn; Rosa Bud also flees Cloisterham to visit Mr Grewgious, where she finds her own sanctuary in the Billickin's letting house, and a fairy-tale setting in the tidy apartment of Mr Tartar; even John Jasper, the book's brooding antihero, finds his solace in the opium den in London, where he can drop the façade he has to maintain in Cloisterham of being a reputable choir-master. The customary viewpoint would be to see the metropolis as the den of vice, and the town as the safe harbour from such evil. After all, it is in London where Fagin's gang operates; it is from London that David Copperfield escapes the indignity of the blacking factory to find the oasis of his Aunt Betsy's house in Dover; Dickens frequently falls back on the idea of safe havens outside of the city, and it is tempting to link this to his earliest impressions of the city – and its debtor prison – compared with happier memories of living outside the city.

But *Edwin Drood* reverses that ideology. Now, the city is a place to long for, to find freedom in, and it is the town which is stifling. The very name Cloisterham implies a claustrophobic feel. Its small size is no longer charming but suffocating. What has changed? Well, for one thing Dickens has now seen more of the world than in his youth, which could explain the changed perspective. Then there is his ongoing relationship with Ternan. Suddenly the size of the metropolis, and that feeling of not knowing all its population, no longer becomes a source of anxiety and isolation, but rather a comforting blanket of anonymity where one can be free of scrutiny; in contrast the town is a place where everyone knows everybody, and where secrets struggle to stay hidden. Dickens evokes the sense of disassociation in his description of people coming back to visit Cloisterham: it perfectly captures that sense of returning to your hometown as an adult:

> A few strange faces in the streets; a few other faces, half strange and half familiar, once the faces of Cloisterham children, now the faces of men and women who come back from the outer world at long intervals to find the city wonderfully shrunken in size, as if it had not washed by any means well in the meanwhile. To these, the striking of the Cathedral clock, and the cawing of the rooks from the Cathedral tower, are like voices of their nursery time. To such as these, it has happened in their dying hours afar off, that they have imagined their chamber-floor to be strewn with the autumnal leaves fallen from the elm-trees in the Close: so have the rustling sounds and fresh scents of their earliest impressions revived when the circle of their lives was very nearly traced, and the beginning and the end were drawing close together.[37]

In this passage Dickens recreates that sensation of coming home to once-familiar haunts, finding the place of our youth now 'shrunken in size'. Again, it is tempting so see some sense of prophecy in Dickens's discussion here of the end of people's time on this earth, 'when the circle of their lives was very nearly traced', as Dickens himself is unwittingly doing the same thing here, reimagining his childhood location as his life draws to a close; in *Pickwick* and *Drood* Rochester provides the background, 'the beginning and the end [...] drawing close together.'

In *Drood* then we see a corrupted nostalgia, a confrontation between our dreams of the past and realisations of the present. Much like Dickens's disappointed reunion with Maria Beadnell, so too the very towns themselves simply do not match the benevolent and exaggerated memories we have of them. This is not the first time Dickens has warned against nostalgia, in *The Haunted House* he makes a similar warning against it by recounting the recurring disappointment of reuniting with schoolfellows:

> I myself had, in later life, turned up several boys whom I went to school with, and none of them had at all answered. I expressed my humble belief that that boy never did answer. I represented that he was a mythic character, a delusion, and a snare. I recounted how, the last time I found him, I found him at a dinner party behind a wall of white cravat, with an inconclusive opinion on every possible subject, and a power of silent boredom absolutely Titanic.[38]

The sense of disappointment that Dickens recounts time and again with any attempt to reclaim the past speaks increasingly about him, rather than the people and sights he is seeing. Dickens, back in Gad's Hill, his supposedly family home (but one in which Catherine was no longer present), the same house he had dreamed of being in when a small boy with ambitions of being a gentleman, was going a little stir-crazy. But his interrogation of nostalgia takes on an extra dimension in *Drood*. The night of the disappearance, the key moment of the text, happens, of all nights, on Christmas Eve. Just as *Drood* returns to Rochester, so too Dickens returns to Christmas, and once again he twists it from the familiar into something altogether more haunting. A great deal more attention is paid to the *appearance* of Christmas rather than its moral message. We are told:

> Seasonable tokens are about. Red berries shine here and there in the lattices of Minor Canon Corner; Mr. and Mrs. Tope are daintily sticking sprigs of holly into the carvings and sconces of the Cathedral stalls, as if they were sticking them into the coat-button-holes of the Dean and Chapter.[39]

There is a sense here of tradition and going through the motions. Houses and homes appear more like Christmas through the presence of decorations. All are 'seasonable tokens.' But as Dickens goes on he emphasises the increasingly commercial aspects of the season. In the *Carol* the Spirit of Christmas Present takes Scrooge on a wondrous tour to unexpected places, from mines to lighthouses, to show how the true meaning of Christmas can be found in the most dismal and unlikely of places. In *Drood*, the narrator takes us on a tour of the shops, to show us what can be bought:

Lavish profusion is in the shops: particularly in the articles of currants, raisins, spices, candied peel, and moist sugar. An unusual air of gallantry and dissipation is abroad; evinced in an immense bunch of mistletoe hanging in the greengrocer's shop doorway, and a poor little Twelfth Cake, culminating in the figure of a Harlequin – such a very poor little Twelfth Cake, that one would rather called it a Twenty-fourth Cake or a Forty-eighth Cake – to be raffled for at the pastrycook's, terms one shilling per member.[40]

This is a surprisingly cynical take on the festive season from Mr Christmas himself. But then, there is evidence of Dickens perhaps growing a little weary with writing about Christmas. In his defence, he had been doing so on a regular basis for nearly 27 years by the time he was writing Drood. After the initial success of the *Carol* in 1843, he had then produced four more Christmas books before commencing the Christmas numbers in *Household Words* and *All the Year Round*. Dickens did not invent Christmas by any means, but he certainly made himself synonymous with it through the regular appearance of the books and numbers each year. Over time, the routine appears to have worn thin. In 1843 he said he produced the *Carol* 'in a white heat' of frenzy, working at a terrific pace in a short time; but by 1867, when he was writing *No Thoroughfare* with Wilkie Collins, the rate of production, along with Dickens's enthusiasm, had dwindled. 'I am jogging on' he told Collins, 'at the pace of a wheelbarrow propelled by a Greenwich pensioner'.[41] By 1868 the well of inspiration had dried up completely:

I have been, and still am – which is worse – in a positive state of despair about the Xmas No. I cannot get an idea for it which is in the least satisfactory to me, and yet I have been steadily trying all this month. I have invented so many of the Christmas Nos. and they are so profoundly unsatisfactory after all with the introduced Stories and their want of cohesion or originality, that I fear I am sick of the thing. I have had serious thoughts of abandoning the Xmas No.![42]

Sure enough, in September of that year a small notice appeared in *All the Year Round* announcing that since 'The Extra Christmas number has now been so extensively, and regularly, and often imitated, that it is in very great danger of becoming tiresome' Dickens had decided 'to abolish it, at the highest tide of its success.'[43] Now, two years later, Dickens was returning to Christmas, for a potential murder. The juxtaposition of the scene and its timing is further heightened by the actual publication date of the episode. The disappearance of Edwin Drood takes place in Chapter 14, in the fourth number of the planned twelve, which was published in the July issue (most likely released on 30 June 1870): the height of summer. In *Pickwick*, Dickens had carefully and astutely linked the adventures of his characters to the publication schedule: the Christmas episode was published at the end of December, Sam Weller's attempt to write a Valentine was published at the end of February. The resulting experience for Dickens's readers was that each month they got an update on what Pickwick and his friends had been doing in that time. Now, Dickens was upending this too. Readers of Drood were thrust into Christmas in July. The time was truly out of joint. But there was a further disjointment of time, unintentional but ultimately most unsettling, for the July issue was the first one to appear after Dickens's death. This was the first time that readers of Dickens would come to his works knowing that the author was no longer with them to finish the story. All the sensation of excitement, optimism and anticipation were now swapped for reflection, regret and loss. This was truly unlike any Christmas Dickens had ever written about before.

But, let me offer a counterpoint. As I have said repeatedly in this chapter, our knowledge of Dickens's death cannot help but impact on the way we think about his last days, even in the very act of referring to them as his *last* days. Yes, Dickens was paying more attention to his own mortality, he was making preparations in his book contracts, and becoming more aware of his failing health: this is called getting old, and anyone who has ever written their will can testify that it does not mean they are planning to pop their clogs the next day, but rather they are taking stock and planning for the future. Did Dickens know he was going to die soon? I strongly doubt it. Was he starting to reflect on the past, and think about the limitations of the future? Absolutely.

Returning to *Drood*, here we have Dickens returning to Rochester, to Christmas, and to the serial novel. There is a sense of circularity in this, and our pressing awareness of *Drood* as his last novel encourages us to see it as looking back, tying up the story of his career and reflecting on all that has gone before. But what if Dickens was not just returning? What if he was reinventing? The portrayal of Rochester and Christmas in *Drood* is new, as is Dickens's inverse use of serialisation to place his readers out of time. If he is looking back upon the themes, traits and methods of his past career, he is also interrogating them, reassessing them and making something new. Forster had called the Italian trip of 1844-1845 a turning point in Dickens's career – the break from his hectic schedule allowed Dickens the opportunity at last to stop playing catch-up and start planning his novels more effectively. It is seen frequently as a development in his career from the early comic novels to grander social panoramas. Well now, thanks to the reading tours, Dickens had just experienced an even longer break than the year in Italy had afforded. It had been five years since *Our Mutual Friend* was published; five years on the road, reworking old material for new readings, getting to know his literary output anew and seeing the reaction of the audience to them. Imagine – just imagine – that Dickens did not die in 1870. In that alternate reality, *Drood* would not have been the last, but the first of a new, third wave of novels. His reappraisal of the past need not be seen as a return back to his roots, but rather a way forward into a new phase: not, as Wilkie Collins meanly said, 'the melancholy work of a worn-out brain', but rather the reimagining of an invigorated mind, ready to return to 'the large canvas and the big brushes' as he had with *Our Mutual Friend*, and start writing again.[44]

Notes

1 Dickens, Letter to F C Beard, 10 June 1865, in Graham Storey (ed.), *The Letters of Charles Dickens*, Volume Eleven 1865–1867 (Oxford: Clarendon Press, 1999), p.49 (p. 49).

2 Dickens, Letter to F C Beard, 10 June 1865, in *Letters*, Vol. 11, p. 49 and p. 49n.

3 Dickens, Letter to John Forster 10 June 1865, in *Letters*, Vol. 11, p. 50 (p. 50); Dickens, Letter to Thomas Headland, 12 June 1865, in *Letters*, Vol. 11, p. 52 (p. 52).

4 Dolby, p. 11.

5 Dickens, Letter to Wilkie Collins, 22 April 1863, in Graham Storey (ed.), *The Letters of Charles Dickens*, Volume Ten 1862–1864 (Oxford: Clarendon Press, 1998), pp.236–239 (p. 238); Dickens, Letter to Georgina Hogarth, 24 January 1869, in Graham Storey (ed.), *The Letters of Charles Dickens*, Volume Twelve 1868–1870 (Oxford: Clarendon Press, 2002), pp. 282–283 (p. 282); Dickens, Letter to John Forster, 29 April 1870, in *Letters*, Vol. 12, pp. 515–516 (p. 515).

6 Dickens, Letter to John Forster, 6 August 1867, in *Letters*, Vol. 11, pp. 407–408 (p. 407).

7 Dickens, Letter to the Editor of the *Times*, 2 September 1867, in *Letters*, Vol. 11, p. 416 (p. 416).

8 Dickens, Letter to F. D. Finlay, 3 September 1867, in *Letters*, Vol. 11, p. 419 (p. 419); Dickens, Letter to Charles Kent, 3 September 1867, in *Letters*, Vol. 11, p. 420 (p. 420).

9 See Nicholas Cambridge, *Bleak Health* (Brighton: Edward Everett Root, 2022).

10 Dickens, Letter to Georgina Hogarth, 21 April 1869, in *Letters*, Vol. 12, p. 339 (p. 339).

11 Cambridge, p. 79.

12 Dolby, p. 416.

13 Dickens, cited in Dolby, pp. 448–449.

14 Anon., *The Athenaeum*; 2 April 1870, pp. 443–444 (p. 443); Anon, *The Times*, 2 June 1870, p. 4.

15 Anon., *The Athenaeum*; 2 April 1870, pp. 443–444 (p. 443).

16 Anon., 'The Mysterious Mystery of Rude Dedwin, *Judy*, 13 April 1870, p. 240 (p. 240).

17 John Forster, *The Life of Charles Dickens*, Volume Three (London: Chapman and Hall, 1870), p. 501.

18 Claire Tomalin, *The Invisible Woman* (London: Penguin, 1993), p. 271.

19 Tomalin, p. 279.

20 Leon Litvack, 'Dickens's Burial in Westminster Abbey: The Untold Story', in Leon Litvack and Nathalie Vanfasse (ed.), *Reading Dickens Differently* (Chichester: Wiley Blackwell, 2020), pp. 15–45 (p. 17).

21 Litvack, p. 41.

22 Dickens, 'Trading in Death', *Household Words*, Volume Six (27 November 1852), pp. 241–245 (p. 241).

23 *The Times*, 10 June 1870.

24 *Daily Telegraph*, 10 June 1870.

25 *Pall Mall Gazette*, June 1870.

26 Anon., 'Charles Dickens', *Punch*, 18 June 1870.

27 Anon., 'Charles Dickens's Legacy to England', *Fun*, 25 June 1870.

28 Anon., 'Charles Dickens', *Punch and Judy*, June 1870.

29 Anon., 'The Magazines', *Illustrated London News*, 9 July 1870, p. 46.

30 R. S., Letter to the Editor, *Daily News*, 14 June 1870.

31 Note from the Publishers, Charles Dickens, *The Mystery of Edwin Drood*, No. 6 (London: Chapman and Hall, 1 September 1870), afterword.

32 For a fuller discussion of Drood theories, see Pete Orford, *The Mystery of Edwin Drood: Charles Dickens' unfinished novel and our endless attempts to end it* (Barnsley: Pen & Sword, 2018).

33 Forster, Volume Three, pp. 425–426.

34 Charles Dickens, *The Mystery of Edwin Drood*, ed. by Margaret Cardwell (Oxford: OUP, 1972), Ch. 3, p. 12.

35 Charles Dickens, *The Pickwick Papers*, ed. by James Kinsley (Oxford: OUP, 1986), Ch. 2, p. 20.

36 *Pickwick*, Ch. 2, p. 20.

37 *Drood*, Ch. 14, p. 121.

38 The Ghost in Master B's room, in Charles Dickens et al, *The Haunted House*, The Extra Christmas Number of *All the Year Round*, 13 December 1859, p. 595.

39 Drood, Ch. 14, p. 121.

40 Drood, Ch. 14, p. 121.

41 Dickens, Letter to Wilkie Collins, 18 September 1867, in *Letters*, Vol. 11, pp. 434–435 (p. 435).

42 Letter to W H Wills, 26 July 1868, in *Letters*, Vol. 12, pp. 158–159 (p. 159).

43 Charles Dickens, 'New Series of All the Year Round', *All The Year Round*, Vol. 20 (19 September 1868), p. 337.

44 Wilkie Collins, 'Wilkie Collins about Charles Dickens', *Pall Mall Gazette*, 20 January 1890, repr. Philip Collins (ed.), *Charles Dickens: The Critical Heritage* (London: Routledge, 1971), pp. 587–588 (p. 588); Dickens, Letter to Wilkie Collins, 25 April 1864, in *Letters*, Vol. 10, pp. 346–349 (p. 346).

Afterword, Afterlife

Dickens's Posthumous Reputation

Focal Point: 1870–now

Case Study: A Christmas Carol

When the final instalment of *The Pickwick Papers* was published in 1837, it may have been the end of the novel, but not the end of Pickwick. The character loomed large in a variety of media: in the unauthorised sequels such as G. W. M. Reynold's *Pickwick Abroad*; in a host of theatrical adaptations and stage shows (including several on horseback); in cigarette cards, playing cards, humorous songs and ditties, and cartoon sketches [see Figure 13.1].[1] Even Dickens could not leave the character alone, and introduced him into the narrative to revive the flagging sales of *Master Humphrey's Clock*. The joy which Master Humphrey feels upon Pickwick visiting echoes the same joy Dickens trusted his readers would feel:

> I endeavoured to express in my welcome, something of that heartiness and pleasure which the sight of him awakened and made him sit down beside me [...] I remarked that I had read his adventures very often, and that his features were quite familiar to me from the published portraits.[2]

What is apparent is that while in theory, Samuel Pickwick is a character contained within the pages of Dickens's novel, in reality the character has a much larger life and presence outside of those pages and in the public imagination. Pickwick does not belong to Dickens, but to everyone. Every reader of the serial, both at the time of its original publication and ever after, has created their own Pickwick in their mind, and despite Dickens's attempts to reclaim control of his characters in the public readings, ultimately the very success of the character relies precisely upon that shared ownership which ensures future generations continue to generate and regenerate Pickwick for their time.

As it is for the creations, so it is for the creator. Dickens may have died in 1870, but we still read and discuss him today. The word 'Dickens' has ceased to refer solely to the author and now applies equally to the works themselves. The adjective 'Dickensian' is readily thrown about with no real agreement on what

The Life of the Author: Charles Dickens, First Edition. Pete Orford.
© 2023 John Wiley & Sons Ltd. Published 2023 by John Wiley & Sons Ltd.

it actually means; for most people it indicates Victorian squalor and work-houses, while those who have actually read Dickens would argue this is the very opposite of what Dickens represents. Just like Pickwick, Dickens belongs to us all, despite his attempts to counter that. Just as he tried to maintain control of his fictional creations, so too Dickens was careful to control his own personal reputation. The disastrous handling of his separation from his wife was born from the need to maintain his public persona; but Dickens did attempt to keep the personal and public separate. In his first tour of America he found the constant attention of the public to be too much, becoming 'more anxious than ever, to travel peaceably' and this public scrutiny of his life would only increase on his return.[3] As his relationship with Ternan developed, Dickens increasingly sought a life away from the public gaze while simultaneously courting the public with his reading tours. The apparent contradiction

Figure 13.1 Assorted 19th and early 20th century *Pickwick* Memorabilia, from The Charles Dickens Museum, London.

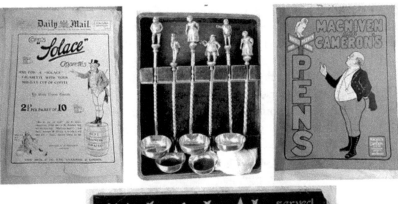

Figure 13.1 (Cont'd)

in this is resolved by recognising that Dickens was thinking of his personal and private life as two separate entities. He could be Charles Dickens, author, and court the public eye as and when he chose, but as soon as he wanted privacy, he could find solace hidden away, either at the family home in Gad's Hill with its secret tunnel, or abroad with Ternan. In his will, Dickens left explicit instructions as to how he wished to be remembered:

> I conjure my friends on no account to make me the subject of any monument, memorial or testimonial whatever. I rest my claims to the remembrance of my country upon my published works, and to the remembrance of my friends upon their experience of me in addition thereto.[4]

Why did he suggest this? With his personal life increasingly open to question and scrutiny, it is a plea to be thought of, at his best, through his works. But there is also a recognition of what the public could and could not reasonably expect: the works were there for all, but Dickens and his life remained his own. Well, this too proved to be untrue. We have built a number of statues and monuments to Dickens now, and we know far more of his life than he hoped to be known to the general public. That final clause of trusting 'the remembrance of my friends upon their experience of me' was likely written with Forster's biography in mind, but in time, those friends who had experience of him would also die, so that the definition of who 'knows' Dickens has evolved beyond the immediacy of his own circle to the subsequent generations of academics and their insights into the works. Dickens, for better or worse, belongs to everyone. This chapter will attempt to understand how we got from 1870 to here. It will look at the posthumous reputation of Dickens, to see how our attitudes towards him have changed, developed and in some cases become entrenched. In doing this I will close, by considering what has become his most enduring – and adapted – work, *A Christmas Carol*.

The Reputation of Dickens in the Late Nineteenth Century

As discussed in the last chapter, the initial responses to Dickens's death were an overwhelming abundance of public grief and professional respect. The success and popularity of the man simply could not be ignored, and even his critics now veiled their concerns among a recognition of his talents and achievements. The obituaries offered early attempts at biographies to celebrate and understand this figure who had come to dominate the literary landscape of nineteenth-century Britain. Soon after, longer works appeared to tell the story of the man behind the stories. George Sala wrote an initial piece for the *Daily Telegraph* which he then developed into a short biography published in 1870; Robert Shelton Mackenzie also produced his *Life of Charles Dickens* the same year, both works coming fast upon Dickens's death to respond to and capitalise upon the moment. But the most significant biography would come in 1872, when the first volume of John Forster's *Life of Charles Dickens* appeared. In Dickens's life Forster had been a constant and steady companion; now that relationship was pushed into the public imagination, with Forster arriving as the authorised biographer of Dickens. For the book to work, it was necessary to emphasise just how close the pair had been, and subsequently we have come to look upon Forster almost exclusively in relation to Dickens, like a supporting role in the story of his life. Forster had written other biographies before on figures as diverse as Oliver Goldsmith and Oliver Cromwell, but this is the book that cemented his reputation for future generations.

However, the importance of the book on its first publication was the impact it had on Dickens, not Forster. This was the first time that the infamous blacking factory incident, and the incarceration of Dickens's father for debt, was made public. Dickens's private shame was known by all. This was not a betrayal of Dickens by his friend, but rather Forster carrying out his friend's wishes. Dickens himself had begun writing an autobiography in the late 1840s which he subsequently abandoned; Forster now continued that work for his friend at a point where Dickens himself did not have to suffer the consequences of people knowing about his difficult childhood. There is of course an element of manipulation here – the 'shame' is, contradiction as it sounds, an acceptable one. Forster's revelation of Dickens's childhood did not actually shame the author so much as make him even more endearing, rewriting the life of the successful novelist as one of triumph against the odds. Truly, Dickens was a man of the people, who understood poverty firsthand and came to be a great gentleman. Revealing his past did not bring humiliation, but humility. It is notable in particular that when Forster produced the next two volumes, no mention was ever made of Ternan. The blacking factory was a 'shameful' secret that worked to Dickens's advantage; the existence of a mistress was not. Was Forster right to suppress the information? It is the fundamental flaw in his biography, and his omission of this in turn raises suspicion over how much we can trust him elsewhere. But this is the very nature of Forster's *Life* – it is, of all biographies, the most illuminating and the one written by one who knew Dickens well. No matter how much research subsequent scholars do, none will ever get as close to Dickens as Forster did. That proximity comes at a cost; Forster had a responsibility not only to his readers but to Dickens as well. His readers wanted the full story, but his friend did not want that story told. Forster told as much as he could without hurting his friend or damaging his reputation. The ideal of Dickens as the great man of the people remained intact – for now.

Accordingly, the reputation of Dickens at the turn of century is buoyed by the emergence of fan clubs and fan writing. In Dickens's own lifetime, shortly after the publication of *Pickwick*, Pickwick clubs had emerged around the country, and then world, and now after his death further groups were established. Dickens's friends and family formed the Boz Club to remember the great man, meeting up regularly to share anecdotes and toast the great inimitable; Dickens's son Henry was one of the founding members, but the driving force was Percy Fitzgerald. The club celebrated Dickens himself as much as his works, and was informed, and chiefly celebrated, by the direct links between its members and Dickens; Emily Bell notes 'the Club's success lay in its personal connection to Dickens: only those who had visited Gad's Hill could recognise the spirit of Boz and have the sense of shared camaraderie.'[5] But such a group had its own shelf-life, for those who knew Dickens before he died must also eventually die too. Forster himself died in 1876, and as the years went by more and more of those with direct experience of Dickens passed away too. As they did, newcomers stepped forward to claim knowledge of Dickens, not through his life, but through his works. This created a tension, seen especially in the rampant field of solutions and theories being proposed to *The Mystery of Edwin Drood*. This is where we see the battle lines being drawn, as the answers being provided by Forster and others did not match the expectations and hopes of Dickens's readers. Increasingly, *Drood* theorists began to disparage Forster, arguing that either he had misunderstood Dickens, or Dickens was lying to him, or Forster was lying to us. There is absolutely no foundation for these claims other than the Droodists' ardent desire to have a more sensational ending than the one which Forster proposed. Dickens's daughter Katey defended Forster on this point, identifying the absurdity of these people claiming to know Dickens's intentions better than his close friend, as well as the hypocrisy that it was 'often those who most doubt Mr Forster's accuracy on this point who are in the habit of turning to his book when they are in search of facts to establish some theory of their own; and they do not hesitate to do this, because they know that whatever views they may hold upon the work itself, or the manner in which it is written, absolute truth is to be found in its pages.'[6]

This tension between those who knew Dickens, and those who knew his works, was replicated in the clubs. In 1902 The Dickens Fellowship was formed, an institution designed to celebrate the life and works of Dickens. This was not like the Boz Club where friends would share anecdotes, but instead a place where fans could talk about the works. Indeed, one meeting of the Boz Club proved disastrous when a speaker talked about the works, instead of the usual merry memories of the man, prompting Marcus Stone to complain:

> At times I think there have been imported into these meetings a little too much of the grave and ponderous element instead of the genial and living one, and feeling, as all his old friends do, and as I think all the whole world does, a specially convinced regard for him, I think we ought to limit ourselves more to that.[7]

But such discussions were becoming limiting indeed, with less people able to contribute direct memories of the man. The new wave of Dickensians were not the people who knew him, but the people who read him. The ownership of Dickens was changing hands.

Dickens and Academia

Ironically, that idea of Dickens as perfect and cosy which Forster's book had secured proved to be both blessing and curse. It allowed for his works to be celebrated by the masses while sneered at by the literati.[8] Trollope's dubbing of Dickens as 'Mr. Popular Sentiment' encapsulates this.[9] The more popular Dickens became, the more ammunition that provided for those who considered themselves to be serious artists. Dickens's cosy, household image excluded his works from academic discussion. Recent scholarship by Michael

Hollington has challenged the preconceived notion that the Bloomsbury group were not fans of Dickens.[10] On the contrary, Virginia Woolf and her peers very much enjoyed reading Dickens – they just did not see him as someone who should be studied. Dickens's popularity was never in doubt, nor was the pleasure of reading him. But in the age of modernism, authors demanded more of their predecessors. They wanted to challenge their readers, not placate them. Dickens offered a reliable and heart-warming read, and the more enjoyable his works, the less seriously they were treated by critics.

This distinction of what was and was not great art was further cemented by F. R. Leavis's *The Great Tradition* (1948). This is a book which regularly draws ire from modern scholars for its condescending and grandstanding sense of importance while it identifies the 'great' literature of the nineteenth century. Leavis's book celebrates all the novels you *should* be reading rather than the novels you *want* to be reading. In much the same way as Oscar-winning films rarely correlate with box office success, Leavis's book looks down upon the popular view to instead dictate to us about what is great art. George Eliot, Henry James, Joseph Conrad – these were all great writers in Leavis's opinion. Dickens, decidedly, was not, being 'a writer at the other end of the scale from sophistication'.[11] In fact, Leavis spends several pages of his introduction explaining why Dickens is not in the book, which somewhat defeats his own purpose:

> That Dickens was a great genius and is permanently among the classics is certain. But the genius was that of a great entertainer, and he had for the most part no profounder responsibility as a creative artist than this description suggests.[12]

The omission of Dickens from Leavis's review of nineteenth-century writers is extraordinary to modern readers for whom Dickens is a fundamental figure in nineteenth-century studies. But Dickens could not have it both ways – he could not be popular and scholarly at the same time. In a later edition in 1960, Leavis would add an appendix which included one solitary Dickens work, *Hard Times*. Yes, *Hard Times*. As wonderful a book as it is, it is not the first that would occur to someone when asked to nominate Dickens's greatest achievement.

While Dickens's work was being dismissed, his life was attracting more scrutiny. More and more details concerning Ternan were beginning to emerge. Gladys Storey had ingratiated herself into the now-aged Kate Perugini's company and over the course of several interviews began to reveal details of Dickens's relationship with the young actress. One might think that the attack on Dickens's character would prove the final nail in the coffin; ironically it provided a lifeline for his works. This darker side of the artist made him much more interesting to his early twentieth-century readers than the jolly Father Christmas figure he had been hitherto thought as. Edmund Wilson's seminal essay 'The Two Scrooges' reimagined Dickens as a haunted man, exorcising his demons through his work, not to demolish Dickens, but to build him anew; Wilson recounted the darker sides of Dickens's life, stating that 'All these circumstances are worth knowing and bearing in mind, because they help us to understand what Dickens was trying to say'.[13] It was a polar opposite to the cheerful figure Dickens himself had tried to represent, but it was the portrayal he needed to make him appealing to a new generation: Wilson lamented that 'of all the great English writers, Charles Dickens has received in his own country the scantiest serious attention from either biographers, scholars or critics.'[14] Focus shifted from the early comic novels which had proved the most popular in his lifetime, to instead celebrate the later darker novels as the moment when Dickens really got serious. Both the blacking factory and Ternan served to show the hidden, *interesting* side of Dickens which readers could now explore in his works. The opportunity arose to reinvent Dickens, for readers to uncover the subversive nature of his writing and find a different Dickens to the one their parents and grandparents had known.

Like all extremes, this view of Dickens as the melancholy man has its fair share of flaws, no less than the idea of Dickens the eternal Pickwick. A counter-revolution reappraised and once more celebrated the earlier works, which had been largely dismissed from critical discussion, as well as celebrating the humour of Dickens. As ever, the truth – malleable as it is – will be found somewhere between the two extremes. Dickens can be funny *and* morose; silly *and* serious; popular *and* academic.

Today Dickens has a relatively firm place in the academy, though it has taken time. Michael Slater recounts the difficulty of finding a supervisor in the 1960s for a Dickens PhD; he notes that at Oxford in 1957 'the University's B.A. English curriculum ended at 1832' because, according to his tutor, 'After that [...] it's only books.'[15] The Dickens scholar Philip Collins helped to establish the Victorian Studies Centre at the University of Leicester in 1962, and worked hard to establish Dickens as a topic for serious academic contemplation. Today there are several academic monographs, journals and conferences devoted purely to Dickens, and plenty more discussion of him and his work in nineteenth-century scholarship. In schools, Dickens maintains a presence as someone children should know about, although in primary schools, especially, the length of the average Dickens novel makes him something of an aspiration rather than a realisation. Frequently it is not the books themselves that are taught, but rather a nod to him and his works during studies of the Victorians. *A Christmas Carol* is a perennial favourite, as is *Oliver Twist* on account of its child protagonist (the same twisted logic which sees *Romeo and Juliet* frequently taught in schools for its relatability, despite most teenagers being blissfully, and mercifully, unable to personally relate to the message of teen marriage and double suicide). In high schools his works make a regular appearance on the UK syllabus. He has not reached the status of Shakespeare, who is compulsory, but instead features as recommended texts in the category of 'Pre-1914 literature'. The most popular works of his to teach at high school are *Great Expectations* and *A Christmas Carol* – it is no coincidence that these are two of his shortest works, nor that they are works with an abundance of screen adaptations available. In an era where increasing concern is being raised about our dwindling attention span, the doorstopper novels can be a hard sell to a new reader. This need not be cause for concern however; e-readers are lighter than the average Dickens book and can help make his works a little more transportable again. More importantly, the digital age allows the presence of a digital community; readers can find like-minded souls online. A number of recent projects have encouraged and initiated online read-alongs, where the pattern of original publication is respected and readers experience Dickens not as one behemoth of a book, but in the far more appealing and sustainable package of smaller weekly or monthly episodes. At a time when television is shifting from the weekly serial to binge-watching on streaming sites, there is a joy in seeing readers of Dickens reverse the flow and find pleasure in reading in parts.

Nonetheless, when a writer becomes embedded in academia and education there is an inherent tension that arises between the perception of them as someone to study, and someone to enjoy. Dickens was a popular phenomenon in his time, but that was over a century and a half ago. As much as any of us enjoys Dickens, we will never quite read him in the way that his contemporaries did: there is simply too much surrounding context and baggage around his reputation and cultural prestige. An interesting comparison is Terry Pratchett, a much more contemporary author and one who, like Dickens, was universally praised, but not currently studied in anywhere near the same amount. Pratchett's works are enjoyable and thought-provoking, and he shared Dickens's concerns with social injustice. We can find several thought-provoking quotes in there: in 2022 Pratchett's passage about boots was cited and recited in the UK by those exploring the imbalance of wealth among the cost of living crisis.[16] Pratchett, like Dickens before him, was one of the great social commentators of our time, which seems remarkable to say now given how little critical acclaim and attention he has received. He never received a Nobel prize for literature, but his books are enjoyed by many. But now imagine people reading Pratchett in 150 years' time: will they still get the jokes? Will they read it as the work of a contemporary, or will the books have gained that inevitable cultural weight (and baggage) of being an old, 'classic', work? Such is the difficult position in which Dickens is now held. His works are great, but the more we impress that, the more we establish his reputation as someone you *should* read – and no-one likes to be told what they should and should not do. But if we leave Dickens to be discovered by each reader individually there is the danger of his reputation dwindling. So Dickensians find themselves in the awkward position of recommending but not insisting; simultaneously defending the relevance and importance of Dickens while also recognising the right of any reader to choose who they read; firmly placing Dickens in the literary canon while also recognising that the canon is only ever a construct and open to reinterpretation; championing Dickens's intellectual worth without making him exclusionary; celebrating his popular appeal without dumbing him down.

Dickens beyond the Page

If reading a Dickens novel can seem overwhelming to modern readers, there is a wealth of adaptations and appropriations of his work in alternative media to offer new ways into his stories. Even in his own lifetime, Dickens's works had a life beyond the page. Theatrical adaptations of his works proved popular, and in an age where copyright law did not prohibit the use of his characters in such works, there was an abundance of different adaptations of the same work which would often dominate the London theatrical scene: I have mentioned previously how when *The Cricket on the Hearth* was published in December 1845, eighteen theatres were all performing adaptations of it that month.[17] During his second tour of America Dickens said 'There are no end of No Thoroughfares being offered to Managers here' and 'They are doing Crickets, Oliver Twists and all sorts of versions of me.'[18] Dickens was simply unavoidable. But what this means is that even after the production of Dickens's writing stopped, the Dickens factory continued. With the advent of cinema, Dickens's works found a new home. The cinematic pioneers Sergei Eisenstein and D. W. Griffith were both fans of Dickens's works; Griffith adapted the *Cricket* for screen in 1909, while Eisenstein wrote an impassioned essay arguing that 'Dickens's nearness to the characteristics of cinema in method, style and especially viewpoint and exposition, is amazing.'[19] Dickens's works, it was argued, were almost custom-made for cinema. The truth of this is perhaps somewhat more nuanced. Dickens himself was heavily inspired by the theatre of his age, and that theatre in turn proved a direct inspiration for the beginning of cinema: several theatrical actors and directors would transfer from stage to screen, so that both the acting and directorial style of early cinema is borne from the theatrical traditions which in turn emerged in Dickens's writing. It is not necessarily that Dickens inspired cinema, but that both Dickens and cinema drew equal inspiration from the same theatrical source, which in turn allowed for perfect compatibility between the two. Subsequent adaptors of Dickens's works for film have found director's notes within his narrative: David Lean's 1946 adaptation of *Great Expectations* takes Pip's inner monologue during his night-time walk through the marshes and shows the reader what Pip is thinking, even down to when 'The cattle came upon me with like suddenness, staring out of their eyes, and steaming out of their nostrils, "Halloa, young thief!"'[20]

Ironically, by taking Dickens's narrative as direction, Lean both amplifies and reduces his voice. We as the viewers see exactly what Pip is imaging as a literal event – the cow talks – but equally we do not have Dickens's own voice, through Pip, describing that to us. In my introduction I explained why I thought Barthes's infamous theory of the death of the author does not apply to Dickens, precisely because his narrative voice is such a key presence in the text; in some respects, the numerous adaptations of Dickens's works, and our own interpretations as modern readers, impacts upon that and allows some potential for the theory to hold. For an adaptation, losing that voice threatens to lose a fundamental aspect of what makes a Dickens story. Yet the fidelity shown by Lean here, and in particular the reliance upon the narrative voice even while presenting the story as a film, argues yet for Dickens's integral role in his own tales.

Of course, the enduring success of Dickens on screen shows that his works can and do survive without that narrative voice, pushing further emphasis upon the characters and plot to define what we mean by the term 'Dickensian'. In the triumphing of Dickens's characters we return again to the nineteenth century mindset and that influx of character-based merchandise. Thanks in part to the illustrations of Phiz and Cruikshank, the characters themselves became instantly recognisable as they were recreated on playing cards and in Toby Jugs. Today, people may not be familiar with the exact details of many Dickens's novels, but they will be familiar with characters such as Scrooge, Fagin, the Artful Dodger, Miss Havisham, and poor little Oliver asking for more.

But people have not simply translated Dickens to the screen; they have adapted and remoulded him. It is no coincidence that many of the characters I just listed as an example come from *Oliver Twist*, which has reached a wider audience through Lionel Bart's 1960 musical adaptation. The proof of this lies in a well-intentioned but misinformed plaque at London Bridge that identifies the location to tourists as 'Nancy's steps', being 'the scene of the murder of Nancy in Charles Dickens's novel *Oliver Twist*'. This, I'm sorry to say, is fake news. In Dickens's novel, Nancy meets Mr Brownlow at the steps, and is then murdered elsewhere; but in Carol Reed's 1968 film version of *Oliver!*, Nancy is indeed murdered on the steps.[21] So here we have a historical plaque identifying a physical location as the scene of a murder in the film of the musical of the book: the innocent attribution of it to 'Charles Dickens's novel' tells us that the plaque writer never even realised they were misquoting the book. 'Of course Dickens's books *came* first (in time)' notes John Glavin, but 'They just don't come first (in meaning) any more.'[22] Dickens is a household word, but the very words that made him so are now reaching a smaller audience than the adaptations and appropriations of both him and his works. The jury is still out on Dickens in the digital age: as mentioned, online read-alongs and open-access resources can increase both the availability of his works and our level of interaction and engagement with them. Fanfiction sites are an unexpected but welcome source of new Dickensian stories and reworkings. Dickens has even made it into video games: when Ubisoft launched the next instalment of their popular video game series *Assassin's Creed* in 2015, *Assassin's Creed Syndicate*, it was set in Victorian London so, unsurprisingly, Dickens featured. While the quests made some links to his works, knowledge of them was not essential. Instead, it was Dickens himself who players could interact with, not his works, playing 'a wise, well-informed commander who sends his troops – or his secret agents – on dangerous missions, as in a James Bond film'.[23] On one hand, it would be almost unthinkable to have a game set within Victorian London where Dickens did not make an appearance. But one must also wonder how much knowledge the average gamer had of Dickens's works before playing. The man himself is famous to a general audience, the works maybe less so.

Dickens in the Modern World

Another tension which Dickens's growing reputation introduces is the extent to which he can, or cannot, be considered a global figure. Just as Leavis tried to dictate the great tradition, so too politicians and practitioners are keen to promote the idea of British authors that should/must be taught. In schools outside the UK this is tied to ideas of cultural exports. Across the world, in countries such as Egypt, Iraq and Nigeria, school children read Dickens in English as an example of great literature, and Dickens thus becomes embedded as part of a student's experience of English culture. In doing so it simultaneously celebrates Dickens as a global export while intrinsically tying him to ideas of his Englishness. To celebrate his Bicentenary in 2012, the British Council organised a Global Readathon across twenty-four countries. Regenia Gagnier notes that the Council 'urged education ministers throughout the world to invite their schools to participate', initially by asking pupils the prompt question 'What would Dickens write today' but eventually refining this to the question 'Where would he be writing from?'[24] This idea of where Dickens would be writing from today has led to well-meaning, but ultimately patronising, pieces in which slums around the world are compared to Victorian London, redefining Dickens's relevance while conveniently (and falsely) assuming that such slums could never possibly be found in Dickens's own country today.

Today our appreciation of Dickens as a man is complicated further by our growing awareness and discomfort with some of his views – the antisemitism of Fagin's portrayal, or the inherent racism portrayed in his 1853 essay 'The Noble Savage' and its attack on the 'howling, whistling, clucking, stamping, jumping, tearing savage'.[25] This article was written in response to the Indian Rebellion of 1857 (commonly referred to at that time, and for some time since, as the Indian Mutiny, which is telling in itself); Dickens's son Walter was serving in India at that time so

Dickens had a personal investment in his attack. Dickens would later apologise for Fagin, and in later edits of *Oliver Twist* the various references to the character as 'the Jew' were replaced with his name. But other moments of attack persisted. Melisa Klimasweski notes there is 'no avoiding the hatred' in Dickens and Wilkie Collins's 1857 Christmas Number *The Perils of Certain English Prisoners*, in which the villain is a 'Portugese Pirate Captain, whose "brown fingers" and other features make him a "man-monkey"'.[26] Klimaszewski posits that the work's collaborative status allowed each author an element of anonymity and deniability to test the boundaries, but argues that it needs to be read in the context of Dickens's other works which are significantly more humane, and that 'the conversation about race, violence and power that courses through [his] individual works benefits from being understood as just that, a conversation, rather than a monolithic, single-authored set of views.'[27] The problem is that while Dickens's works, en masse, celebrate the human condition and champions the underdog, there is little positive commentary on other races to balance these other examples of attack; Grace Moore notes that 'very few colonised others actually appear in Dickens's fiction'.[28] Tantalisingly, the closest Dickens got to a sympathetic portrayal was the Landless twins in his final novel *The Mystery of Edwin Drood*. Perhaps, given longer, Dickens might yet have come to redeem himself from his earlier views.

Nor is racism the only difficulty for modern readers of Dickens to overcome; they must needs reconcile their love of his work with their disproval of his actions when separating from his wife. It is not only his life that raises concerns about sexism; much criticism has been made in turn of Dickens's depiction of women either as perfect angels or comic grotesques, though this criticism is increasingly being challenged as the complexity of some (but not all) of his female characters is now being recognised.[29] Nonetheless, these underlying concerns of both racism and sexism sit at odds with what we would hope to find in a global, universal, cultural icon. Many readers still long for Dickens to be the same embodiment of Pickwick that his nineteenth and early twentieth century readers believed him to be. Rosemarie Bodenheimer ponders whether the constant ambiguity of Dickens's character places a responsibility on us to recognise that split in order to fully appreciate him; that 'the perfect reader of Dickens would embrace both the disturbing and the self-comforting fantasies with equal humanity.'[30] In belonging to everyone, Dickens cannot please everyone all of the time. But we should not expect the people to tear down his statues just yet; although Dickens would probably thank them if they did. In his own lifetime he contended with the expectations of the world, balancing the brand of Dickens with his own desires and frailties as a man. Though he courted celebrity, he resented the intrusions into his private life, and far preferred to let the works speak for themselves. With Dickens now dead, he can no longer hide nor defend his private actions, leaving the works themselves as his sole defenders and advocates.

Case Study: *A Christmas Carol* without Dickens

As the *Carol*'s success beyond the page has continued, there has developed what Paul Davis defines as 'two texts, the one that Dickens wrote in 1843, and the one that we collectively remember.'[31] The second text, which Davis dubs the culture-text, is a version of a story understood by society which stands separate to the actual text itself, much like the musical version of *Oliver Twist* inspiring the plaque at London Bridge. Everyone *knows* what the *Carol* is about, but not everyone has *read* it. Inevitably, changes occur and people do not even realise that the story in their mind is not the story Dickens wrote: 'we are still creating the culture-text of the *Carol*'.[32] For example, one aspect of his tale which is frequently and readily changed is the confusing time-travel narrative behind the visitation of the spirits. In the original text, we are told that Scrooge is visited by Marley's ghost on Christmas Eve, then sleeps through all night and the rest of the day before being visited by the Spirit of Christmas Past:

> To his great astonishment the heavy bell went on from six to seven, and from seven to eight, and regularly up to twelve; then stopped. Twelve! It was past two when he went to bed. The clock was wrong. An icicle must have got into the works. Twelve![33]

After the Spirit of Christmas Past leaves him, he is then visited by the Spirit of Christmas Present an hour later, who takes him back in time to see Christmas Day, then after the Spirit of Christmas Yet to Come visits, Scrooge awakes to find it is Christmas morning AGAIN. Scrooge thus exists in the same Christmas day three times over: asleep the first time after Marley's visit, then visiting with the Spirit of Christmas Present, then again after the Ghosts have visited in order to rewrite the day again. No wonder he has to ask the small boy out his window what day it is. This all seems unnecessarily complicated, and adaptations have understandably simplified it to have all the ghosts appear in one night – Christmas Eve. Sometimes the changes are so apparent that we immediately recognise they are not in the original – clearly, Bob Cratchit is not a puppet frog in Dickens's text. However, we are so focused on the obvious changes in an adaptation like *The Muppet Christmas Carol* (1992) that other changes go by unnoticed – there are a surprising number of people who were unaware that there is only one Marley, having seen Waldorf and Statler haunt Michael Caine's Scrooge as the Marley brothers in that film many a time.

The Muppet Christmas Carol has long since evolved from guilty pleasure to an adaptation readily acknowledged and celebrated by Dickensians. It seems strange to talk of an adaptation with talking pigs and frogs as authentic, especially when Dickens is played by Gonzo the Great. The answer lies in transparency.

Clearly, we can see the film is not trying to portray the actual Dickens, and so we are more willing to accept the changes that occur because there is no 'trick'. The irony, as said, is that we are so busy looking at the obvious changes that others can pass us by; but equally it has to be said that *The Muppet Christmas Carol* is, on the whole, rather faithful to the original. A great deal of the dialogue is unchanged, and Michael Caine insisted on playing his character straight through the whole film despite the surrounding case of rats and talking vegetables. It is not a parody of the *Carol* at all, but a heartfelt and earnest retelling of it. For an older generation the classic adaptation is *Scrooge*, the 1951 adaptation starring Alastair Sim, which is a very fine film indeed. The exclusive presence of human actors in *Scrooge* might lead us to assume it is a more direct adaptation than the Muppets', but here again there are significant deviations, especially in the fleshing out of Scrooge's past. The Sim film dramatically expands on this, showing us the deaths of both Scrooge's sister and Marley, and more of their lives too, to impress upon an audience the impact these two people had on Scrooge's development for better and worse. It is, and is not, *A Christmas Carol*.

Adaptation studies have increasingly impressed upon the idea that fidelity to the original text should not be the sole criterion by which to judge an adaptation. While there have been many adaptations of the *Carol* that have attempted the illusion of fidelity, there are many more which have brazenly and cheerfully worn their deviations for all to show. In addition to the Muppets, the *Carol* has been adapted by Mickey Mouse, Batman (twice, in fact), Barbie, Mr Magoo, The Flintstones, Daffy Duck (in *Bah Humduck!*), and Blackadder to name but a few. It is by far the most adapted of all Dickens's stories. Again, we can thank its brevity in part for this, but we should also recognise the impact of its seasonal tone (which also allows for the same songs to dominate the chart year in, year out) and for the simplicity and clarity of its structure. Attempting to summarise *Bleak House* in a few sentences is a Herculean task, but the *Carol* is remarkably straightforward: a miser is visited by three spirits who show him his past, present and future in order to change his ways. The structure in particular is very helpful for adaptations and appropriations as it gives a clear framework which they can add details to whilst maintaining the overarching sense of the original story. Often these appropriations test the limits of what can and cannot be called the *Carol*. Some of them are not set at Christmas – the 1995 Batman story *Ghosts* by Jeph Loeb reimagines the events happening on Halloween, with Bruce Wayne learning how to be a better and less secretive person when not wearing the cowl; David Zucker's 2008 film *An American Carol* sees a spoof character based on Michael Moore learning to be more patriotic and right-wing; and Disney's straight-to-video 2003 film *Springtime for Roo* sees Winnie the Pooh and his friends help Rabbit to discover the true meaning of Easter. Even without the Christmas setting, all three of these stories see the protagonist visited by spirits of the past, present and future to effect a necessary change in their character. Each one owes a close debt to Dickens, even while avoiding what many might assume to be a key facet of the story. Another deliberate deviation is seen in the 1988 Christmas special of *Blackadder* called, inventively enough, *Blackadder's Christmas Carol*, in which the protagonist starts the story as the nicest man in Victorian London, only to be shown images of his mean-spirited ancestors and descendants to help him realises that 'bad guys get all the fun'.[34] The joke of the show is precisely that the Christmas spirit's intervention goes wrong, and while he is supposed to be going around convincing misers to do good, he inadvertently takes a good man and turns him bad. What these appropriations all assume is that we know the original story, and rely on that knowledge for their adaptation to make sense. Each one is therefore a testament to the success and fame of the original, as well as a means by which to perpetuate that success and fame. Many people will never read the *Carol*, but be familiar with the core elements of the story nonetheless.

And how does all of this impact on Dickens himself? Earlier I raised the difficulties of Dickens's nineteenth-century views in a twenty-first century multicultural world. The works remain open to adaptation and updating, and Dickens himself is equally reinvented on a daily basis by both fans and critics as we grapple with understanding him in a modern context. This brings us to the decision to include Dickens among the cast of characters in *The Muppet Christmas Carol*, played by Gonzo the Great, 'A blue furry Charles Dickens who hangs out with a rat'.[35] There is your Dickens for the masses: colourful, larger than life and wearing a top hat. Gonzo would never leave his wife or write the violated letter, heaven forfend! He is truly a symbol of diversity, going beyond race and sex to present Dickens as not even human. Yet as far removed as he may be in looks, the characterisation is very familiar and nostalgic. Gonzo's portrayal takes us back to the jolly Dickens persona of the nineteenth and early twentieth centuries. Even in questioning Gonzo's credentials as Dickens, his friend Rizzo emphasises the positive qualities of the author, telling him that 'Charles Dickens was a nineteenth century novelist – a genius'.[36] The scholars and academics can consider his demons and inconsistencies, but as a brand it will always be the jolly, genius Dickens that gets most approval from the marketing department. Other modern Dickens have focused primarily on recreating the original: Simon Callow has performed a number of one-man readings of the *Carol* to great effect, standing in for Dickens – very much so in fact when he was then cast as Dickens in a *Doctor Who* episode.[37] Similarly, Dickens's great-great-grandson Gerald Dickens also performs one-man readings of his ancestor's texts, the appeal being, much like the original reading tours, that sense of proximity to the original. Gonzo the Great is therefore something of a departure: a blue furry Charles Dickens signals the departure from historical authenticity which one might assume would make him less relevant to Dickensians, but in advertising that departure from reality it offers us the Dickens we want.

Returning to the idea of global Dickens, one of the most recent portrayals of Dickens, of sorts, was in Armando Iannucci's 2019 film of *David Copperfield*. Here, David opened the story while doing a public reading, telling his story just as Dickens told his. While the 1997 BBC adaptation of *David Copperfield* emphasised the link between author and character by showing David with the iconic beard by the end of the series, Iannucci's took a notable departure by casting Dev Patel in the role of David, alongside several other non-white actors in the supporting cast. This prompted the predictable mix of applause and condemnation at 'woke' casting. Iannucci's defence was simple: he was picking the best actors for the job, and to him Patel best captured that sense of naïve innocence he wanted in his Copperfield: 'Armando always knew he wanted Dev'.[38] The film was a great success, and welcomed by Dickensians – the image it presents of Dickens's fictional persona played by a non-Caucasian actor is a welcome intervention in the argument of Dickens's wider legacy. Producer Kevin Loader explained how the casting of different ethnicities allowed Dickens's London to reflect the London of today:

> I was standing on the side of the set the other day, watching a scene between three of the younger characters. I suddenly realised I was watching three young black British actors in a Dickens adaptation, none of which were written as black characters. And it didn't seem odd. It's just another scene in the film.[39]

If Dickens is to belong to everyone, then he really must belong to *every*one. The author, like his works, stands to be reinterpreted by each new reader and generation. Learning about the life of Dickens offers us a great opportunity to better understand him, his works and their inspirations; but as time goes on we must equally recognise and celebrate the ability of those works to stand independent of their author. The man Charles Dickens lived and breathed from 1812 to 1870 and his story is told within the pages of this book, but the author Charles Dickens lives and breathes still, forever being told and retold to fit to the society he is being read in.

This book has attempted to provide information and insight on Dickens's life, but that story is not over, and you as reader have just added a new page to it. Your impression of him, of his works, and what you do next with it will in turn contribute to the perception of Dickens today. He maintains a presence in schools, universities, libraries, bookshops, theatres, television, cinema and online: some of those may dwindle, others may expand, but one thing it certainly shows is the adaptability of Dickens's works and reputation. We do not know what future generations will be saying about Dickens, but if we are uncertain about the content, we can be certain nonetheless about the action itself: whatever it is they say, people *will* be talking about him, for some time to come.

Notes

1 For more information on equestrian acts in the nineteenth century, see Paul Schlicke, *Dickens and Popular Entertainment* (London: Unwin Hyman, 1985), pp. 157–163.

2 'Master Humphrey's Visitor', *Master Humphrey's Clock*, No. 5 (2 May 1840), pp. 49–53 (p. 51).

3 Dickens, Letter to George Putnam, 4 March 1842, in Madeline House, Graham Storey and Kathleen Tillotson (eds.), *The Letters of Charles Dickens*, Volume Three 1842–1832 (Oxford: Clarendon Press, 1974), pp. 98–99 (p. 99).

4 Dickens, Last Will and Testament, 12 May 1869 and 2 June 1870, in Graham Storey (ed.), *The Letters of Charles Dickens*, Volume Twelve 1868–1870 (Oxford: Clarendon Press, 2002), pp. 730–734 (p. 733).

5 Emily Bell, 'Changing Representations of Charles Dickens,1857–1939', Unpublished PhD Thesis, University of York, 2017.

6 Kate Perugini, *Pall Mall Magazine*, June 1906.

7 Marcus Stone, cited in Bell, pp. 134–135.

8 For a full discussion of Dickens's academic reputation, see Laurence W. Masseno, *The Dickens Industry: Critical Perspectives, 1836–2005* (Rochester: Camden House, 2008).

9 Anthony Trollope, *The Warden*, ed. by Robin Gilmour (London: Penguin, 1984), Ch. 15, p. 131.

10 See Michael Hollington, 'Mansfield eats Dickens' in Sarah Ailwood and Melinda Harvey (eds.), *Katherine Mansfield and Literary Influence* (Edinburgh: EUP, 2015), pp. 155–167; Michael Hollington 'Dickens and Lawrence' in Leon Litvack and Nathalie Vanfasse, *Reading Dickens Differently* (Chichester: Wiley Blackwell, 2020), pp. 113–124.

11 F R Leavis, *The Great Tradition* (London: Chatto & Windus 1960, p. 18).

12 Leavis, p. 19.

13 Edmund Wilson, 'Dickens: The Two Scrooges', *The Wound and the Bow: Seven Studies in Literature* (Cambridge: Riverside Press, 1941), pp. 1–104 (p. 10).

14 Wilson, p. 1.

15 Michael Slater, 'Dickens in my life', *Dickensian*, Vol. 115, December 2019, pp. 246–251 (p. 248).

16 Alison Flood, 'Terry Pratchett estate backs Jack Monroe's idea for "Vimes Boots" poverty index', *Guardian*, https://www.theguardian.com/books/2022/jan/26/terry-pratchett-jack-monroe-vimes-boots-poverty-index, 26 January 2022.

17 Malcolm Morley, '"The Cricket" on the stage', *Dickensian*, 1 January 1852, pp. 17–24 (p. 17).

18 Dickens, Letter to Wilkie Collins, 24 December 1867, in Graham Storey (ed), *The Letters of Charles Dickens*, Volume Eleven 1865–1867 (Oxford: Clarendon Press, 1999), pp. 520–521 (p. 521).

19 Sergei Eisenstein, 'Dickens, Griffith and the Film Today', in Sergei Eisensten, *Film Form: Essays in Film Theory*, trans. by Jay Leyda (New York: Harcourt, 1949), pp. 195–255 (p. 206).

20 Charles Dickens, *Great Expectations*, ed. by Margaret Cardwell (Oxford: OUP, 1993), Ch. 3, p. 17.

21 I am indebted to Jeremy Clarke, Education Officer for Medway Council, who first made me aware of the plaque and its error during his talk 'Innocent Places and Imposters: Curating and Creating Dickens' for the Dickens Fellowship Annual Conference held online 17 July 2021.

22 John Glavin, 'Introduction', in John Glavin (ed.), *Dickens on Screen* (Cambridge: CUP, 2003), p. 5.

23 Francesca Orestano, 'Dickens as Icon and Antonomasia in *Assassin's Creed: Syndicate*', in *Reading Dickens Differently*, pp. 207–222 (p. 217).

24 Regenia Gagnier, 'The Global Circulation of Charles Dickens's Novels', *Literature Compass*, Vol. 10, No. 1 (2013), pp. 82–95 (p. 83).

25 Charles Dickens, 'The Noble Savage', *Household Words*, Vol. 7, 11 June 1853, pp. 337–339 (p. 337).

26 Melisa Klimaszewski, *Collaborative Dickens: Authorship and Victorian Christmas Periodicals* (Athens: Ohio University Press, 2019), p. 95.

27 Klimaszewski, p. 99.

28 Grace Moore, *Dickens and Empire* (Aldershot: Ashgate, 2004), p. 58.

29 Since the 1980s, a number of works appeared to counter the criticism of Dickens's female characters, including: Michael Slater, *Dickens and Women* (London: J. M. Dent and Sons, 1983); Patricia Ingham, *Dickens, Women and Language* (London: Harvester Wheatsheaf, 1992); and Brenda Ayres, *Dissenting Women in Dickens's Novels* (London: Greenwood Press, 1998).

30 Rosemarie Bodenheimer, *Knowing Dickens* (Ithaca: Cornell University Press, 2007), p. 205.

31 Paul Davis, *The Lives and Times of Ebenezer Scrooge* (New Haven: Yale, 1990), p. 4.

32 Paul Davis, p. 4.

33 Charles Dickens, *A Christmas Carol*, in *A Christmas Carol and other Christmas Books*, ed. by Robert Douglas-Fairhurst (Oxford: OUP, 2008), Stave 2, p. 26.

34 Richard Boden, *Blackadder's Christmas Carol* (BBC, 1988).

35 Brian Henson (dir.), *The Muppets Christmas Carol* (Jim Henson Productions, 1992).

36 *Muppets Christmas Carol*.

37 'The Unquiet Dead', *Doctor Who*, BBC, First aired 9 April 2005.

38 Kevin Loader cited in Cath Clarke, 'Why Dev Patel in Dickens could change film forever', *Guardian*, 17 August 2018, https://www.theguardian.com/film/2018/aug/17/why-dev-patel-in-dickens-could-change-film-for-ever.

39 Loader, cited in Clarke.

Index

Note: All references to Dickens literary outputs can be found listed under 'Dickens, Charles – WORKS'. Literary works by other authors, and film adaptations of Dickens's works, are listed by title within the main index.

The Life of the Author: Charles Dickens, First Edition. Pete Orford.
© 2023 John Wiley & Sons Ltd. Published 2023 by John Wiley & Sons Ltd.

Printed in the USA
CPSIA information can be obtained
at www.ICGtesting.com
LVHW010930211223
766828LV00012B/90